ALPINE SKI TOURING

Selected ski tours in the European Alps

By Bruce Goodlad et al.

Contributors: Martin Chester, Al Powell, Mark Charlton, Andy Teasdale, Tim Blakemore, Jonny Baird, Graham Frost, Terry Ralphs, Rob Collister, Olly Allen, Cain Olsen, Andy Perkins and Mike Austin

First published in Great Britain 2019 by Pesda Press
Tan y Coed Canol
Ceunant
Caernarfon
Gwynedd
LL55 4RN

© Copyright 2019 Bruce Goodlad et al.

ISBN: 9781906095666

The Author asserts the moral right to be identified as the author of this work. All rights reserved. No part of this publication may be reproduced, stored in a retrieval system, or transmitted, in any form or by any means, electronic, mechanical, photocopying, recording or otherwise, without the prior written permission of the Publisher.

Maps by Bute Cartographics

Maps based on OpenStreetMap (Open Database License) licensed as CC BY SA
with SRTM topography data and local information sources
© OpenStreetMap contributors, SRTM topography data 2018

Printed and bound in Poland, www.lfbookservices.co.uk

Acknowledgements

The idea for this book came about sitting in the cabin of a boat while on a ski and sail trip in the Arctic which I do each year. Dave Crichton, one of the most regular ski clients and a good friend, suggested a selected ski touring guide to the Alps. Over the years Dave has skied most of the Alpine Arc, so we started chatting about what areas would be included and what we would leave out. As the wine flowed I started making notes and, as is usually the case after a few drinks, the whole thing seemed like a great idea and we would have it done over the summer.

In the cold light of an Arctic dawn the enormity of the project struck me – apart from the amount of work involved, the intimate knowledge of each area required to produce a guidebook goes way beyond one quick ski tour in perfect weather. I felt it was too much so parked the idea, but my subconscious wouldn't let it go. One day the idea popped back in there again, but instead of me writing the whole book I would ask a number of my colleagues if they would contribute one or two tours. I would then pull the whole thing together.

A summer had now elapsed and I was sitting in a lodge in Japan (on the floor as there are no chairs). I got my laptop out and started to pull the idea together, asked Franco at Pesda Press if he was interested in the idea, and put a plan together. I also started speaking to guides to see if they would be interested in contributing and which tours they would be happy to submit.

The criteria would be classic ski tours at a variety of grades spread through the Alps, with some venues that were well known and others that were not really on the radar for British ski tourers. In many respects the list is a starting point for the reader to get a feel for the Alps; then they can head out and explore, putting their own tours together.

When choosing who to ask to be involved, there was only so much space in the book, so I focused on friends who I have skied with, guides who spend most of their winters on skis, and guides who friends and clients have enjoyed skiing with. If we had infinite space I'm sure we could have expanded further, maybe there is space for another volume.

When you start reading the book you will see that it is genuine collaboration between fourteen guides. The team has been incredible in their attention to detail, with everything from the text through choice of photographs, through to checking the edits and making sure the maps allow the reader to orientate themselves with the real map and get a feel for an area.

One of the criteria for involvement was that the guide had done the tour recently, so while conditions vary from year to year, and global warming has had a massive effect on the Alpine glaciers, the information is as current as you will find in a guidebook.

I could go through and name each author individually but I won't as their contributions are all equally valued and I owe a massive debt of gratitude to them for their hard work.

I also need to thank Don Williams at Bute Cartographics who has drawn all the maps – this was an area of the book that was a big challenge to both of us. To bring the mapping from four countries all with different scales together into a common base map, then decipher the scribblings and vague lines drawn on maps then photographed with a smart phone, has been a tour de force. Don may never look at another foreign map again, but he can be proud of this achievement and I am very grateful to his hard work for pulling everything together.

About the author and contributors

Franco and the team at Pesda Press have been a pleasure to work with for the third time. Even though the team is spread round the globe it works seamlessly: if ever there was an advert for a virtual office this is it. Thanks for all your support and patience.

Finally, can I thank my wife Kate. When we finished *Ski Touring*, just as our son was born, she thought books were a thing of the past. Since then we have had a daughter, reprinted *Alpine Mountaineering* and produced a second edition of *Ski Touring*. I promise no more – for a bit at least. Thanks for your patience, tolerance and all the fun days we have had on skis together.

Photo acknowledgements

Photos in the first part of the book are by Bruce Goodlad, unless otherwise captioned. Photos of the tours are by the contributor, unless otherwise captioned.

About the author and contributors

A pen portrait of the author and each of the contributors can be found in the description of the first of the tours they have written.

Brian O'Connor on his way to Mont Rogneux.

Introduction

Ski touring / ski mountaineering is one of the best ways to enjoy the winter mountains. What other sport can open access to un-tracked wilderness, where you can lay your own trail as you climb up, then whoop with joy as you carve magnificent turns down through soft untracked snow?

In recent years ski touring, or as it seems to be increasingly referred to 'backcountry skiing', has undergone a revolution. Kit is lighter and easier to use, avalanche and weather forecasts are more sophisticated, and the advance in digital mapping on smart phones and GPS has made the winter mountains more accessible than ever. Accessibility does come at a price: it is easier to access wild remote places and so it is easier to get yourself into trouble if you don't have the skills to match.

This book is a selected guidebook to ski touring in the European Alps. While we will remind you of a few key skills, kit considerations and what avalanche skills you should have in the coming chapters, it is not an instructional manual, and the author assumes that you are comfortable with the skills outlined in his previous book *Ski Touring*.

This is a unique collaboration between a number of guides who have volunteered to contribute some of their favourite ski tours; you will see from their bios that we have accessed an incredible knowledge base, with decades worth of ski touring experience. The great advantage of being able to access this knowledge base is that the guides who have written up each tour have an intimate knowledge of the routes and have skied them recently so the information is correct and as up-to-date as possible.

This guidebook by its nature is selective; we have asked all the guides involved to share some of their favourite tours – there are many other ski tours out there but hopefully this book will help you explore the Alps before discovering your own favourite areas.

Contents

Acknowledgements	3
About the author and contributors	4
Introduction	5
Contents	6

Ski Touring in the Alps ... 9
When to ski tour in the Alps	10
Travelling to the Alps	10
How to use this book	11
Maps	11
Ski tour grading	12
Ski mountaineering	12

Ski Touring Kit ... 13
Ski kit	13
Avalanche rescue kit	15
Crevasse rescue kit	15
Mountaineering kit	17
Clothing	17
Miscellaneous	18
Extra kit for hut trips	18
Group kit	19
Specialist equipment	20

Skills Check ... 21
Uphill skiing skills	21
Downhill skiing skills	22
Movement on foot / crampons	22
Glacier skiing	22

Avalanche Safety and Rescue ... 23
Get the gear and know how to use it	23
Companion avalanche rescue	24
Get educated	25
Get the avalanche forecast	26
Get feedback from the mountain	26
Get out of harm's way	26

Tour Planning ... 27
Your tour plan	28
Timing	28
Alternatives	29
Evacuation plan	29
Using mountain huts	30
Rescue plan	31
Calling for help in the mountains	32

Contents

The Ski Tours
The tours are described from south to north in an arc around the alps.

Val Maira Day Tours by Martin Chester	35
Briançon and Queyras Day Tours by Al Powell	45
Mont Thabor by Mark Charlton	55
The Haute Maurienne by Andy Teasdale	61
Vanoise Traverse by Tim Blakemore	71
Gran Paradiso National Park by Andy Teasdale	81
Miage by Andy Perkins	91
Mont Blanc Ascent by Mark Charlton	101
Chamonix Day Tours by Jonny Baird	107
Chamonix-Zermatt Haute Route by Graham Frost	117
Mont Vélan by Bruce Goodlad	127
West Oberland Ski Haute Route by Terry Ralphs	133
Bernese Oberland Tour by Al Powell	145
Arolla Day Tours by Graham Frost	153
Val d'Anniviers Tour by Rob Collister	161
Monte Rosa Summits Tour by Olly Allen	169
Tour de Soleil by Olly Allen	177
Albula Alps Traverse by Bruce Goodlad	185
Ortler: The Cappuccino Tour by Mike Austin and Bruce Goodlad	193
Adamello by Cain Olsen	201
Stubai by Andy Perkins	209
Circuit of the Tofana – Dolomites by Martin Chester	217

Appendices ... 227
Appendix 1 – Variations on the Manuel Genswein Training Module ... 227
Appendix 2 – Kit list ... 228
Appendix 3 – First aid kit ... 230
Appendix 4 – Ski touring spares kit ... 231

Index ... 232

The Author and Publisher of this book would remind the reader that:
Ski touring and ski mountaineering are activities with a danger of personal injury or death. People participating in these activities should be aware of and accept these risks and be responsible for their own actions.
Every effort has been made to ensure that the content and instructions in this book cover all aspects of personal safety skills and techniques required in ski touring at beginner and up to intermediate level. The Author and Publisher cannot accept any responsibility for any accident, injury, loss or damage sustained while following any of the techniques described within.
If you feel that you need additional instruction in order to use this book then it is advised that you employ a suitably qualified and experienced mountain guide.

Heading for the Col Pale Rosse below the Grand Zebrù in the Ortler.

Ski Touring in the Alps

We can ski tour anywhere there is enough snow on the ground, and ski touring is happening all over the world. As a guide I have ski toured from the Arctic to the Antarctic and have been lucky enough to visit places as diverse as Japan and Armenia all on skis. So you may ask what is so unique and special about the European Alps? The answer is that there is no other mountain range on earth that has the incredible hut network and accessibility to high mountains that the ski areas in the Alps provide. There are many mountain huts in the world, but there are few other places where you can enjoy a hearty breakfast (well, bread and jam), wave goodbye to one guardian, and then eight hours later arrive at another hut, having had a great day's ski touring, to be greeted by a steaming cup of tea and then sit down to a three course dinner and wine, before settling in for a good night's sleep.

This hut network allows the ski tourer to travel up, over and through the mountains unencumbered with anything on their back other than their ski touring kit and essential safety equipment. Not having to carry any supplies other than the food for a day means you can glide through the mountains for days at a time with the minimum of effort. This allows the skier to enjoy the ups, as well as having the leg strength left to enjoy the downs.

When to ski tour in the Alps

Traditionally ski touring happened in the high mountains in the spring. This was because of a combination of factors. After the first big thaw and associated avalanche cycle the snow pack was much more stable, and as much of the touring was on glaciated terrain, we waited until later in the season when the glaciers were well covered in snow and the snow bridges were at their strongest. To a degree this is still the case in the high mountains, with the huts opening in early March when the glaciers have much of the winter's snowfall already lying on them.

However, this does not mean that you have to wait for the spring to go ski touring. As soon as the snow hits the ground you will see people out skiing; they just have to think about where and when they can tour.

It sounds obvious, but if the first few feet of snow in a season land on a hillside covered in big boulders then it will need a lot of snow to cover the boulders and allow you to ski. If the same snowfall lands on a grassy hillside then you will need far less snowfall to allow you to ski tour. When the first snow arrives I will look to go ski touring on the lower mountains where the ground allows us to ski without a huge depth of snow. This also has the advantage of generally more pleasant skiing conditions. The high mountains early in the season can be very cold, windy places, whereas the lower mountains with trees can be a much more pleasant place to start the ski season.

Brian O'Connor skiing cold winter snow on the descent from Mont Rogneux.

Early season ski touring is predominantly day tours, but the huts in some areas like the Queyras and Val Clarée open as soon as there is enough snow to tour, so in an average season this can be from early January or even December onwards.

As the season progresses, the more rocky areas will fill in, and many classic day tours are possible from January onwards. If you are looking to the higher mountains, the Silvretta huts in Austria open mid February, then the higher glaciated huts open from early March, most of them staying open until early May. The highest huts in areas like the Bernese Oberland stay open until the end of May or even into June, and the best ski touring conditions on the highest peaks like Mont Blanc can be mid April onwards, depending on the season.

Travelling to the Alps

It is always best to travel hopefully but have a plan B and C at the ready. So when you are planning your trip, think about how you will rearrange your logistics should the weather and conditions not let you carry out plan A. The key to this is not only having plan B and C, but being able to get to it.

Ski Touring in the Alps

I once had a trip booked to do a ski tour starting in Meiringen in northern Switzerland. I met the team there with a terrible forecast that was going to kick in after the first day. Luckily we had enough cars that we could change the plan. We spent the first day doing a brilliant day tour in good weather, then with a strong, disturbed northerly airstream we drove five hours south, escaped the weather and skinned to the Benevolo hut in the Gran Paradiso. We spent the rest of the week skiing great snow in the sun, whereas if we had stayed put we would have achieved very little. This relocation did require having enough vehicles, as doing it by public transport would have been almost impossible. I am not suggesting that you should drive from the UK, or always hire a car, but it is worth thinking about how to relocate should the weather dictate.

Mateo Maino skiing down from Mont Vélan in perfect spring snow.

How to use this book

The objective of this book is threefold: to inspire you to get your skins and skis out of the cupboard and get into the mountains; to make sure you have the skills you need to ski tour effectively and safely; and to suggest some amazing places to go ski touring.

Each ski tour has been selected by a mountain guide who has done the ski tour and has shared their experiences of the tour with the reader. Each tour includes a brief description of the tour, an overview map, its highlights and an overall flavour for the area. It then goes on to outline the best time of year to ski the tour, where you can find hut and accommodation information, weather and avalanche forecasts and other useful information. There is then a day-by-day tour description, with each day broken down into its key sections. We will not lead you by the nose through the tour; the description needs to be studied with a map. There are no GPS coordinates, so you will need to study the tour and put your own tour plan together. While it may seem as if this is the information that should be supplied in this book, it is only by studying the map that you will become intimate with the tour and its possibilities, making your life easier when on the mountain. (See also Tour Planning.)

Maps

We have included an overview map for each tour. This is not intended to replace the local topographic map for the tour, but it has enough detail to give you an overview of the area and help you to orientate the map. You will notice that the maps use a variety of scales; this has been necessary so that each tour will fit on a page or double page spread, so it is essential that you look at the local maps as some of the scales will not be ones that you may have come across before.

Ski tour grading

Most guidebooks use a grading system to help you select an appropriate tour for your experience, the weather and conditions. Any scale is extremely subjective and the same tour will never feel the same on any two days – the grading is given for 'average conditions'. Average conditions would mean the average conditions that a particular ski tour would be done in, so for example, if it's a glacial tour then mid season with a good covering of snow on the glacier.

There are a number of tour grading systems out there that all end up in roughly the same place, so rather than presenting the systems we can look at the terrain and then give the grade that will match. The three grading scales we will look at are the Blanchère, Traynard and that used by the Swiss Alpine Club (CAS). The latter can be particularly confusing if you are a mountaineer, as they use the same nomenclature as the Alpine Mountaineering grading system. To make life easier we will describe the terrain then mark up all the possible grades that it may equate to, though the Traynard scale is usually used to describe the steepest section of skiing on a tour and is often combined with the Blanchère. I have included the Blanchère in French, German and Italian as these are the languages that many of the ski texts are in.

Ski mountaineering

When you move into ski mountaineering terrain where you will need crampons, ice axe, use of a rope and crevasse rescue knowledge, the Blanchère Scale extends to:

	Terrain up to 30 degrees with basic mountaineering skills	SAM – Skier Alpiniste Moyen MAS – Mittlere Alpineskifahrer MSA – Medio Sciatore Alpinista
	Terrain 30 to 35 degrees and more advanced mountaineering terrain that may require short pitches of climbing.	BSA – Bonne skier alpiniste GAS – Gute Alpineskifahrer BSA – Buon Sciatore Alpinista
	Terrain over 35 degrees and necessary use of mountaineering techniques such as abseiling.	TBSA – Tres Bonne Skier alpiniste SGAS – Sehr Gute Alpineskifahrer OAS – Ottimo Sciatore Alpinista

Ski touring kit takes us to amazing places – ski touring in the Vallée Blanche.

Ski Touring Kit

Ski touring kit has changed massively in recent years making it more accessible than ever for people to go into the backcountry. We are not going to look in depth at kit, but just run through a checklist with a few key considerations.

Ski kit

Skis
A classic mid fat-ski in the 90–100mm width range is probably the most versatile all-round ski as it will cope with off-piste skiing as well as touring in all conditions. If you go wider you may find the ski a bit awkward in firm snow conditions; if you go narrower the ski will be lighter but may be more challenging in deep, soft snow.

Dynastar Mythic a classic all-round ski.

Ski Touring Kit

Bindings

These can be split into pin or frame bindings. Pin (or low tech) bindings are much lighter and give a more natural stride when skinning, but with a few exceptions do not offer an adjustable toe release. Frame bindings will work with downhill boots and any ski boot without tech fittings, but they are much heavier and not as easy to use.

A Dynafit pin binding.

Boots

Modern touring boots range from Alpine boots with tech fittings to allow the use of low tech bindings, to boots designed for ski mountaineering racing which are so light you can run uphill but they are a challenge to ski downhill in. Have a think about what is most important to you, performance downhill or weight uphill; you need to marry this to your ski ability. If you are a pretty basic skier then a lightweight boot will make the skiing more challenging, so when you are buying boots be very honest with the boot fitter about your ability and aspirations.

A selection of touring boots. Left to right: soft and light to heavier and stiffer.

Skins

Lots of ski manufacturers now sell skins pre-cut for their own skis. If you can't get pre-cut skins, then a shop will do it for you, or it is pretty easy to shape them yourself. One consideration is the choice of attachment. Most skins now have a tip and tail, but there is a choice of adhesive between a traditional glue or the new silicon compound which is meant to be easier to look after. I have considered all these options and keep coming back to glue, as it is easier to maintain in the field and I have had multiple sets of silicon skins fail completely year after year when touring in Japan (cold conditions with lots of snow).

Putting skins on.

Ski crampons

This a piece of kit that you will carry for years, then try to put on somewhere really awkward when you should have put them on much earlier. So make sure you take them with you and put them on in plenty time. Watch how the team in front is coping, as this will be a guide as to when to put yours on.

Poles

I would not get too hung up on having adjustable ski poles as they often decide to adjust when you don't want them to, but it's nice to have the option to extend them for poling or skating down a long, flat valley. Fixed length poles are cheaper and stronger. Some grip tape below the handle, to make them easier to hold on a traverse, is a worthy addition.

Using ski crampons.

Ski Touring Kit

Avalanche rescue kit

Avalanche rescue kit will not stop you from getting avalanched. Only a solid avalanche skill set and sound route planning will help you do this, but regular practise will mean that if you are involved in an incident, rescue will be as swift and smooth as possible. Remember that for a good chance of survival you need to have the victim on the surface in less than 15 minutes.

Transceiver, shovel, probe and skins.

Transceiver
All transceivers work on the same frequency so they are compatible. I would strongly suggest only using a three-antenna beacon, as these have been around for a few years and are the units that will save lives the fastest. Start every tour with a battery over 90%.

Shovel
Only use a metal shovel as anything else won't dig in real avalanche debris.

Probe
Take a 240cm minimum alloy probe – if it's carbon, unless it has a wide cross section, it will be deflected in the debris. The styles that lock with a single pull when deployed are the fastest to get ready.

Airbag
Airbags have become lighter and lighter in recent years and you will see people touring with them, but they are still generally difficult to pack and there is a significant weight penalty. Personally I prefer good avalanche mitigation and a lighter pack when touring, but everyone must make their own decision.

An inflated airbag.

Crevasse rescue kit

It is essential to have two sets of crevasse rescue kit and two ropes in any party. If the team decides to skimp on weight and only takes one rope, you are going to feel pretty silly if you are carrying the rope and you are in the bottom of the crevasse.

There has been a move to thinner, no-stretch or 'hyperstatic' ropes in crevasse rescue. These are great because they are lighter and take up far less room in your rucksack, and the fact that they do not stretch also means that hauling out a victim is more efficient. There are of course drawbacks, as a 6mm rope (such as the Petzl RAD system) can only be effectively gripped using mechanical devices such as a Petzl Micro Traxion and a Petzl Tibloc. Normal prusik loops and knots are very unlikely to bite on this

Ski Touring Kit

type of rope, so your kit should match the rope you are carrying. If you do choose a hyperstatic rope make sure you have practised with it, and be very aware that its static nature (unlike a standard climbing rope which stretches to absorb impact) means that it cannot be used in a lead climbing situation due to the forces that can be generated. Personally, I will carry one 30m hyperstatic rope and one 30m 8mm standard climbing rope in the party. This allows most situations to be covered.

Full crevasse rescue kit – two per team

Each person carrying a rope should carry this kit.

- Rope – 30m rope (see discussion above).
- Mechanical devices – Petzl Micro Traxion (with screw-gate karabiner) and Petzl Tibloc (carried on a DMM Revolver), this allows thin ropes to be used, as well as reducing friction and increasing mechanical advantage. You can use a prusik in place of these to save money and a bit of weight, but make sure they work on your rope.
- DMM Revolver karabiner – this reduces friction in a pulley system.
- 2 ice screws – if you can reach ice this is the strongest anchor. Carry them on a single snapgate karabiner.
- 2 x 8ft (120cm) slings with snapgate karabiners – the type of sling like an Edelrid Aramid does not absorb water and so is easier to untie if it has been loaded with a knot in it.
- 3 x screwgate karabiners – I usually carry two HMS (also known as pear-shaped) models and one standard model.

Crevasse rescue kit.

Personal glacier travel kit

Should you fall into a crevasse unroped, this will allow you to place an ice screw in the sidewall and attach yourself so you are safe while awaiting rescue.
- Harness – there are some great lightweight models designed for ski touring.
- Ice screw – on a snapgate karabiner.
- 8ft (120cm) sling – see notes above, on a snapgate karabiner.
- 2 screwgate karabiners.

Personal crevasse rescue kit.

Ski Touring Kit

Mountaineering kit

Many of the tours in this book do not require anything other than ski touring kit, but to ascend some of the summits covered you will need to add an ice axe and a pair of crampons, with the knowledge how to use them.

Crampons
A clip-on pair that will fit easily onto your ski boots. My personal favourites have a steel front part and an aluminium rear, which is a good balance between robustness and weight. Having an anti-balling plate (stops snow build up) makes them easier to use.

Crampons on a ski boot.

Ice axe
A short (50cm) lightweight ski touring axe is easier to carry on your pack than a longer, heavier more traditional ice axe.

Clothing

The layering system is the most versatile for ski touring, especially in the spring when the mornings can be cold, yet by early afternoon, when you are heading back to the hut, it can be really warm. I am a big fan of softshell as it is really comfortable to ski in, being weather resistant, breathable and more flexible than a hardshell.

The following is a spring ski touring list. If I am touring in the early part of the winter I will add beefier hardshell trousers that will be worn all day and more layers on my top half.

A ski touring axe.

Starting at the feet
- Socks – most blisters can be traced to poor sock choice. In my experience a good quality, pure wool sock is the best. Don't be afraid to throw them away when they get worn or baggy as this can cause blisters. If you think you are prone to blisters, tape preventatively before you go out the door; it's much easier than doing it on the hill.
- Softshell trousers – models with vents are the most versatile.
- Hardshell trousers – to wear on top of your softshell should the weather be really bad. Should be as light as possible as they will hopefully spend much of their time in your rucksack.
- Base layer top – merino wool is amazing for this as it doesn't smell, a real consideration on a week's hut-to-hut trip.

James Thacker ski touring in softshell near Mont Thabor.

Ski Touring Kit

- Softshell top with hood – if it is cold I will wear a thin fleece under this.
- Hardshell jacket – with a hood.
- Down or synthetic insulated jacket – this should fit on top of everything else.
- Gloves – A thin pair for skinning and a thicker pair for skiing. If the forecast is cold I will add a pair of mitts. Wrist warmers can be a great way of adding warmth to your glove system. The blood supply to the hand is very close to the surface at the wrists, so wrist warmers helps keep these, and hence your hands, warm.
- Hat – warm hat and sun hat.

Miscellaneous

- Sun glasses – I will usually carry a spare pair with orange lenses as these are really good in flat light.
- Ski goggles – if you can find a stiff case they will last a lot longer.
- Sun cream – I use a high factor all the time 30+ SPF as a minimum.
- Lip protection – as above.
- Water bottle or flask – I use a 1 litre Thermos for much of the season, then in the spring I use a 0.5 litre Thermos and a 1 litre flexible bottle for water. Having a flexible bottle makes it easier to pack.
- Insurance certificate – even a photocopy will make life much easier should you have an accident.
- Camera.
- Rucksack – depending on the length of trip you may need to vary this – I have a 35 litre sack that I use for everything from day tours to a week's hut-to-hut adventure. The style I find best has a safety pocket for shovel and probe (these should **never** be on the outside of your pack as they will be ripped off in an avalanche) and multiple attachment points for skis. See the Avalanche rescue kit section for a discussion on airbags.

Extra kit for hut trips

When going on a hut trip there are a few extra bits of kit to bring along.
- Sheet sleeping bag – this is a requirement in most huts for hygiene reasons, but they also give a better night's sleep should the blankets be itchy. Silk models pack the smallest.
- Headtorch – even if you are not planning to be out in the dark you may end up doing so by mistake; and you will need it to find the toilet in the hut in the dark.
- Toothbrush and paste – it is worth finding out if the huts you will be visiting have running water or even a shower. If they do I will add in a small wash kit.
- Moisturiser for face and lips – this helps recovery after a long day in the sun.
- Book or Kindle – I like reading in the evening in a hut so having a book is a nice thing. A Kindle or e-reader is about the same weight and means that you should never run out of something to read.
- Wet wipes – while not particularly environmentally friendly they can make a tour without running water significantly more pleasurable. Having said that, when I took some to Greenland, they froze solid at the start of the trip and thawed on the way home.
- Clean T shirt – having a dry, non-sweaty T shirt to change into at the hut is a nice luxury if you have the space.

Group kit

This can be spread out in the party.

Group shelter
Should you be caught out this will save your life! You should have enough capacity for everyone in your group. There are some amazing lightweight models available now so there is no excuse for not carrying one.

First aid kit
This need not be elaborate but should have some barrier gloves, wound dressings, crepe bandage to sort out a knee, some tape for blisters (and many other things), and some pain relief. Israeli bandages are superb as they come in a foil packet so they survive in your rucksack – search online. (See Appendix 3 at the back of this book.)

A group shelter protecting a skier with a broken leg while waiting for rescue.

Spares kit
You need enough kit to get you home should you break a binding or have a ski problem. I usually carry: a selection of strong cable ties, some wire, a metal scraper, roll of physio tape (duct tape goes brittle and doesn't work very well in the cold), some emergency skin glue, a couple of spare binding screws and a couple of nuts and bolts to cobble together some minor ski boot repairs.
Multitool – used for everything from cutting cheese to repairing ski bindings. They are quite heavy so one in the team should be fine.

Navigation equipment
Ideally there should be two sets of this in the party so you can check each other's navigation. Options include map, compass and GPS with digital mapping. There is some great mapping software available for smart phones which is really quick and easy to use on the hill, as the phone will fit easily into your pocket. I would just make sure you have the paper map in your bag and have at least one phone switched off and away, should you need to make an emergency call. Personally I use phone-based mapping a lot for its convenience, and have a satellite phone in my pack as a back-up.

Secondary communication
This is worth consideration. Cell phone coverage is pretty impressive in Europe, especially if you can see a ski area, but some areas like the Écrins have no coverage at all, so it is worth thinking about how you will call for rescue should you need to. I carry a satellite phone, but this is a big investment and an alternative is a VHF radio with the emergency channel (Channel E) programmed into it. If there is no cell phone coverage make sure you have discussed an emergency plan as part of your tour planning.

Ski Touring Kit

Specialist equipment

Should the weather be really bad, or there is no phone reception and someone has an injury, you may need to evacuate the casualty yourself, or at least be able to move him or her to a place where you can await rescue. A good exercise is to see if you can make a useable stretcher using the kit you have with you. If not, consider augmenting your spares kit to have the stuff you may need. A selection of rubber ski straps is one of the most useful bits of kit you can carry – if everyone in the team has one then you are sorted.

One piece of specialist kit I carry all the time is the BCA Shaxe. This clever piece of kit is a metal-bladed shovel with a really strong, well-designed blade, whose handle can be removed and fitted with an ice axe head. This may sound like a gimmick but it is actually a really good ice axe, one that I have used for the last couple of winters ski guiding. Should you need to make a stretcher, you can bolt the shovel blade onto the front of a pair of skis, then the shaft across the tails, then cross-brace using ski poles and ski straps and you have a usable stretcher. K2 skis come with pre-drilled holes so you can do this, but it is a really easy job to drill a hole in the tip and tail of your skis, then seal the edges of the hole with epoxy. The hole only needs to be big enough to fit the bolts that come with the kit and makes no difference to the skis' performance. Once drilled and sealed I fill the hole with ski wax to make sure there won't be any water getting into the ski. (On really remote tours I add part of a Brooks-Range sled system, as this makes it easier to transport a casualty should you need to travel any real distance.)

A BCA Shaxe system.

Ski touring near Les Contamines.

Skills Check

This isn't a how-to section – all these skills are covered in great detail in *Ski Touring* – but a check that you are comfortable with the key skills you will need to undertake any of the tours in this book. We have split them into groups to make it easier for you to access them.

Uphill skiing skills

An ability to skin effectively and carry out smooth and efficient kick turns is an essential part of any ski tourer's skill set. I am constantly amazed by the number people I see in the mountains who can't make an effective kick turn; the only reason I can fathom is a lack of willingness to take the time to practise. If you aren't very good at them find a slope and practise.

The use of ski crampons is another area where people seem reluctant to engage with the kit they are carrying. It is almost an unwritten law that people wait until they are exposed on a steep icy slope before they try and put on their ski crampons. Look at the terrain ahead and get clues from how other parties are moving. If the snow looks firm, icy or you can see other people slipping about, put your ski crampons on where it is easy and comfortable to do so.

Kick turn.

Skills Check

Downhill skiing skills

An ability to ski downhill in most snow conditions is to my mind an essential for enjoying ski touring safely. That is not to say that you can't go ski touring with lesser downhill ski experience and ability, because you can, and many people do, but their enjoyment of the downhill element of the ski tour is massively diminished. In addition, poor downhill ski technique greatly increases the chance of injury with all the associated issues of rescue and long-term withdrawal from the sport as your body heals.

Neil Stevenson skiing downhill in touring kit.

While all time spent on skis improves your ability to move around the mountain effectively, the only way to improve your downhill technique is by skiing downhill with some good quality coaching. Alison Thackers's chapter in *Ski Touring* will give you some good pointers, but book learning is no substitute for time on snow. Many people think because they can get where they want to go they have had enough instruction, but many very experienced skiers, myself included, take regular ski lessons, as there are always areas of our skiing to work on and we will never stop learning.

As a minimum you should have coping strategies to deal with most types of snow including breakable crust. Even if the strategy is just traverse and downhill kick turn, at least you have a strategy.

Movement on foot / crampons

If you are from a ski rather than a mountaineering background, one of the most intimidating things you can do is to take your skis off and move about on foot. If you want to extend your ski touring into what could be described as ski mountaineering, there will come a point where you have to leave your skis and climb to a summit in boots. If the snow is icy, you will need to attach crampons to your boots so that you can reach your summit.

Trying to climb a 4000m peak in the middle of the Bernese Oberland is not the best place to learn how to put crampons on for the first time, so make time to practise these skills. You may even want to consider a course where you can develop these skills before taking them into the bigger mountains.

If you want to move onto more exposed summits, you may need a rope, and if you are going to use a rope ask yourself the question "What is this rope adding to our safety?" If you can't answer this question, or the only thing you can rationalise is that the rope will ensure that you all die if someone slips, then you need to have a think about how to use a rope, or ask someone who knows to teach you.

Glacier skiing

Many of the tours in this book involve skiing on glaciers; this is an incredibly beautiful place to ski and is one of the unique features of skiing in the high mountains. Skiing on glaciers does have inherent risks – glaciers have crevasses and some of them are incredibly deep; deep enough that if you fall in one they may not even be able to recover your body. While glaciers are to a degree a little bit predictable as to where you will find crevasses, there is always a rogue crevasse where you didn't expect it, so you need to be sure about reading terrain and not be afraid to ski on a rope if the visibility is poor or you just aren't comfortable.

Skiing on glaciated terrain does require the knowledge to be able to rope up, ski with a rope on in ascent (relatively easy) and descent (really difficult), and rescue someone from a crevasse should they fall in (roped and unroped).

A natural avalanche in Tignes.

Avalanche Safety and Rescue

Mike Austin and Bruce Goodlad

This is a massive topic that we explored in some detail in *Ski Touring*. We will not repeat that here, but would like to give you six key things to think about before and during your tour planning and while on tour. This is based on the widely used Know Before You Go avalanche awareness program developed in the US (check out www.kbyg.org).

Get the gear and know how to use it

I will not leave a controlled ski piste with anyone who does not have a three-antenna avalanche beacon, a metal shovel and an avalanche probe at least 240cm in length. This is the basic off-piste safety equipment everyone should carry. If you do anything but ski within easy access of a piste or lift I would add a set of skins to my essential safety kit. If you have skins and you arrive somewhere you don't like, you can climb out. No skins and you are committed to going downhill.

Essential avalanche safety equipment.

Avalanche Safety and Rescue

Carrying the safety kit is nothing without the knowledge and the practice to use it. Even if you know how to use it, make sure your ski partners do as well. If they don't you can give them some basic training in as little as 15 minutes (see Appendix 1). Even if you ski with your avalanche safety kit all the time you need to keep practising with it. A great tool is to set up scenarios for each other in awkward terrain, this is much more fun and more realistic than the practice you see most people doing.

A selection of modern transceivers.

Companion avalanche rescue

If anyone in your team is avalanched you have 15 minutes to rescue him or her, so you need a practised rescue strategy. Here are some key points. If you see the avalanche make sure you watch where the victim goes and lock into your brain where the last point they were seen is.

1. Appoint a leader to coordinate and direct.

2. Ensure it is safe to get involved.

3. All but the searchers turn off their beacons.

4. Start searching from the last seen point using a search pattern that ensures the entire debris is covered on the first pass.

5. Communicate. Do you have a signal? What distance? etc.

6. Once you have a signal locked on, follow it in while the others get out shovels and probes.

7. Start probing at the lowest reading, remember to probe at right angles to the surface.

8. When you get a positive probe strike leave the probe in place.

9. Move downhill and dig out the victim using strategic shovelling.

If you didn't see the avalanche you need to get the number of victims and the last seen point by interviewing any witnesses.

Unless you have spare manpower, you cannot afford the time to call for rescue until all victims have been dug out.

Avalanche Safety and Rescue

Rescue search pattern. Illustration – AvalancheGeeks.

Get educated

Avalanche hazard evaluation is not learnt by osmosis from being in the mountains; the victim or their party triggers 90% of avalanches involving humans, so you need to learn about avalanches. If you don't know what the avalanche problem is going to be on any given day, then you need to go and learn about the avalanche phenomenon and how we interact with it as backcountry skiers.

Avalanche education is not book learning, you need to mix theory with practice so you can understand at least basic snow stability and probably most importantly, terrain.

There is great quote from avalanche forecaster Drew Hardesty, "If snow stability is the question, then terrain is the answer". If you can recognise safe, low consequence terrain then you can spend your entire ski career keeping safe with very limited knowledge of snow pack stability. If you don't understand terrain or snow stability you are playing Russian roulette every time you go into the mountains.

So, educate yourself either by going out with more experienced hill goers or by taking a course.

Taking an avalanche class.

Avalanche Safety and Rescue

Get the avalanche forecast

Getting the avalanche forecast is one thing, but making sure you read and interpret it and relate it to where you are thinking about going skiing is a whole lot more.

It is essential to remember that an avalanche forecast is just that, a forecast. It is based on observations and a weather forecast, so if the weather forecast is wrong then the avalanche forecast may well be wrong.

When you head into the hills you need to remember that the forecast covers a region, not a specific slope, and that the longer you are from the forecast date the less accurate it will be. The question I always ask myself when I go skiing is, "Does what I'm seeing on the ground relate to the forecast?" By asking this simple question you can start to gauge the accuracy of the forecast.

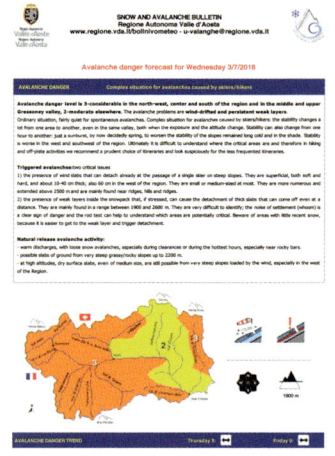

An avalanche forecast from the Val d'Aosta.

Get feedback from the mountain

What can you see on your drive to the mountain or when you are looking out of the window of the hut while eating breakfast? Is there any wind? Is there any snow moving about? If so, where is it going? Is there any new snow either by wind transportation or new snowfall? When I get out of the car or come out of the hut, I am asking myself: how cold is it, what are the clouds doing, does it look like we may get new snow? I am constantly questioning everything I see and adding the information to my data bank about the snow pack and hence its stability. When on the mountain I am then looking for Red Flags that are key signs of instability – recent avalanche activity, sudden collapses, whoomfing sounds and shooting cracks.

With the wind blowing the snow across the ridge and depositing slab on the north-east side, it was pretty obvious where we shouldn't ski.

Get out of harm's way

When we ski around the mountains, as well as looking at clues to stability, I ask myself, "What if?" The snow I am standing on is connected to a big slope above me; what's keeping it there and if it did slide where would the snow go and what would happen to me? Sounds really obvious, but sometimes people lack a bit of imagination. With lots of new snow and wind there is going to be a wind slab avalanche hazard on lee slopes, but if you don't know what a lee slope is it is going to be pretty hard to avoid. Standing at the bottom of one, while a bunch of muppets who know even less than you do about avalanche hazard evaluation ski onto the slope above, isn't a great idea. I will be looking to get myself out of harm's way, either altogether or hiding behind, or on, an island of safety until the muppets have passed.

If you are in any doubt about the stability adopt safe travel techniques; ski one at a time spotting one another. Only use islands of safety if they really will protect you in the event of an avalanche. If the slope is big and there is nowhere to hide then ski the whole thing one at a time then get out of the way.

Mike Austin spots the author skiing in avalanche terrain.

Bruce Duncan and Mike Austin execute a well-planned ski tour above Tignes.

Tour Planning

As I mentioned earlier in the book, we have deliberately not given you any GPS coordinates or downloads where you can plug a tour into a GPS and follow it blindly through the mountains. Studying the map and identifying the overall route, then highlighting key places that may need extra attention, is an essential part of tour planning. At the planning stage you should be able to identify everything, from where you may be able to leave your car to how are you going to escape from this deep, narrow avalanche-prone valley when it has just snowed 60cm.

Our tour descriptions give you enough information to be able to plot your route through the mountains in conjunction with the local map, and any key pieces of information about the route and what equipment you may need. It will also point you in the direction of accommodation providers in the area, as well as sources of avalanche forecasts and any other useful pieces of information. Armed with all this information you should be able to put a thorough tour plan together. In many areas there are other guidebooks available, which may give some additional information. While we strive to have the most up-to-date information, it doesn't do any harm to have more.

Tour Planning

Your tour plan

If you have never done a tour plan before don't worry, the concept is simple. Before setting out on the tour you want make sure you have studied the map and description in enough detail that you have a good idea about what is going to be around every corner when actually on the tour. You will have plotted the route on your GPS, so that anywhere you need a little navigational aid it is easy to access. On the map you have already plotted the route and marked on the compass bearings, so when the visibility is poor and the wind is strong you just need to read them off the map, dial them into your compass and go. You will also have worked out how long each stage will take, so you will know what time of day you need to be at key stages. Knowing all this will ensure that you start at the right time and have built in a margin of safety.

You will also have highlighted areas of concern, or 'key places', where you need to be extra vigilant or the decision-making needs to be spot on.

Timing

Timings are a key element to any tour, and pretty difficult to estimate accurately as there are so many variables. If the weather is nice, the snow good, you are feeling fresh and there is a well-set track to follow, then you will fly along. If you have to break trail and navigate then it is unlikely that you will travel at the same speed. As outlined above we have made a conscious decision not to include this information with each tour. It is an essential part of any tour plan that you study the terrain in enough detail to calculate approximately how long each stage of your tour will take.

There are all sorts of complicated ways of calculating the timings. Personally I find a good rule of thumb is about 300m of height gain per hour, unless it is a long, horizontal distance with not much up, then I use about 3km per hour. In descent I usually allow 1000m per hour unless the terrain is complicated. If there is a short descent I don't count it. I then adjust it once I see how we are moving.

This is way too vague for lots of people, so if you prefer you can use a more scientific method, developed by Werner Munter. His system involves breaking your tour into legs, which you will do anyway when looking at the navigation. He assigns units for distance travelled and height gained or lost:

- One unit is assigned for each 1km travelled horizontally.
- One unit is assigned for each 100m of height – gained or lost.
- Add the units up to gain a total for ascent and descent.
- Divide the uphill total by 4, and multiply by 60 (minutes) to get an uphill time.
- Divide the downhill total by 10, and multiply by 60 (minutes) for a downhill time.

Example in ascent

If we use an example of a ski touring leg where we skin for 2km with a height gain of 300m, then we have total of 5 units. Divide this by 4, to give us 1.25, then multiply this by 60 (minutes) to give a time, in this case 75 minutes.

Example in descent

We are going to ski down 400m over 3km, so 7 units divided by 10, which is 0.7, multiply by 60 (minutes) is 42 minutes.

Tour Planning

You do this for all the legs, then add them together to get a time for your day out. The conditions and the team will affect the timing dramatically, so these numbers are just a starting point that you can then vary as you develop a sense of your speed through the mountains.

It is always worth building a contingency into your timing. Planning to finish the tour as it gets dark doesn't leave any margin for error. If you plan to finish an hour or so before dark you will have that time spare if you need it.

Alternatives

A big part of my tour planning is tracking the snow and avalanche conditions in the area you are going to visit. This is really easy in the Alps using the internet, so you should have a good idea about the snow pack before you arrive in the area. A bit of a dig about in the snow on arrival is always useful to confirm what you think should be there. When you have this knowledge you can decide, given the weather as well as the avalanche forecast, if your tour is viable. There is nothing wrong with arriving in a valley, having a look at the snow pack, and deciding this is not for me this year. As part of my tour plan I will have identified a number of alternatives so it is really easy to slip into Plan B or C. If you don't have a Plan B or C you will probably push on regardless. With a high avalanche hazard the alternative may be as simple as skiing around the local ski resort, but at least it is a plan that you will have discussed before arriving in the area.

Fatmap

There are some amazing tour planning aids – one of my favourite is Fatmap. You can access digital maps from around the world, enabling you to plot your route on the map then shade areas over 30 degrees (perfect avalanche terrain); you can highlight details such as altitudes etc., and you can even 'fly' through your route so you have a good idea about what you are going to see on the ground. It is also possible to download a GPX file of your route and upload it straight onto a GPS. This even works in really remote parts of the world, so even if you are skiing somewhere with no maps you can get a good feel for the terrain prior to arrival.

Tour planning using Fatmap.

Evacuation plan

A big part of this tour planning should be, "What am I going to do if someone breaks a leg and I can't get a mobile phone signal, or the weather is too bad for a helicopter to fly?" If you don't have a plan or the kit to enact one then you need to make one. (See also Rescue plan below.)

Tour Planning

Leaving the Pizzini hut heading out for a day's touring.

Using mountain huts

As we have discussed earlier, the hut network in the Alps is one of the things that makes the Alps so unique; it is worth knowing a little bit about how huts work. An Alpine club (Swiss, French, or Italian etc.) owns most of the huts – there are also a number of private ones. The general financial arrangement is that when you pay the bill, the accommodation part goes to the Alpine club, and the restaurant part goes to the hut guardians. The busy popular huts then pay a levy that goes to support the more remote, less frequented, huts.

When planning a tour it is essential to pre-book the huts. This is especially the case if you are planning to ski a popular tour like the Haute Route or ski at a busy holiday time. If you book well ahead of time then change your plans because of weather or snow conditions, the hut guardian will not mind you cancelling, as long as you do so as soon as you make the decision not to come. Calling at lunchtime on the day you were meant to arrive to say you are going elsewhere is not good, as the guardian will have already started to prepare dinner for your team and this food will go to waste.

If you have booked a hut and can't make it, or decide to change your plan, it is essential that you do cancel your reservation. If you don't turn up, the guardian may assume that you got into difficulty and call a rescue. In certain countries, particularly Switzerland, you will be liable for the cost of the search, which may prove to be rather expensive. If this does occur your insurance company may choose not to support you or pay.

While all mountain huts are slightly different, they all run on the same principles. When you arrive, there will be somewhere to store your skis, either indoors or on a rack outside. There will then be a boot room where you can change from ski boots to hut slippers; most huts provide these, but check the hut descriptions for any extra information. It is worth splitting the labour here, so while someone sorts the skis, someone else can change their footwear and check in with the hut guardian. While doing this it is worth leaving your sack and all sharp objects in the boot room! When you arrive they will register your team and the guardian will assign you bed spaces for the night; this may be specific bed spaces or just a room. They will let you know what time dinner and breakfast are (usually dependent on your plan for the next day). The guardian will also let you know where skins and other pieces of kit can be dried and where sharp objects like ice axes should be left.

Some huts are really busy, so keep an eye on where you leave your kit – with so much stuff lying about the wrong kit can easily be taken in the morning. It is worth swapping a boot with a team member so no one can take one of your boots by mistake. When kit is drying, as soon as it is dry, pack it away in your rucksack so it won't get lost or confused with someone else's stuff. Write your name on skins and other kit and keep track of it.

When ordering extras like water, beer or lunch, some huts will want you to pay for everything as you go, and some huts would prefer that you pay for everything together the night before you leave. You just have to go with the system in each hut. Some huts will have no running water and only sell you boiling water by the litre, which isn't too expensive, or bottles of mineral water, which can be pretty expensive. A top tip is to bring your own tea bags and coffee sachets – that way you can just buy hot water, which is much cheaper than buying individual teas and coffees.

Most hut guardians will have their own idiosyncrasies, so while they may be frustrating at times you just have to run with it; it's their hut and they have designed a system that makes it work 'efficiently' for them. A popular hut on the Haute Route may have 130 guests per night passing through, who all want to be fed and watered, so be patient if the guardian looks a little fraught around dinner time.

Rescue plan

In the mountains you should always hope for the best and plan for the worst, so that you can enact any rescue plan easily. We have already discussed improvised stretchers and communications, but having a phone signal is no use unless you know what number to call.
For rescue numbers see below.
When you do call make sure you have the following information ready:
- Location, including grid reference
- Number of casualties
- Nature of injuries
- Number in party
- Your phone number (they will probably get this from their system)
- Weather at the scene – most mountain rescue in the Alps happens by helicopter, so local weather is really important.

When someone is injured it is amazing how quickly they and everyone else will get cold. Have everyone put on more clothing straight away and as soon as it is practical to do so get everyone into a group shelter. Not only is a group shelter surprisingly warm, it is also a great boost for moral.

If, as you read this, you are asking yourself what you would do with someone with a broken leg, maybe it is time to go on a mountain first aid course.

Tour Planning

Calling for help in the mountains

If you do need to call for outside assistance, you need to have the means to do this and the correct numbers available. A cell phone is great in most situations, but you need to be aware that if you don't have line of sight on a mast then you are unlikely to get a signal. Most ski areas have masts on top of the higher lifts so it is surprising where you can get a signal. When you are planning your tour it is worth thinking about your options if you can't get a signal. I carry an Iridium satellite phone, but this is an expensive 'piece of mind'. The standard rescue number from a mobile phone in Europe is 112 but this doesn't work in every country – for example if you are in Italy the number is 118, if you are in the Valais region of Switzerland the number is 144. I have outlined the numbers below country by country, they are correct at the time of going to press but it is worth checking. An alternative if you are on a hut-to-hut ski tour is to call the nearest hut. This can often save time as they can often best explain to rescue services where you are.

When I was an aspirant guide, I had to call a rescue on the Weissmies. After losing about 500m in altitude in order to get a phone signal, I called the Almageller hut, explained the problem and asked them to call for a rescue. I explained that there was no phone reception at the site of the accident and that would re-ascend to the casualties. They then called and helped coordinate the rescue services.

France
In France the Gendarmerie du Haute Montagne (PGHM), which is the police, carries out rescues. The service is completely professional with their own helicopters. You can dial 112 and ask for mountain rescue, or better still, dial one the direct rescue numbers outlined below. This number will put you through to the rescue centre directly; the numbers are different for specific parts of France.

Savoie
PGHM de Modane: +33 4 79 05 18 04
PGHM Bourg St Maurice: +33 4 79 07 01 10

Haute Savoie
PGHM de Chamonix: +33 4 50 53 16 89
PGHM Annecy: +33 4 50 09 47 47

Hautes Alpes
PGHM de Briançon: +33 4 92 21 58 58

Isère et Drôme
PGHM de Grenoble: +33 4 76 77 57 70

Switzerland
In Switzerland rescue is coordinated by REGA which employs local guides to perform the rescue. In some areas they use their own helicopters and in others they use local companies e.g. Air Zermatt or Air Glacier in the Valais.
144 in the Valais
1414 for Swiss Rescue Service REGA
REGA has also produced an app that will allow you to request assistance and automatically sends your

Tour Planning

GPS position (assuming you have phone reception).
iREGA for iPhone http://itunes.apple.com/ch/app/irega/id415358154
iREGA for Android https://play.google.com/store/apps/details?id=ch.rega.Rega&hl=en

Italy
The rescue services in Italy use a variety of agencies depending on the region.
118 (except for Valle d'Aosta)
Valle d'Aosta +39 0165 238 222
You need to **keep the '0'** of the area code when calling Italian phone numbers.

Austria
112 for general emergencies
140 for Austria Mountain Rescue Services
144 in Vorarlberg

> There is an excellent app called Echo 112, which can send your location and call for help to the local rescue services. Switzerland is particularly keen on this system.

Helen and Iain Muir in the Val Maira.

Helen Muir enjoying some great powder in the Val Maira.

Val Maira Day Tours

By Martin Chester

Area overview

Val Maira is nestled in the bulge on the Italian / French border, about 100 miles south-west of Turin. It is just south of Monte Viso, with the Queyras over the border to the north-west. To the south-west is the Mercantour National Park and we are to the north of Isola 2000 on the main Alpine frontier chain. While it might be a long way south, the snow conditions are remarkably reliable here, with a wacky micro-climate dumping plentiful powder on this side of the range throughout the early winter.

Val Maira is a long, curving valley, running mostly east-west for 45 kilometres before curving north at the end. There are numerous side-valleys that shoot off the main feature, all adding up to provide a plethora of ski touring options on every aspect. With the valley floor at 1000 to 1600 metres above sea level, and the summits ranging from 2300 to 3400m, the valley is the perfect scale for day tours – from the mellow to the adventurous. Typical days out will involve at least 1000m of skinning, but you can usually ensure a greater descent by choosing a linear trip from a high starting point to a lower pick-up at the end of the day.

Within this relatively small corner of the Alps you can find almost every type of terrain imaginable. Wide, open slopes offer amazing spring snow to the north of Elva and Acceglio. The major peaks of the frontier ridge offer everything from classic couloirs to exposed ridges and mountaineering summits. But if the snow keeps falling and the avalanche risk mounts up, you can always find easy-angled, tree-covered slopes up as high as 2500m – so there is always something safe and enjoyable to do, whatever the weather gods throw at you.

A number of day tours are described, to demonstrate the variety of the area. As such they can be adapted and undertaken in any order to suit the conditions.

Val Maira Day Tours

Grade
A collection of day tours with a range of difficulties – see the description for each day.

Season
Ski touring is possible here from the first snows of the winter to the early spring. The season is usually at its best here from early February to mid March.

Map
Esquiar en Val Maira 1:20000 sheet by Bruno Rosano. This excellent map has all the classic ski tours marked on it with colour grading.

Kit
These peaks are not glaciated, so lightweight ski touring day packs are adequate. Mountaineering equipment (rope, harness, crampons, axe etc.) can be added to suit the requirements of any mountaineering or steep skiing objectives.

Weather forecast
www.meteomont.gov.it/infoMeteo/index.do?inglese=true and your favourite weather app!

Avalanche forecast
www.arpa.piemonte.gov.it/englishversion
www.meteomont.gov.it/infoMeteo/index.do?inglese=true

Hotel information
The Hotel Londra is a popular choice, run by ski touring enthusiast Alessandro Bolfi.
Info@hotel-londra.eu
Another popular choice is the Pensione Ceaglio
www.ceaglio-vallemaira.it/index.php?lang=GB
Both hotels offer plenty of information regarding routes, conditions and transfers.

Useful information
Val Maira tourist information
www.vallemaira.org/en/tag/tourist-information/
Sort any ski rental equipment before you come, either in Cuneo www.ravaschietto.com/ or in the UK at Outdoor Hire www.outdoorhire.co.uk/snow.php

Alternative guide books
The excellent guide book, *Charamoi mai en Val Maira* by Bruno Rosano is a true labour of love. It is only available in Italian and German, but with photos, illustrations and details this good, it hardly matters.
It is complemented by a superb annotated map *Esquiar en Val Maira* that gives you a lifetime's worth of information in one magnificent 1:20000 sheet.
At the time of writing, these are readily available in the valley, but not so easy to pick up in the UK.

Val Maira Day Tours

Iain Muir descending Monte Ruissas.

Day tour 1 – Monte Ruissas

Grade F S2 SM	Starting altitude 1510m	
Aspect SW	Ascent 1230m	Descent 1230m

The north peak of Monte Ruissas is a great first day for any visitor to the valley. The route is obvious and uncomplicated, the open slopes give expansive views all the way to the summit (which provides a great viewpoint across the rest of the valley), and you return by a variation on the skinning line.

Start at the end of the cleared road in Lausetto (1510m) and follow the snow-covered road until it meets the river (1590m). Cross over and loosely follow the line of the summer road (as snow conditions dictate) to the first collection of buildings. Here you can follow the line of least resistance to the collection of buildings at Gr Durazza Sopra (1815m). Skin across open slopes, heading towards the top corner of the obvious stand of trees. The slopes ease in angle and open up to reveal the faint summit of Monte Cappel. Pass this on the right (leaving the high point on your left) to gain the broad col below the twin peaks of Monte Ruissas. These upper slopes are often ravaged by wind and sun, so pick the line of best snow cover to gain the ridge, and the marginally higher north peak. In descent, follow the rough line of skinning track or, if spring snow conditions prevail and your timing is right, traverse under the south peak to access the open south-facing bowl below. From c. 2500m traverse diagonally right (west) to regain the broad col and pass the high ground of Monte Cappel. From here the open slopes await and you can straighten out the line of ascent to enjoy a great ski back to Durazza to pick up the road back to the valley.

Val Maira Day Tours

The final skin on the traverse of the Col d'Enchiausa.

Day tour 2 – Traverse of the Col d'Enchiausa

Grade PD S3 PD	**Starting altitude** 1485m	
Aspects NE, WNW and N	**Ascent** 1260m	**Descent** 1210m

An ideal second day in Val Maira is to complete one of the classic tours of the valley. The traverse of the Col d'Enchiausa is a long journey that allows you to explore the wealth of options in the area, and proves there is more to skiing in Val Maira than day tours to bag summits. From the car park in Chialvetta, a veritable hub of the valley where a great number of tours begin, skin up the frequented track to the hamlet of Pratorotondo. Follow the main skinning track (in common with many routes) past Viviere to pick up the switchbacks in the summer road. Follow the route of least resistance to point 1840m, where a prominent flattening in the gradient of the path coincides with an obvious bend and a summer trail sign to the Valle and Col d'Enchiausa. Take care not to blindly follow the wrong skinning track from here on, as many routes diverge in this area.

Skin up and over the flat plateau, taking care to identify the ridgeline of Arpet and the prominent feature of point 2285m. At 2130m, three paths fork, so be sure to take the central fork into the bowl of the true Valle Enchiausa. Skin up the right-hand flank of the hanging bowl above, to access the upper valley by passing to the right of Bric Mouliniere. The valley now stretches out again before you, with obvious route finding, to steepen and access the Col d'Enchiausa (2736m) at last.

A short, steep descent quickly eases to give mellow skiing on north-west facing slopes into the Valle d'Apsoi. A prominent roll (short steepening) at 2530m marks the start of the long descending traverse to the right (north) to reach the prominent shoulder above the north-east tip of Lago Apsoi, and traverse round above the Bonelli bivouac hut. Keep enough height on the traverse and it should be possible to easily ski to the east, to crest the edge of the flat area without too much effort. The shallow valley (and broad ridge to its left) is north-facing and often contains fantastic snow, shaded by the ridgeline above. Ski, with pleasure, down the slopes to Visaisa Sopra. Then either, keep enough height and stay left with enough speed to gain the Visaisa lake, or milk every last roll through the trees and pole down the track. The lake will often be frozen, but make a judgement whether to skin around or across on the day (1900m).

Any hotel you are staying in should be able to organise a taxi pick-up.

Day tour 3 – Bric Boscasso

Grade PD S3 BS	**Starting altitude** 1485m	
Aspect NW	**Ascent** 1110m	**Descent** 1110m

You will, by now, have realised that the main focal hub in the valley is undoubtedly the bustling hamlet of Chialvetta. This is a starting point for a huge number of routes and gives you the best range of options on a day when you cannot decide. Just set off and let the conditions (and the other parties) dictate where to go, or where to avoid. Most teams head for the classic peaks of Bric Cassin and Monte Vanclava, which are great, leaving the quieter summits of Soleglio Bue or Bric Boscasso for those seeking fresh tracks.

Follow the common start from the previous route, to the bridge before Pratorotondo. Turn left across the river, widely passing the small Cassin chapel. Locate the open slope between the two streams. A prominent rocky crag will be obvious before you. Pass to the left of this to gain La Bandia Longa. Skin gently through trees and clearings. As you come out of the trees for the last time

Enjoying some great powder on Monte Midia Sopra.

(c. 2300m) the wide, open bowl will funnel you towards the ridge of Bric Boscasso. After gaining the prominent col where you can leave your skis, a short bootpack up the narrow ridge yields a rewardingly small summit with excellent views.

From the ski depot, you have a choice of descents: down the far side to Preit (if you have arranged a taxi); return by the route of ascent; or the best route in good snow is to descend the Cumbal Vallonetto (described below), taking a parallel line to the south of the ascent route.

Pole and push south along the ridge to gain the col at 2534m. A number of lines are possible, so let the conditions and best snow dictate the best line into the wide bowl. All tracks funnel together to the prominent stream junction and small flat area where two valleys meet at c. 2100m. From here, loosely follow the line of the stream, staying on the left bank as the stream bed deepens. When you reach the next stream junction (c. 1850m) be ready to break out left into more open slopes. A steepening at 1750m will bring you back to the line of the stream. It is easy to be drawn down the riverbed all the way – but some steep, rocky steps make this challenging in this lower section. Once past the craggy spot height (c. 1800m) on your right, the tight valley quickly opens out to regain the mellow pastures of the ascent. Ski back to the bridge and follow the tracks back to Chialvetta.

Day tour 4 – Monte Estelletta and Monte Midia Sopra

Grade F S2 SM	Starting altitude 1401m	
Aspects N and E	Ascent 1000m	Descent 1000m

Sooner or later you are bound to get a day of bad weather. When you do, be reassured that the Val Maira has a number of routes that provide superb tree-skiing (in well-spaced mature larch forest) on easy-angled slopes. Furthermore, being so far south, the tree line reaches up to 2350m in places. An ideal choice is the ascent of Monte Estelletta, continuing to the summit of Monte Midia Sopra if conditions and aspirations allow.

From the car park in Ponte Maira (in front of the café) cross the ski de fond area, past the pavilion, to enter the woods. There is a faint summer track which is often followed on snowshoes, but this is not such a good skinning line. Work your way up by any route to pass the farm buildings of Grangia Rossetto at 1534m. From here you take the line of least resistance between the stream beds, generally keeping right (west) to avoid most of the steeper rolls and occasional crags in the woods. Resist the temptation to swing left too soon as the skinning is easier on the open slopes to the right, and this will leave the good snow for the descent. Undulating and fiddly terrain soon yields to the open slopes above the forest as the slope eases, and you come out of the trees to skin the final, open slopes to Monte Estelletta.

Ski off to the north, following the broad ridge after a short step before putting the skins back on. The keen may ski a few pitches down the enticing meadows before going back up for more. The ridge-line of Monte Midia Sopra has a flat area, where you can leave your skis (at 2300m), before a short, sharp and exposed ridge leads, on foot, to a summit cross. If you are here on a clear day, the views from these summits (and especially down over the valley to Acceglio) are stunning.

From the ski depot, savour the meadows below before descending into the trees. It is possible to straighten out the line of ascent a little to get fresh tracks, but be sure to get across the Rio Selletta before too long to join the environs of the skinning track. Great skiing in well-spaced trees leads back past the farm buildings for a well-earned beer at the café and car park.

Val Maira Day Tours

Matching turns on the descent from Monte Soubeyran.

Day tour 5 – Monte Soubeyran

Grade PD S2 BS for the easiest line; S3-S4 for the steeper descents		**Starting altitude** 1539m
Aspects W, N and S	**Ascent** 1160m	**Descent** 1160m

This is a great trip weaving through some spectacular terrain, providing a number of options for steeper descents on return.

Park near the bridge just north of the lake beyond Saretto (1539m). An easy skin over open slopes soon leads to the steeper switchbacks of the road past Sorgente Pausa (1920m). Take time to check out the conditions of the appealing couloirs above and left of you as you skin this section – they are options for the way down. Let the valley (and road, if obvious) funnel you upwards to the flat area below Grangia Pausa. From here, hug the left flank to curl around Point Bessie to the south, then east of you. The slope eases again before a switchback up a steeper roll to gain a flat shoulder above the first of the prominent couloirs.

Cresting another small rise, head SSE toward Punta le Teste and the end of this mellow valley. Near the end, curl right (west) to gain the final bowl under Rocciasetto to gain the col at 2539m.

Skin diagonally up the right-hand slopes of this open bowl, aiming to gain the ridge below Monte Soubeyran at c. 2650m before the final 50m climb to the summit. You may have to do this on crampons depending on the conditions.

From the summit, there are a number of options for the descent, depending on conditions and ski ability. The easiest line is to return via the skinning route without difficulty or surprise.

A lofty traverse under the summit ridge to the north will give access to the col between Monte Soubeyran and the Aiguille de Barsin (2627m). From here, a steeper descent to the north-east will soon regain the skinning line at the prominent flat area above 2350m.

From this point where both routes come together, you can re-evaluate your options: continue via the route of ascent; or take one of the enticing couloirs spied on the ascent at the start of the day. The left-hand (north-westerly) is the least serious of the two and gives a great ski. Cruise easily northwards down the upper bowl, to gather at the start of the steeper ground. An initial roll hides the terrain from view, but not for long. Ski the obvious line of the couloir (35 to 40) knowing you are able to pass either side of the rocky divide halfway down. All too soon you will regain the switchback road and the skinning line, to ski the scrub-covered slopes back to the car.

Day tour 6 – Monte Cervet

Grade PD S2 BS	**Starting altitude** 1631m	
Aspect S and NW	**Ascent** 1350m	**Descent** 1350m

At the head of the valley, above Chiaperra, the terrain starts to feel much more rugged and wild. From here, the quintessential peaks of Monte Eighier, Monte Cervet and Monte Freide come into reach. These are great days out, and feel longer and more serious than those lower down the valley. With the right conditions and the correct timing (with an early start) this tour on Monte Cervet can provide powder and spring snow in equal measure.

From Ponte Soubeyran, the rocky ridgeline of Rocca Provenzale is obvious. Work your way up to gain the hanging valley to the right (east) of this feature. Follow the easiest line (usually on the right side) but being careful to recognise the threat from the slopes of Monte Boulliagna above and right. Before the angle eases to the col (at about 2150m), turn right to skin up the faint bowl, which steeply guards access to the hanging valley above. Quickly gain the plateau of the lake at 2461m before curving round to the right. Follow the obvious valley south-east at a steady gradient to the Passo di Cervet at 2861m. From the col turn left (north) away from the south ridge, taking the easiest-angled terrain across to the north-west ridge. These slopes are often hammered by the wind, and you may need to proceed on foot, depending on conditions. Follow the easiest line up the ridge (increasingly rocky) to gain the summit. Again – this is a stunning viewpoint.

For the descent, follow the line of ascent to gain the Passo di Cervet. Enjoy the great skiing in this north-west facing bowl, before carefully turning left. You are now heading onto steep south-facing slopes, so be aware of the temperature and increased risk if you are late or it is especially hot. Once in the south-facing valley, it is often possible to enjoy fine spring snow back down to the car at Ponte Soubeyran.

Possible variants or alternatives

There are endless variations and combinations in this valley, so buy the local guide book and map, then let conditions and local knowledge steer you.

Val Maira Day Tours

About Martin Chester

www.martinchester.co.uk

As an International (IFMGA) Mountain and Ski Guide, kayak coach, and previously the Director of Training at Plas y Brenin (National Mountain Centre), Martin is one of the most experienced and highly qualified professionals in the outdoor industry. While he may be a jack-of-all-trades across the spectrum of adventure sports, skiing is his primary passion and self-confessed 'desert island' activity. Martin originally fell in love with skiing as a way to explore the Alps in winter – exploring the nooks and crannies of the mountains with his wife to be. Exploration and adventure has been a constant theme since, leading guided ski trips from the obscure corners of the Alps to the Himalaya, and everywhere in between.

Martin has a passion for helping others to fulfil their potential in challenging environments, and has played a key role in the development of coach education and leadership awards for numerous National Governing Bodies of sport. He is now the Coaching Development Officer for Mountain Training UK, has been involved in developing UK avalanche education, and been a technical expert for both the BMG and BBC following avalanche incidents. Martin wrote, produced, and presented the educational *Off Piste Essentials* DVD for the British Mountaineering Council, provided the climbing expertise and coaching for Hidden Talent on Channel 4, and has made numerous appearances as a subject matter expert for the BBC on TV and radio. He is the backcountry editor for Fall-line Skiing magazine and has been a regular contributor to the outdoor press.

Martin now enjoys a diverse range of work – all connected by making great things happen in the great outdoors. Whether that is as a Guide with a wide range of private clients, or as an industry expert helping organisations fulfil their potential. He can be found via www.martinchester.co.uk and is always up for a great adventure or interesting project.

Blue skies and fresh powder, another great day in the Queyras.

Briançon and Queyras Day Tours

By Al Powell

Area overview

There are arguably more ski tours within an hour of Briançon than any other region in the Alps, and as a consequence the area has an active population of local ski tourers who are out skinning all winter long. Lying in the southern French Alps, larch forests predominate in the area, making it an excellent venue for early season powder touring; this is why I start my ski season down here every winter! The following tours just scratch the surface of what's available, but are a number of good, local tours that offer reliable skiing in a range of conditions. Local conditions forums are a great place to find out more.

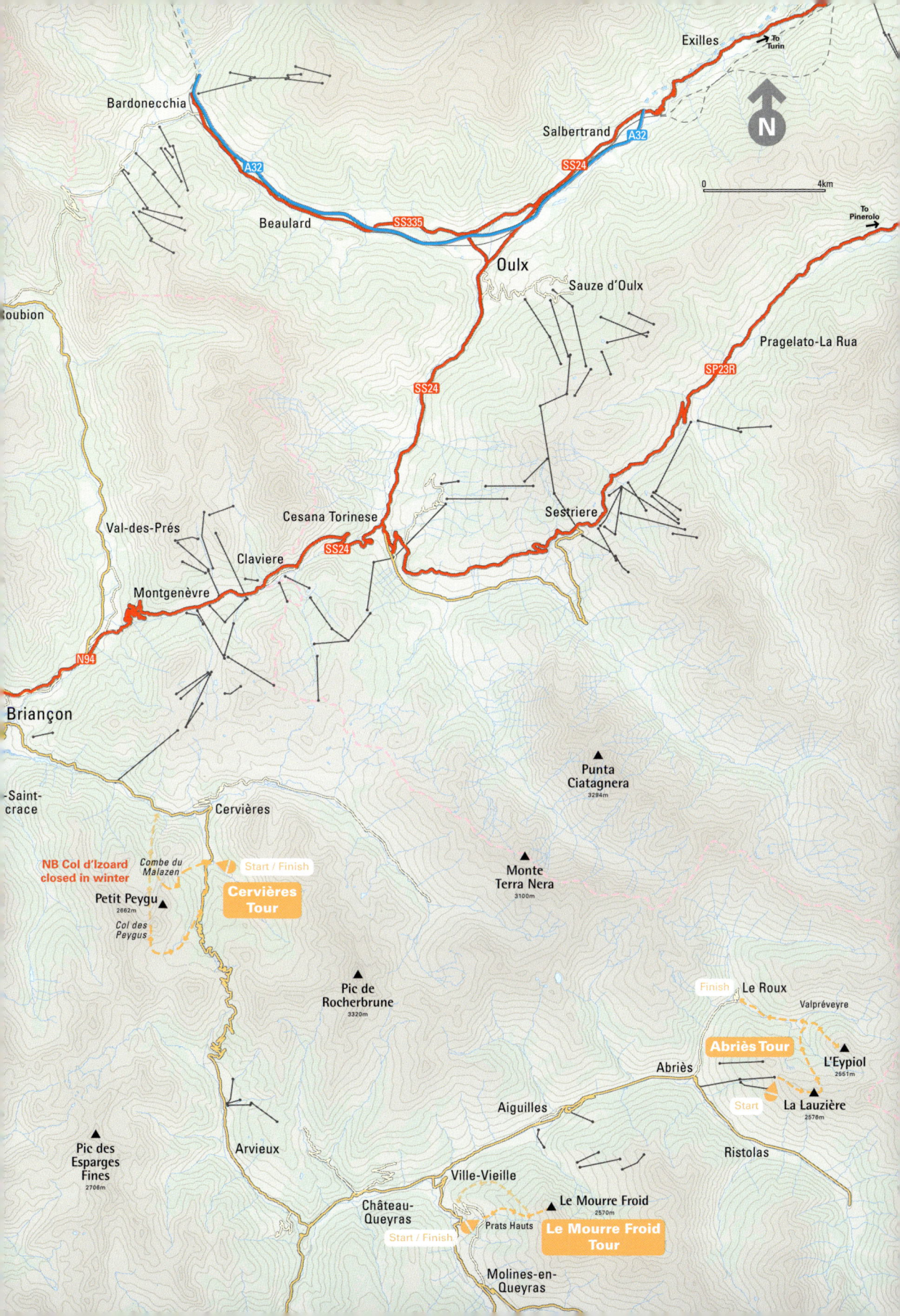

Briançon and Queyras Day Tours

Grade
Various – see individual tour descriptions.

Season
December to May

Maps
IGN Briançon 3536 OT, IGN Valloire 3435 ET, IGN Meije Pelvoux 3436 ET, IGN Orcières Merlette 3437 ET and IGN Mont Viso 3637 OT

Kit
Classic ski touring kit – ice axe and crampons are only needed where indicated in the tour description. Glacier travel and crevasse rescue kit are not required.

Weather forecast
www.meteofrance.com

Avalanche forecast
www.meteofrance.com

Useful information
www.camptocamp.org – excellent source of information about local ski tours and current conditions in the region.
www.gites-refuges.com – information about gites in the region.
www.queyras-montagne.com – Queyras tourist information

Alternative guide books
Ski de Randonée Haute Alpes – Editions Olizane (French Language)
Queyras - Toponeige

Day tour 1 – Col du Lautaret – Pic Blanc du Galibier (2955m)

Grade PD S3-S4 BS	**Starting altitude** 1980m	
Aspect SE	**Ascent** 975m	**Descent** 975m
Season December to May	**Map** Valloire 3435 ET	

With a high start point and long season, this classic ski summit is justifiably popular and gets skied all through the winter, offering great summit views of the nearby Écrins Massif to the south and a distant Mont Blanc to the north. The tour only takes half a day, so if you've got energy to spare, there are numerous other half-day tours starting at the Col du Lauteret.

Park 1.5km before the summit of the Col du Lautaret on the Briançon side, just past the gite at Les Sestrières and before the large bend and paravalanche shelter. A reasonably early start is required, as the decent faces south-east.

Head north for 1km following the Torrent du Galibier to point 2176m, before crossing the stream and branching leftwards (heading NW) up into a small valley overlooked by steep cliffs (potential terrain trap). Cross the summer road at point 2451m and continue in the same direction, heading to the final, steeper summit slope. **Attention:** this final slope starts at 35°, rising to nearly 40° at the top and is exposed when icy – ski crampons and/or boot crampons may be needed to reach the summit. The descent follows the same line as the ascent – take care on the initial steep slope and don't forget to visit the café at the Col du Lautaret!

Alternatives

Col du Galibier (2624m)

| Grade PD- S3 BS | Aspect S | Ascent 650m | Descent 650m |

Park as above. A shorter, less steep alternative to the Pic Blanc. Only the final slope up to the col is above 30°. Start as per the Pic Blanc, but continue directly north up to the Col du Galibier.

Col de Laurichard

| Grade PD S3-S4 BS-TBS | Aspect N and E | Ascent 600m | Descent 600m |

Park at Col du Lautaret. Head south from the Col du Lautaret, climbing a steeper section (30°) to gain the Combe de Laurichard. Skin up this (**attention:** large, steep slopes above you to the right) to a final short, steeper section (35°+) leading up to the col.

Vallon de Combeynot and Col des Clochettes

| Grade F-PD, S2-S4 BS-TBS | Aspect N, W, E | Ascent 300-400m | Descent 300-400m |

Park at Col du Lautaret. Head south-east from the Col du Lautaret – the lower reaches of the Vallon de Combeynot are sub 30° and a safe spot to ski in most conditions. The Col des Clochettes to the east (near point 2549m) is steeper (S3-S4) and in stable conditions offers a great descent down its east side S3-S4 – eventually arriving at the road 4km below the col.
Note: two cars are useful if you do this tour.

Day tour 2 – Cervières – Col des Peygus and Combe du Malazen

Grade PD S3 BS	Starting altitude 1750m	
Aspects all	Ascent 700-1100m	Descent 700-1100m
Season December to April	Map Briançon 3536 OT	

Set in a high dead-end valley, Cervières is a wonderful and peaceful spot to enjoy a day's ski touring. The tours described can either be done separately, joined together, or via a good variation if you have two vehicles available (or you don't mind a bit more hiking at the end of the day!).

Park at the road-end hamlet of Le Laus, 2km south of Cervières, which lies 10km east of Briançon on the D902 road to the Col d'Izoard (closed in winter). Finding the right road out of Briançon is the hardest part! Follow signs to Col d'Izoard, then drive 2km past Cervières to Le Laus – car park on the right just before the buildings.

Briançon and Queyras Day Tours

Approaching the Col des Peygus.   *Powder slopes on the north side of the Col des Peygus.*

Combe du Malazen

| Grade PD- S2-S3 BS | Aspect NE | Ascent 700m |

An excellent, shorter half-day tour with good skiing, hence it's popular. Skin west from Le Laus up into the woods, then south-west up the Combe du Malazen. A steeper section at about 2200m is turned by joining a spur on the left, which then leads up to a flatter section at the top of the forest. Finally, head rightwards (NW) up the steep top slope (over 30°) to the ridge at point 2426m. Ski down the same way.

Col des Peygus

| Grade F+ S2 BS | Aspects all | Ascent 850m |

An easy-angled tour through lovely scenery – combining this with the Combe du Malazen (or variations), makes it a longer, more interesting tour. Skin south up the road for 4km to just beyond point 2117m, where a path on the right leads up out of the forest to the Chalets d'Izoard. Continue 1km west across easy-angled ground, before climbing (avoidable) steeper slopes and turning right to head north up to the Col des Peygus at 2612m (all sub 30°).

Descents

South face

| Grade S2 | Aspects S and E | Descent 850m |

Ski back down the same way – easy-angled skiing all the way.

North face via Combe du Malazen

| Grade S3 | Descent 1100m |

Ski down the north side of the Col des Peygus (30° – **attention:** steep slopes above you on the left) then continue down north for 2km to just beyond point 2279m. Put skins back on and climb east (steep slope 35°) onto the Crête de la Lausette. The old fort here is worth a visit, before climbing south up the ridge to point 2426m and joining the Combe du Malazen descent back to Le Laus.

North face via Combe de la Lause

Grade S3 **Descent** 850-1100m

A great tour if you have two cars (or don't mind the hike back up to Le Laus!). Ski north off the col as for above and continue down north into the forest. The steeper section below point 2131m is 35°+, but sheltered and partly in trees. At point 1892m, if cover is good continue straight down to point 1514m, otherwise take the old military road past point 1806m just to the west. Cross the bridge at point 1514m and either walk and skin back up to Le Laus, or split two vehicles ready for the return.

Alternatives

There are numerous other good ski tours in this area; visit www.camptocamp.org or see the *Queyras Toponeige* guidebook for details.

Day tour 3 – Puy-St-Vincent – Col du Bal and Crête de Reychard

Grade PD S3 BS	**Starting altitude** 1400m	
Aspects N and E	**Ascent** 600m	**Descent** 1900m
Season January to March	**Maps** Orcières Merlette 3437 ET, Meije Pelvoux 3436 ET	

Puy-St-Vincent is small family ski station 15km south-west of Briançon. However, it also has some of the best freeride terrain in the area and a great lift-assisted day tour.

Drive south on the N94 from Briançon and take either the D4 back road to Les Vigneaux, or the D994E up from L'Argentière-la-Bessée and follow signs to the lower ski station, Puy-St-Vincent 1400. Park here, buy a pass and don't forget to pick up a piste map.

Head up through the lift system (plenty of good off-piste terrain) to the top of the highest lift, La Pendine. From here, hike or skin 10 minutes to the summit of La Pendine (2749m). Now, ski WSW for 1km down and along the Crête de la Pendine to the Col du Bal. **Note:** this ridge can be serious and exposed in icy conditions and occasionally requires crampons – take care. From the Col du Bal, drop due north down long, open slopes (S3, 300m at 25-35, superb in powder) into the Combe de Narreyroux. Stay on the left side of the valley to Narreyroux d'Amont. **Note:** If avalanche or snow conditions on the Col du Bal are of concern, then the same point can be reached more safely by skiing northwards past the top of the Téléskis des Lauzes, then dropping left off the ridge and skiing north down through the forest. From Narreyroux d'Amont, skin north up to Serre la Barre, then south-west up the Crête de Reychard. Most teams stop at the top of the forest at about 2300m, but you also can go further.

Descents

If the snow level is low and you have two cars, position one in the valley floor near Vallouise at the start of the day, then ski right down to the valley floor at 1200m – this is a superb descent! It may also be possible to organise a taxi / bus for return – speak to the tourist information office.

Otherwise, ski down through the forest to no lower than 1900m altitude, then traverse rightwards back down to Narreyroux d'Amont. Cross the stream in the valley floor and skin / pole / hike along the return run track to a fork in the path just beyond an uphill clearing. Take the lower track down to Le Rouchas and the road at La Balme, hike 200m up the road, and rejoin the piste where it passes through a tunnel under the road and ski back down to Puy-St-Vincent 1400.

Day tour 4 – Crête de la Seyte

Grade PD S3 BS	Starting altitude 1250m	
Aspect NE	Ascent 1350m	Descent 1350m
Season January to April	Map Orcières Merlette 3437 ET	

A long and reliable tour with a good north-facing descent. Don't be put off by the apparently low starting altitude; because the lower section follows forest roads, the tour can usually be completed both early and late in the season.

Drive 15km south from Briançon to L'Argentière-la-Bessée, then just after the railway bridge take the small road leading up into the Fournel valley – this is usually ploughed up to the car park near l'Eychaillon.

Skin up the road for 1.5km and cross the bridge to the south side, then just beyond a second bridge, head left up a forest road. Follow this past the first two bends, then near point 1386m head north-west up through the forest. If snow cover is thin, continue up the road to 1600 or 1700m before joining the ridge on the left.

Carry on up through the forest past point 1952m, eventually reaching open ground at 2200m where a cross becomes visible on the ridge above. Either head up to the cross, or go diagonally rightwards to join the snowy ridge beyond and skin up this as far as possible (around 2600m). This final section is about 30° – possibility of wind slab.

Descents

Ski back down the same way. If snow cover is thin, rejoin and follow the forest road on the lower section.

Alternatively, the steep Combal des Prés lies directly below the summit and gives a good descent in stable conditions (300m at S4). Ski down to 2100m where the angle eases, then traverse diagonally right and rejoin the normal route at about 1700m.

Day tour 5 – Le Mourre Froid (2570m)

Grade F S2 MS	Starting altitude 1780m	
Aspects E and N	Ascent 800-1000m	Descent 800-1000m
Season December to April	Map Mont Viso 3637 OT	

Located in the heart of the Queyras, the Mourre Froid has all the ingredients of a good ski tour – reliable conditions, a quiet location, steady ascent, great views and excellent skiing.

The tour starts at the tiny hamlet of Prats Hauts. Drive to Guillestre 25km south of Briançon, then follow the D947 up into the Queyras as far as the roundabout at Ville Vieille. Turn right here heading for St-Veran, then after 2km take a sharp left up the small road leading to Prats Hauts. Park on the left at the edge of the village.

Skin NE up meadows behind the village, heading for a ridge in the woods above. Follow this and continue east up the fall line to the top of the forest and a flat spot at 2200m. Above, the summit slopes just reach 30° in their steepest part, before easing off near the highest point.

Descent

Either ski back down the same way, or far better, ski down to the flat spot at 2200m, then turn right and drop into the north-facing Forêt de Chanteloube. Head WNW down 'vallons' and bowls as far as the

Briançon and Queyras Day Tours

La Lauzière powder.

forest track at point 1605m. Turn left, put skins on and follow the track back around the hill to the road at point 1592m, before skinning or hiking back up to Prats Hauts. Note: With two cars, one can be left at the first bend above Vieille Ville (point 1434m) to enjoy an even longer descent.

Alternative – La Gardiole (2786m)

| Grade F S2 MS | Aspects E and NE | Ascent 1000m |

La Gardiole lies 1km south of Le Mourre Froid and can be climbed either from Prats Hauts, or starting from Gaudissart 2km to the south. Both routes give excellent skiing down long, open, sub 30° slopes.

Day tour 6 – Abriès – La Lauzière and L'Eypiol

Grade F S2-S3 MS	Starting altitude 1550m	
Aspects S,N and W	Ascent 850m	Descent 1550m
Season December to April	Map Mont Viso 3637 OT	

A great lift-assisted day tour, with two excellent north-facing descents. L'Eypiol is known locally as a safe place to tour after a large dump of snow. Likewise, if a large storm is ongoing, then the off-piste tree skiing at Abriès is some of the best in the Alps.

The tour starts at the small ski station of Abriès. From Briançon, drive south to Guillestre, then follow the D947 up into the Queyras to Abriès. Drive through the village and park just past the lifts.

Buy a forfait 'ski de rando' and pick up a piste map. First take the chairlift, then the Téléski de la Collette (in front of you on the right). From the top of the lift, skin up and right along the south flank of the Crête de Gilly to the Sommet de la Lauzière (steepest sections approaching 30°). From the summit, ski down the ridge beyond for 300m to just before small knoll. Drop left here onto the north-facing slope (30° to start) and ski down through woods and glades keeping to the left (W) of the Torrent d'Urine. Either cross the stream at around 1900m or rejoin the piste temporarily down to Valpréveyre. Now skin east up through the forest, then open ground above to the flat-topped summit of l'Eypiol (the top section is usually wind affected). Ski back down to Valpréveyre and follow the piste down to the road below le Roux. Here, a shuttle bus takes skiers back to Abriès (check times before you set off).

Alternative

If avalanche risk is of concern, the Sommet de la Lauzière can be bypassed by skiing the upper part of the black piste leading down to Valpréveyre. Pass through the col, then leave the piste just past here on the right, and either make a traverse or a short skin to pick up the descent off La Lauzière at the Clot de Besseys (point 2304m).

About Al Powell

www.alpine-guides.com

Al is a ski touring specialist and head ski guide for the guiding company Alpine Guides Ltd. He has lived in the mountains his whole life, both parents having been keen alpinists, which lead to a strong interest in winter mountaineering, alpinism and expeditions.

Like many climbers, skiing initially began as a means to access winter climbs, but while going through the guides' scheme Al began ski touring more seriously and eventually delved into the world of ski mountaineering racing, where he has competed at numerous internationals and two world championships.

Now older and (possibly?!) wiser, his skiing is still almost exclusively human-powered, touring throughout the winter with both clients and his two sons, who are both keen ski tourers.

Al has also kept up a running career, with highlights including winning the Elite course on both the LAMM and OMM Mountain Marathons and being the first Briton to run the Tour du Mont Blanc in under 24hrs (102 miles and 9000m ascent – that hurt!). More recently he has moved back to orienteering, having won the Veteran Home Internationals for Wales and numerous night orienteering races.

In the summer months he guides in the Alps and the rest of the year he lives in Yorkshire with his wife and family, where he maintains the company website while trying to spend as much time bouldering, running and riding bikes as possible.

Mateo Maino heading for the Rocher de la Grande Tempête above the Drayères hut.

Mont Thabor

By Mark Charlton

Tour overview

The Thabor Massif, situated on the French / Italian border between the Vanoise and the Écrins Alps, is one of those unknown ski touring destinations for the average British ski tourer. It offers some great skiing, pleasant huts and no glaciers. While to some people the attraction of skiing in the Alps is glaciated skiing, the lack of crevassed terrain allows you to ski with a lighter rucksack and extends the touring season, as you only need enough snow to cover the rocks, not fill in the holes.

The Névache side of the area which gives access to the Val Clarée offers some great touring on slightly lower peaks and has a whole hut network of its own, so is worth a look if you are not sure about committing to a circular tour. This circuit is accessible from three valley bases: Valfréjus, Névache and Bardoneccia, but the uplift at Valfréjus gives the best descent for effort.

Grade
AD S3 BS

Season
Mid February to end of April

Map
IGN 3535 OT Névache / Mont Thabor

Kit
Classic ski touring kit. There are no glaciers on this tour so you can ski with a lighter pack. It would be worth taking an ice axe and crampons.

Weather forecast
www.meteofrance.com then look up Montagne – Valfrejus

Avalanche forecast
www.valfrejus.com
www.meteofrance.com then go through Bulletins – Montagnes – Alpssud – Haute Alpes – Thabor

Hut information
Refuge du Thabor – www.refugeduthabor.com – +33 0479 203213
Refuge des Drayères – www.refugedesdrayeres.ffcam.fr – +33 0492 213601
Refuge I Re Magi – www.iremagi.it – +39 0349 6112920
(You need to **keep the '0'** of the area code when calling Italian phone numbers.)

Useful information
www.valfrejus.com – to check on lift opening

Alternative guide book
Vanoise Ski Touring by Paul Henderson, Cicerone

Day 1 – Valfréjus – Refuge du Mont Thabor

Grade PD S2 BS	Starting altitude 2731m	
Aspects all	Ascent 900m	Descent 1144m

Using the ski lift system at Valfréjus, with a one-way (Randonneurs) ski pass to the Punta Bagna, allows for an effortless ascent to 2731m. An easy leg-loosener on the piste follows, to just below the Col de Fréjus (2515m).

Here is the first climb of the tour to the Punta Nera (3046m) in a south-westerly direction.

The descent from here is in a large S-shape going from west to south and finally north around the rocky spur of Le Grand Argentier to around 2100m, one kilometre south of the Fontaine Froide. Skins are on from here.

A rising traverse NNW above the Fontaine Froide, leads to a level area where a swing left leads to a broad spur at 2290m. Follow this to the south-west, passing the Col de la Replanette (2338m) and point 2383m to the Col de la Vallée Étroite. A right turn SSW leads to the Refuge du Mont Thabor 2500m.

Mont Thabor

Leaving the Mont Thabor hut early in the morning.

Day 2 – Mont Thabor and the Refuge des Drayères

Grade AD S3 BS   **Aspects** S, E and N   **Ascent** 800m   **Descent** 1010m

The ascent of Mont Thabor starts with regaining the Col de la Vallée Étroite. From here, a descent south then south-west, takes you down to 2400m, where it's skins back on and a westerly ascending direction leads to the Lac du Peyron (2453m).

The rising cliffs on the south side of this vallon need to be passed on their eastern extremity and turned to follow the shelf of Les Chances du Peyron west to the Col des Méandes (2727m). Still in a westerly, then north-westerly direction, passing a cross at 2810m, you reach the Chapelle du Mont Thabor. This is an ideal place to take a rest before the summit, which is only a short distance away.

The descent passes back past the chapel before heading south into the combe to the east of the Pointe des Angelières (3093m), then gaining the Col de la Chapelle 2943m. A traverse below and on the north-west side of the Roc de Valmeinier leads to the Col de Valmeinier. Some skinning or a boot is needed here.

From the col, keeping a high traverse west then south, below the Roche du Chardonner (2950m), leads to point 2882m. Usually some pushing and sidestepping is required! Travel south down to the Col des Muandes (2828m).

From here, it's downhill in a south-westerly direction past point 2611m, past the Lac des Muandes (2580m), continuing west down the valley of the Muandes and eventually arriving at Refuge des Drayères from the north side. The last time I undertook this descent, it was on one ski, due to a binding / ski failure. A good tool kit at the refuge allowed the ski to be drilled and the binding relocated to finish the tour … but there was one tired leg!

Mont Thabor

John Dallinson and Dave Creighton arriving at the chapel on Mont Thabor.

Day 3 – Refuge des Drayères – Refuge I Re Magi

| Grade PD S2 BS | Aspects all | Ascent 900m | Descent 1320m |

An easy ski down the Val Clarée to the Refuge de Laval (2000m) should allow a gentle warm up before the 935m of ascent. From here it's skins on. Ascend in a north-easterly direction to 2200m, bear SSE past point 2228m and turning east at point 2205m to reach point 2304m. Head north-east from here, passing points 2430m, 2686m and 2725m and eventually reaching the Crête des Gardioles at the Pas du Lac Blanc (2935m).

Choose your line of descent according to snow conditions down to Lac Blanc (from between here and Pic du Lac Blanc at 2980 m). A slight push / side step leads you past the exit to the Lac Blanc and slightly north-east to Col du Vallon (2645m). Continue on due north down to point 2392m, then north-east below the Tête du Chien on its north side, passing point 2216m, also on its north side. Continue south of the footbridge at point 2118m, then south passing some buildings. Go east through breaks in the trees to the bottom of the valley and follow this down in a generally southerly direction to the Refuge I Re Magi (1785m).

Although still in France, with a typically great 'apero' time before dinner, the atmosphere in this hut is distinctly Italian. A strange border position after the 1st and 2nd World Wars has left this refuge in French territory, although it is on the Italian side of the mountain watershed and much more accessible from the Italian side via Bardonècchia.

Hot water and showers are available at the refuge.

Mont Thabor

Day 4 – Refuge I Re Magi – Valfréjus

| Grade PD S2 BS | Aspects S, NW and N | Ascent 700m | Descent 1500m |

Retracing the valley back to the Pont de la Fonderie and then heading due north up the valley base, brings us back towards the Col de la Vallée Étroite (2326m). Head ENE to reach the Col de Fontaine Froide (2509m).

From here it's downhill back to Valfréjus and the beginning of the tour.

If you have any energy left, the ascent from the Col de Fontaine Froide to the Col de la Bagna (2990m) to the south-east is a fun climb and ski. You may need to carry your skis for the final few hundred metres of ascent. Retrace your line of ascent and continue in a northerly direction past point 2458m and Fontaine Froide, eventually picking up the piste back to the station of Valfréjus.

Additional days

At four days this is a great outing making a very natural circuit. However it is also very easy to add in additional day tours and summits. The beauty of all of these extra tours is that you will be returning to the same hut so you can ski with a light pack. Peaks worth considering are:

From the Refuge du Mont Thabor – Pointe de Terre Rouge.

From the Refuge des Drayères – Rocher de la Grand Tempête or Roche Château.

About Mark Charlton

www.bmg.org.uk/guide/?mark-andrew-charlton#bio

Mark was born in the North East of England and was fortunate in having early access to skiing, as both his parents were teachers and they ran the school ski trips. So, early forays into Austria and Italy developed his love of adventuring. At the age of five on holiday in Austria, he managed to find his way off-piste, back to the hotel. Eventually his worried parents found him enjoying a strudel and hot chocolate, completely unaware of their concerns going on outside. These trips kindled a passion for all places wild.

As a teenager he climbed locally on the crags of County Durham, Northumberland, the Lake District and Scotland, progressing quickly to the bigger mountains of the European Alps and greater ranges by the age of 19.

Skiing remained a constant through these years as a pleasure in its own right, but also as access to more adventure.

The journey into a professional career started at Plas y Brenin in North Wales and Glenmore Lodge in Scotland through the mid to late 80s, culminating in achieving the full IFMGA carnet in 1990.

Working as a guide for nearly three decades, including training others to guide, has given him opportunities to mountaineer on all the continents of the world, exploring both local and faraway places.

He is currently President of the British Mountain Guides Association and he mainly lives in the Western Alps ... still exploring.

John Naismith descending from a col above the Glacier du Grand Mean.

The Haute Maurienne

By Andy Teasdale

Tour overview

The Haute Maurienne is far enough from many public transport hubs to require a little extra effort to get there. This worthwhile journey will deliver you to one of the nicest parts of the Alps in terms of ski touring, tranquillity and scenery. Bordering the Gran Paradiso National Park in Italy, the Haute Maurienne is home to a very special ski tour.

Starting from Bonneval-sur-Arc, this circuit visits three huts, crosses wild glaciers, peaks and passes before finishing in Bessans. It is possible to access each hut via high or low level routes, depending on snow and weather conditions. Late winter snowfall and wind can make certain areas avalanche prone, but these can all be avoided by lower level alternatives. Spring snow conditions later in the season can provide safer and more reliable conditions.

The tour described here spends two nights at the Refuge du Carro, one night at the Refuge des Evettes and two nights at the Refuge d'Avérole. This allows for some great day tours as well as some superb high-level glacier and mountain traverses.

Grade
AD S3 BS (maybe touching S4 if you ski everything, but you can climb down a bit here and there to make it S3)

Season
Mid March to mid May. The mountain huts don't usually open until the middle of March. Snow and weather stability is often very good from early April onwards.

Maps
IGN Tignes, Val d'Isere, Haute Maurienne 3633 ET
IGN Val Cenis, Charbonnel 3634 OT

Kit
Usual ski touring equipment, suitable for glacier travel and mountaineering up to Facile in standard. Ice axe, crampons, rope, crevasse rescue equipment and ski crampons.

Weather forecast
www.mountain-forecast.com
www.meteoblue.com
www.meteofrance.com/previsions-meteo-montagne/bonneval-sur-arc/73480
The tourist information offices in Bessans and Bonneval-sur-Arc have very detailed and up-to-date weather and avalanche forecast information from Meteo France.

Avalanche forecast
www.meteofrance.com/previsions-meteo-montagne/bulletin-avalanches/savoie/avdept73

Hut information
Refuge du Carro, mid March to mid May. Hut bookings are best made through the ffcam website.
www.refugeducarro.ffcam.fr – +33 (0)4 79 05 95 79
Refuge des Evettes, mid March to mid May. Hut bookings are best made through the ffcam website.
www.refugedesevettes.ffcam.fr – +33 (0)4 79 05 96 64
Refuge d'Avérole, mid March to mid May. Hut bookings are best made through the ffcam website.
www.refugedaverole.ffcam.fr – +33 (0)4 79 05 96 70

Useful information
www.lepetitbonheur-bessans.fr This is a wonderful gite and a good starting and finishing point for the tour. Well-placed, clean and very friendly. You can safely leave baggage here for a week.
www.bonnevalsurarc.fr/pdf/horaires-skibus-ligne1-2016.pdf This free shuttle service needs to be booked before 7pm the night before you need it.

Alternative guide books
Vanoise Ski Touring by Paul Henderson, Cicerone

The Haute Maurienne

Day 1 – Bonneval-sur-Arc – Refuge du Carro

Grade PD S2 BS	Starting altitude 1835m	
Aspect E and S	Ascent 950m	Descent 0m
Map Haute Maurienne 3633 ET		

An early bus from Bessans will drop you within easy walking distance of the track that leads from Bonneval to L'Écot. This is usually snow-covered until the middle of April, sometimes later. It's a gentle start to the day, soon leaving the quiet resort of Bonneval-sur-Arc behind. Beyond L'Écot you head north-east into the upper Arc valley. Lots of safe places exist along this valley for transceiver training before heading onto steeper ground at La Duis. Here you leave the main valley and head deeper into the mountains. Crossing the Ruisseau de Léchans can provide fun before entering a small bowl, above which you will find the Refuge du Carro. The final slopes of this approach are steep and at an altitude that you are likely to notice.

The refuge is run by very friendly people, and it has a great balcony overlooking large parts of the tour ahead, including L'Albaron. You can scope out some of tomorrow's day tour options easily from the hut; Levanna Occidentale and the Aiguille Percée glow beautifully in the evening light.

Day 2 – Grande Aiguille Rousse

| Grade PD S2 BS | Aspects S, SW and N | Ascent 1000m | Descent 1000m |
| Map Haute Maurienne 3633 ET | | | |

This is a wonderful outing from the Refuge du Carro. Leave the hut via a short walk or skate to the slopes that traverse directly below the south side of the Ouille de Gontière. Eventually you will decide that it's time for skins, then head gently north-west towards the Col du Montet. A direct approach to the col from the south can be quite brutal and a nicer alternative lies a little to the west, where you can round a band of cliffs easily and head back east to the col. Longer, but much nicer. The Col du Montet can be accessed via skis or crampons depending on snow conditions.

From the col you can either traverse north-east to round point 3343m, or enjoy a short ski descent before making your way up to the col between the Petite and Grande Aiguille Rousse. You are on a glacier here, so be aware of how close together you travel and don't remove skis unnecessarily. The final slopes to the summit can be icy, so again, crampons and axe might be required.

Descent options are either back the way you came, or down the much steeper south face. The

Gary Palmer on the south face of the Grande Aiguille Rousse.

face has a south-east to south-west aspect, so a good line can be chosen to get good snow or a preferred slope angle. From the flat ground at the bottom of this section near point 2956m you can either head home via your line of ascent, or skin up the short distance to the Col de Gontière. From here you can enjoy a fun, and often untracked, journey back to the hut.

Alternatives

Levanna Occidentale via the Col des Pariotes and flanks of the west ridge
This is a fairly easy journey, but care is required if the upper slopes are rocky. The Glacier de Derrière les Lacs can provide a superb ski descent. It can also be re-ascended to the col below the Aiguille Percée for a bit of extra mileage, followed by a fun, steep finish down to Lac Blanc near to the Carro refuge. An advantage of this tour is that you get a good look across at the Col de Trièves and the slope leading to it, tomorrow's objective.

Day 3 – Refuge du Carro – Refuge des Evettes

Grade AD S2 BS   **Aspects** NW, S and W   **Ascent** 900m   **Descent** 1330m
Map Haute Maurienne 3633 ET

Good visibility is advisable for this day. The descent from the Col des Pariotes to below the Col de Trièves can be complicated and the crossing of the Glacier du Mulinet has some big crevasses. An hour of simple skinning will get you comfortably to the Col des Pariotes. From a post at the col you head south, then south-west above a band of cliffs until you can pass below these and head across slopes in a south-easterly direction, aiming for a distinctive square boulder on a large flat section.

From here, easy and fun slopes lead down to the upper valley of the Source Supérieure de l'Arc. Heading in a south-westerly direction, you now traverse slopes and snow-covered moraine banks until you arrive below the Ouille de Trièves and the steep slopes leading to the Col de Trièves. In stable snow conditions this slope is fine; however strong wind and snowfall can load this slope with wind slab very quickly. It is advisable to check with the hut guardian before leaving if you are not sure. If you do not like the look of this slope it is possible to descend to L'Écot, enjoy a coffee in the tiny café there and then ascend to the Refuge des Evettes from there.

The lower steep slopes are soon passed and the upper slopes lead nicely to a ridge with a prominent rock pinnacle at its eastern end. A col beyond this pinnacle leads easily to the Glacier du Mulinet at about 3100m. Although short, the crossing to the Col du Grand Méan is very crevassed. I do not hesitate employing a rope here if visibility is poor. The Col du Grand Méan has a very steep slope on its southern side, where a small valley has formed. It is best to traverse to the left for a short distance, keeping a high line, to the broader snow crest that runs west from the Tour Bramafan. It is possible to ski directly onto the Glacier du Grand Méan from this col, or better, continue skinning up to the border with Italy at a col below the Tour Bramafan. This gives a nicer line onto the glacier, as well as a few extra turns!

Head south past the west ridge of Pointe Francesetti until you reach a series of gullies that lead west, eventually leading to the Plan des Evettes. Locating these gullies in poor visibility can be tricky. The 3050m contour is useful. The gullies are good, but better still are the glaciated slopes on the north side of the Pointe de Bonneval. When the snow is good, this descent is wonderful and it is possible to head directly to the Plan des Evettes, or take more of a traversing descent to a point in the valley nearer the hut. It is likely to be very warm by the time you get here, so the traverse reduces the amount of

The Haute Maurienne

Teams crossing the Glacier du Mulinet.

skinning required to get to the hut. The Refuge des Evettes is a wonderful hut, often busy but beautifully located in a tiny south-facing bowl with amazing views to L'Albaron and surrounding peaks.

If this journey is not possible, for weather or avalanche reasons, it is likely that you can descend from the Refuge du Carro back to L'Écot and ascend to the Refuge des Evettes from there.

Day 4 – Refuge des Evettes – Refuge d'Avérole via L'Albaron

Grade AD S3-S4 BS-TBS   **Aspect** N, NE, S and W   **Ascent** 1050m   **Descent** 1500m
Map Haute Maurienne 3633 ET

Start before daylight if you can, as it is important that you get over L'Albaron and down the steep south-facing slopes just beyond L'Albaron's summit before the afternoon heat softens the snow too much. This is a wonderful journey, one of the finest ski touring days in the Alps and worth waiting a day for if the weather dictates.

The easy skin south across the Plan des Evettes is a nice warm-up, followed by a short ascent up the eastern side of the icefall leading to a large flat part of the Glacier des Evettes below the Petite Ciamarella. The icefall has changed a lot over recent years and is much less threatening than it used to be. Head to the south-west corner of this bowl, from where you start zigzagging your way up steeper slopes towards L'Albaron. An obvious ice cliff threatens this slope, so I wouldn't recommend taking too long over this section, although it does appear that debris will collect in a small bowl before spilling over onto the line of ascent. Use caution and common sense here.

The Haute Maurienne

The south-east ridge of L'Albaron.

Above, the line is obvious; you are heading for the Selle de l'Albaron, an easily accessed flat section on the south-east ridge of L'Albaron. Transition to crampons here. You will need to carry your skis. The ridge is graded Facile, it is straightforward, but deserving of its grade. It is best to stay on the crest as much as you can. There is one section about half way along where you traverse on the west side below a small rock tower, re-ascending to the ridge beyond it. This is exposed. Beyond here the crest is straightforward, but avoid the temptation to venture too far onto the east side, which is a bit loose and shaly, especially near the top.

The summit plateau of L'Albaron is a welcome reward and a great place to enjoy the views. The descent to the north is initially on a very steep rock band. A fixed rope usually protects this section, but careful cramponing might be required to reach the start of the fixed rope. Parties coming up from the other side will require consideration. It is a 'one at a time' journey on the fixed ropes with a lack of passing places.

With skis back on, the descent heads south-west at first, then south onto the Glacier du Colerin. Care is required on the steep upper section here, especially if the snow has become too soft. You will now be grateful of the early start! Delightful slopes lead down and southwards. Once at the south side of the Glacier du Colerin, it is best to gently traverse the slopes southwards aiming for the impressive rock ridge running west from the top of La Bessanèse. Eventually you will see the Refuge d'Avérole and once in the bowl to the west of the Glacier des Grandes Pareis it is safe to head directly to the hut. The skiing is fun around here with lots of lovely rolls and bowls to cruise around. The Refuge d'Avérole is a wonderful mountain hut. If the pipes feeding the hut have thawed there will be plenty of flowing water to quench your thirst, along with a good selection of locally brewed beers! Enjoy.

The Haute Maurienne

Day 5 (day tour) – The Ouille d'Arbéron

| Grade AD S2-S3 BS | Aspects N and W | Ascent 1360m | Descent 1360m |
| Map Cenis, Charbonnel 3634 OT | | | |

If your legs allow, another long day gives you one of the best day tours in this region. The Ouille d'Arbéron dominates the view at the head of the valley and if you don't ski it today, you must ski it tomorrow!

Leave the hut and head down to the valley of the Ruisseau de l'Oney, which runs down from the Col d'Arbéron. The valley is narrow, quite steep in places, but steady. Sometimes it is worth breaking out of the valley and on to the slopes a little to the east. You can't see the col until the very end though, so be careful not to venture too far east. (If you do, however, you might be able to join the Glacier d'Arbéron and follow this to a higher point on the west ridge of the Ouille d'Arbéron.) The west ridge of the Ouille d'Arbéron is reached via a curving descent and re-ascent from the Col d'Arbéron to a small col beside the 3152m spot height.

The west ridge can be skied completely to the summit, or taken on foot if the snow conditions dictate. It is easier than L'Albaron, with very little exposure except the odd steeper section. Be aware of cornices that can grow on the crest of the ridge. The summit is a wonderful viewpoint.

Skiing down from the top is possible; although reasonably steep initially, it soon eases into another wonderful descent. You can get onto the Glacier d'Arbéron at the first prominent flattening of the ridge in descent, at about 3250m. This leads to some lovely slopes and a fun journey back to the Col d'Arbéron. Various descent options exist from here. The valley itself is good, but often tracked. The slopes out to the east are also very good, with more variety and it is possible to rejoin the main valley line in many places. Once back in the valley bottom of the Ruisseau de l'Oney, a short skin is required to get back to the hut.

Skinning up to the Col d'Arbéron.

Alternatives

You have plenty of alternative objectives available from the Refuge d'Avérole.

Col d'Arbéron
See the Ouille d'Arbéron description as far as this col.

Col d'Arnès
Another nice col and viewpoint, bordering Italy. Steep slopes leading out of the Ruisseau de l'Oney valley provide the main challenge of this journey. Boot crampons are sometimes required, ski crampons definitely. More details of this journey can be found in the following Pointe Marie description.

The Haute Maurienne

Pointe des Audras or the Col des Audras

Head east from the hut onto quite steep and frozen slopes. Ski crampons and care are required, especially with finding a suitable route. Lots of nice looking slopes feel a little bit more exposed when frozen in the early hours of the morning. These west-facing slopes won't soften until later in the morning, when of course they are a delight to ski down! It is worth heading for the Col de la Bessanèse, then working your way north towards the Pointe des Audras.

The Col de la Bessanèse

As for Pointe des Audras, but then head directly to the col when you can see it.

Day 6 – Pointe Marie (day tour) and out to Bessans

Grade PD S2 BS	Aspects NW and N	Ascent 1123m	Descent 1123m to the refuge
Map Cenis, Charbonnel 3634 OT			

Pointe Marie makes for a wonderful day tour, either as an easier alternative to yesterday, or as a prelude to skiing out to Bessans.

You need to head into the same valley as you did to go to the Col d'Arbéron, but soon after starting the ascent you break out left and head onto a short, but steep slope. The route does not follow the line of the Ruisseau d'Arnès, but along the line of a stream bed immediately to the south of point 2587m. It is quite steep, often requiring crampons, and leads to a broad col just south of point 2587m. From here a few alternatives lead up the valley in the direction of the Col d'Arnès. Losing some height and skinning along the valley bottom on the left is as good a way as any. Traversing the slopes ahead also works, but is less comfortable.

Once on the Glacier d'Arnès start to head south-east, heading for the Ouille d'Arbéron. Pointe Marie (3313m) is the highest and most easily accessible snow summit below the Ouille d'Arbéron. Beware of summit cornices, but enjoy the views.

The slopes which lie close to the northern flanks of the Ouille d'Arbéron often hold cold snow, so you can have some great skiing descending in this direction. You need to head for the valley holding the Ruisseau d'Arnès which, when full of snow, gives a great descent. If this looks too lean, then aim for the slope next to point 2587m and enjoy the ski down there instead. Both are great, but the Ruisseau d'Arnès can be bare of snow late in the season. Check this on your way up.

It is wise to re-ascend to the Refuge d'Avérole from here as this will give you the safest way down to the main valley and Bessans. You can also pick up overnight kit left behind in the morning, allowing for a lighter day tour. From the hut, follow the slopes north, aiming for the main track at the Plan du Pré. From here you might be lucky enough to enjoy complete snow cover all the way to Bessans, or it might be that you have to walk parts of this route. At La Goulaz, you can cross the river and follow the ski de fond tracks through the woods and open fields more directly back to Bessans. Taking skis off at the road, right opposite the gite, isn't uncommon!

About Andy Teasdale

www.themountainphotographycompany.com
www.andyteasdaleguiding.com

Andy grew up in Devon, where his love for the outdoors developed. Ten Tors on Dartmoor and various school-organised outdoor activity holidays helped set his sights on a career in the outdoors. Climbing, walking and fell running were Andy's earliest outdoor passions. Winter climbing, Alpine climbing and skiing soon followed, along with photography, which is a great way to enhance and capture outdoor adventures.

Living and working in the Lake District, Antarctica and Snowdonia helped Andy decide that he wanted to become a Mountain Guide. He gained a full IFMGA carnet in 2001 and has spent his working life shared between the Alps and Snowdonia since then. Andy guides on skis in winter and enjoys a full summer of mountaineering in the Alps. In Snowdonia, climbing, walking and photography keep Andy busy.

Family life is also very important to Andy. Mini outdoor adventures with his wife and son are a regular occurrence during the year often involving rock climbing, Alpine climbing, skiing, bird watching and photography.

The two chapters written by Andy for this book are of his two favourite ski touring areas in the Alps. Not only are they both great areas for touring, but they can be blessed with wonderful wildlife and are often quiet. A must for a special mountain experience!

Short roping above the Refuge de l'Arpont.

Vanoise Traverse

By Tim Blakemore

Tour overview

The Vanoise National Park was France's first, established in 1963. We should be grateful for this, as the development of ski stations was rapid in the 1970s, and surely would have otherwise encroached further into this massif.

I like this area as it's accessible, though retains its 'sauvage' aura. Many times I have skied here where the decisions, in both ascent and descent, are yours to make alone. Like many ski tours, the Vanoise should be skied in good visibility and stable snow – it's 'big country'. Depending on snow conditions you may be skiing powder or spring snow, or both!

The area can be accessed from the north via the Three Valleys, Pralognan or Val d'Isère, or from the south via the Modane valley, or Aussois. The variations are only limited by your imagination, and circuits or linear tours are all possible. This variation starts in Pralognan-la-Vanoise and finishes in Val d'Isère.

The main feature of this tour is the crossing of the Vanoise Ice Cap. Unusual in the Alps, it is some 12km long and should be done in good visibility as it is quite committing in terms of escape options. Like many of the glaciers in the Alps it is suffering from retreat and change, and 'blue dotted lines' on the map may just mean it was where the route 'used' to go! As ever, ask a guide or guardian for up-to-date information.

Lastly, the flora and fauna are a delight here. You may find yourself skiing into the tree line amongst spring flowers, and marmot, fox, chamois and bearded vulture are all regularly found here.

Vanoise Traverse

Grade
AD S2 BSA

Season
Early March to late April

Maps
IGN Les Trois Vallées, Modane, Parc National de la Vanoise 3534OT
IGN Tignes. Val d'Isère, Haute Maurienne, Parc National de la Vanoise 3633ET

Kit
Classic ski touring kit including an ice axe, crampons and glacier travel / crevasse rescue kit. Swimwear for the Roc de la Pêche.

Weather forecast
www.meteofrance.com/previsions-meteo-france/pralognan-la-vanoise/73710

Avalanche forecast
www.meteofrance.com/previsions-meteo-montagne/bulletin-avalanches/vanoise/OPP10

Hut information
Central booking portal – www.refuges-vanoise.com/
Refuge de la Femma – www.refugelafemma.com/ – +33 (0)9 80 08 68 02 or +33 (0)4 79 05 45 40, out of season +33 (0)4 79 20 33 00
Refuge l'Arpont – +33 (0)9 82 12 42 13/+33 (0)6 62 05 54 32
Refuge Le Roc de la Pêche – +33 (0)4 79 08 79 75
Refuge Le Col de la Vanoise – +33 (0)4 79 08 25 23/+33 (0)6 77 11 23 41
Refuge Le Fond d'Aussois – +33 (0)4 79 20 39 83/+33 (0)6 70 46 52 94

Useful information
www.vanoise-parcnational.fr/EN

Alternative guide books
Vanoise Toponeige by Leïla and Volodia Shahshahani
Savoie Ski de Randonée by Emmanuel Cabau

Vanoise Traverse

Skinning towards the Col d'Aussois.

Day 1 – Refuge du Roc de la Pêche

Grade F S1 BS **Starting altiude** 1592m
Aspect N **Ascent** 340m **Descent** 0m
Map Les Trois Vallées, Modane, Parc National de la Vanoise 3534OT

This first day is easy and very much a warm up. If you're fresh out and just getting back into it, a day practising kick turns, skinning and avalanche rescue drills is time well spent. An alternative is given later.

Start in the village of Pralognan-la-Vanoise. In a normal winter the road is blocked here and you follow the left-hand branch of the road in ascent (skier's right) to avoid the large, steep slopes above.

If you're feeling strong, a diversion can be made from Les Prioux (sometimes the road is clear to here) towards either the Col des Thurges (2680m) or Roc du Blanchon (2748m), depending upon the type of snow you are seeking out.

The hut deserves a comment being the only refuge (that I know of) that has a working jacuzzi! This may be too much for some (and in some ways it's too early on in the trip) but a swimming costume should be carried if you wish to partake.

Day 2 – Refuge du Fond d'Aussois via the Pointe de l'Observatoire

Grade PD S2 BSA	Aspects W, N and S	Ascent 1080m	Descent 592m
Map Les Trois Vallées, Modane, Parc National de la Vanoise 3534OT			

From the refuge skin along the flat valley towards the obvious gorge (near where the track divides at 1972m) where you start skinning steeply up hill. In some conditions it may be quicker to carry your skis here.

A flattening at around 2200m is a good place to spot chamois on the hillsides above while enjoying a mid-morning break before the next pull. Steep skinning (kick turns essential) lead you inexorably up towards the Col d'Aussois. You can start the descent to the refuge from here, but it's not too much more effort to head on up towards the peak of the Pointe de l'Observatoire. You will have to leave your skis at some point and enjoy the final, last rocky scramble to the top.

The ski down can be on either powder or spring snow. The marked line on the map goes way out to skier's right to avoid the cliff bands. This works well, though avoids quite a lot of the fall line skiing and is sometimes prone to wind slab. In good visibility I like to descend directly down the fall line onto the clean south-west facing slopes where enjoyable short pitches can be had.

The refuge is a traditional CAF one and is more basic than many of the others (though perfectly adequate). It is currently home to two habituated foxes that eat from your hand.

Day 3 – Refuge de l'Arpont via the Col de Labby

Grade AD S3 BSA	Aspects S, W, NE, E and N	Ascent 1100m	Descent 1080m
Map Tignes, Val d'Isère, Haute Maurienne, Parc National de la Vanoise 3633ET			

This is the first of two days that are needed to traverse the Glaciers de la Vanoise and, like much of the tour, the terrain is a little more complicated than it appears on the map. From the hut a shallow valley is followed until the Lac du Génépy. The Col de Labby is located well up and left from here above some cliff bands. The Col du Moine is the more obvious col above you here, make sure you don't climb it by mistake. Depending upon the snow you may well carry your skis over the last section towards the Col de Labby. The decision to climb this section using crampons or not should be taken early, as the traverse goes over some steep ground where it may be difficult to change from skis to crampons. On the other side of the col the terrain is easy, so you can make an easy transition back to skis.

Now head down and right to access the right-hand (E) branch of the Glacier de la Mahure. This is skied until a rocky section with some serac threat at 2800m. From here a long traverse leads you eventually to a flattening around 2710m where skins can be put on again. A shoulder is gained at around 2800m where a steep (40°) pitch must be skied. From here the hut is seen, but the way can be complicated and your line must be chosen carefully. Eventually an old moraine is followed to the hut.

The hut has recently been renovated and is modern and clean. It currently features a resident pet rabbit called Roger!

Ascending the Glacier du Dôme de Chasseforêt.

Day 4 – Refuge du Col de la Vanoise via the Dôme de Chasseforêt

Grade AD S3 BSA	Aspects E, S and N	Ascent 1300m	Descent 1200m
Map Tignes. Val d'Isère, Haute Maurienne, Parc National de la Vanoise 3633ET			

Another big and crucial day. There are two ways to ascend the Dôme de Chasseforêt. The first is to head steeply up slopes a little above the hut (you will probably carry skis at the top) and then on to the Glacier du Dôme de Chasseforêt. This has receded a lot and you wind your way between old ice and rock by the best line possible. The other (and perhaps preferable) way is to head back to the Lac de l'Arpont and skin your way up the glacier above. A bit longer, but more straightforward.

From the peak (you boot up the last summit section) the views are incredible. In descent, head out towards the Dôme des Sonnailles (some nice north-east slopes here) before dropping down to a flat section – the Col du Pelve. Re-ascend here, steeply at first, then increasingly flat, to the Col du Dard. If in doubt here (poor visibility) go further north-east on the Glacier de la Roche Ferran, the danger being dropping too early before the obvious catching feature of the Rochers du Génépy.

The terrain is now complex and in poor visibility the hut can be hard to find. In good visibility you wind your way through nice slopes and re-entrants and wonder what all the fuss is about. In poor visibility I can attest that it is a different matter! If in any doubt ski down to the Lac des Assiettes, swallow your pride and put your skins back on for a short re-ascent. The hut is a busy one and petty theft can be a problem here. Be sure to put all your shiny equipment (screws, carabiners etc.) out of sight in the baskets provided.

Vanoise Traverse

Refuge de la Femma.

Day 5 – Refuge de la Femma via Pointe 3081 Roc Blanc

Grade PD S2 BS	Aspects E, N and S	Ascent 640m	Descent 500m
Map Tignes. Val d'Isère, Haute Maurienne, Parc National de la Vanoise 3633 ET			

Head south-east from the refuge, skinning, skating and poling towards point 2448m. To descend to the Torrent de la Leisse in good conditions, head north-east across large slopes and above cliff bands. A long, descending traverse can be followed here until beyond point 2201m. The marked route on the map is just as steep, though much shorter (but will leave you with a much longer skin). After a break at the Torrent de la Leisse, don skins and head towards the Col de Pierre Blanche. Before you get there, head south-east to ascend (quite steeply) the north ridge of point 3081m. This gives commanding views over the Vallon de la Rocheure. Another long, descending traverse can be followed here (above the blue marked line) before finally skiing wonderful spring snow through marmot burrows to the hut.

Day 6 – Val d'Isère via the Pointe de la Sana

Grade PD S2 BS	Aspects S, E and N	Ascent 1080m	Descent 1630m
Map Tignes. Val d'Isère, Haute Maurienne, Parc National de la Vanoise 3633ET			

The final day! Ski crampons are likely to be needed here as you re-ascend frozen snow towards the Col des Barmes de l'Ours. The blue line on the map is more a descent route, and in fact the normal ascent heads more in a north-easterly direction, avoiding and traversing over rock bands. At the col, slopes open up and a nice rhythm is gained, as after a week's touring the team is normally moving well! There are two tops to this peak and I prefer the more technical and quieter one behind the ski peak (you may need to don crampons for it). Sooner or later the fleshpots of Val d'Isère call and you ski back to the col. From here follow the Ruisseau du Pisset through, at times, some tight and steep terrain (keep spaced). As you near the resort you ski under some large slopes prone to spring slides (space again) marked Rochers des Lauses and Rocher du Charvet, before finally skiing into the resort of Val d'Isère.

Possible variants or alternatives

Day 1 – A descent of the Gébroulaz Glacier via the Col de Thorens is often done for a first day to this tour (quite nicely linking Val Thorens and Val d'Isère). It certainly gives a lot of skiing to ascent ratio, but is ambitious for a first day if conditions are not perfect, you start late, have bad visibility or in fact any other reason!
Day 2 – Instead of staying at the Fond de l'Aussois, the Dent Parrachée is only a small (200m) ascent away. It is a private hut but often quite busy.
Day 3 – The Col du Moine is often done in error when looking for the Col de Labby! It involves a steeper descent (sometimes a short abseil) but in some ways is easier to find.
Day 4 – You can bypass the Dôme de Chasseforêt entirely by heading north after the initial steep slopes from the hut and then accessing the Glacier du Pelve. This is quicker (less ascent) but by no means an easy alternative. Good visibility will still be needed.
Day 5 – A classic day from the Col de la Vanoise refuge is to go over the Col de la Grande Casse and ski under the north face of that peak and then out to Champagny.

Skiing below the Col de la Grande Casse.

About Tim Blakemore

www.alpinemountainguides.com

Tim Blakemore is a high mountain and ski guide based year-round in Les Houches, France. His skiing has taken him around the world and he has visited Antarctica, Alaska, Greenland, Svalbard, Arctic Norway and more recently Uzbekistan. His passion is touring in wild, unspoilt areas and he has a particular love for the Southern French Alps where life seems ... simpler.

His background is working with young people in outdoor education and his career started in Northumberland more than 20 years ago. Skiing and adventure travel have maintained this early passion and each season brings new adventures and destinations to explore with a band of loyal and fun clients.

Tim was an early advocate of exploring the psychology of decision making (having published articles on decision making in avalanche terrain) and is involved in the training and assessment of mountain guides. He is a past Director of the British Mountain Guides.

He has reached the exciting stage in his career where he has forgotten more than he knows and is currently re-learning all his lessons for a second time.

Tim has one son, Michael, who shares his passion for outdoor adventure.

A team skinning up towards the Punta Galisia.

Gran Paradiso National Park

By Andy Teasdale

Tour overview

A tour in the Gran Paradiso National Park is a must for all ski touring enthusiasts. Whether you follow the tour outlined below, or add and remove sections, it doesn't matter; this national park is a wonderful place to tour. The mountain huts and hotels are very friendly, the skiing and scenery are fantastic, and every day there are chances of amazing wildlife encounters.

The tour I have described starts in the Val di Rhêmes, enjoys a couple of day tours on the way and finishes with an ascent of the Gran Paradiso. There are many ways to add to or vary the route I have described. One is to start further west in the Valgrisenche. The reason I have chosen not to do that is because this valley is very steep-sided and the risk of avalanche can be high in poor conditions. At other times it is perfectly safe and a worthwhile starting place. Common sense and judgement are required if you choose to start this way. In fact, the steep nature of many parts of the Gran Paradiso National Park means that judgement is often required to avoid avalanche-prone slopes during the winter. Talk to the hut guardians if you are not sure.

Another pleasant aspect of this tour is a night in a comfortable hotel in Pont at the head of the Valsavarenche. This option can be avoided by going directly from the Chivasso hut to the Vittorio Emanuele hut, but it allows for a nice break from huts and an opportunity to see some of the area's wildlife at a closer range. Both Italian and French are spoken in this region and place names can appear on maps in either language.

Gran Paradiso National Park

Grade
PD S3 BS

Season
Mid March to mid May. The mountain huts don't usually open until the middle of March. Snow and weather stability is often very good from early April onwards.

Maps
L'Escursionista Editore 1:25000 Valgrisenche Val di Rhêmes Carta Sci Alpinistica. This brilliant map can be quite hard to find, but it details ski routes and will get you as far as the Chivasso hut.
Alpes Sans Frontières 1:25000 Vanoise Gran Paradiso Sheet 14. Another hard to find map, but worth looking for.
Istituto Geografico Centrale 1:25000 Valsavarenche, Val di Rhêmes, Valgrisenche Sheet 102
Istituto Geografico Centrale 1:25000 Gran Paradiso, La Grivola, Cogne Sheet 101

Kit
Usual ski touring equipment suitable for glacier travel and mountaineering up to Facile in standard. Ice axe, crampons, rope, crevasse rescue equipment and ski crampons. I also recommend ski leashes for glacier travel.

Weather forecast
www.mountain-forecast.com
www.meteoblue.com
www.yr.no/place/Italy/Aosta_Valley/Gran_Paradiso/

Avalanche forecast
www.appweb.regione.vda.it/dbweb/bollnivometeo/
www.snow-forecast.com You can use this site to check conditions in Courmayeur or Pila to get a feel for the area. This site is good for a weather forecast as well.
The huts can also get good weather and avalanche information,; so don't be afraid to ask the guardians about conditions.

Transport
Taxi – www.taxi.aosta.it
Bus – www.savda.it

Hut information
Hut opening dates vary from season to season. Some of them offer a weekend service after the main ski touring season has finished. You might need to book ahead for this.
You need to **keep the '0'** of the area code when calling Italian phone numbers.
Rifugio Bezzi, mid March to mid May.
www.rifugiobezzi.com – rifugio@rifugiobezz.com – +39 0348 2641927 (mobile phone number)
Rifugio Gian Frederico Benevolo, mid March to mid May.
www.rifugiobenevolo.com – info@rifugiobenevolo.com – +39 0165 936143
Rifugio Chivasso, mid March to mid May.
www.rifugiochivasso.altervista.org/ – rifugiochivasso@email.it – +39 0124 953150
Hotel Gran Paradiso, Pont. Open all spring.
www.hotelgparadiso.com/en/ – info@hotelgparadiso.com – +39 0165 95318.

Gran Paradiso National Park

Rifugio Vittorio Emanuele II, mid March to mid May.
www.rifugiovittorioemanuele.com – info@rifugiovittorioemanuele.com – +39 0165 95920
Rifugio Frederico Chabod, mid March to mid May.
www.rifugiochabod.com – info@rifugiochabod.com – +39 0165 95574
Hotel Beau Sejour, Leverogne, Val d'Aosta. This is a great hotel if you want to start and finish the tour in the Aosta valley and use public transport or taxis to get to and from the start and finish.
www.beausejourhotel.com – info@beausejourhotel.com – +39 0165 99031
Hotel Granta Parey, Rhême Notre Dame. Situated near the roadhead of the Val di Rhêmes, this hotel offers great food and accommodation.
www.rhemesgrantaparey.com –info@rhemesgrantaparey.com – +33 0165 963104

Alternative guide books
Orizzonti Bianchi, Italian topo guide to Alpine ski tours in the Aosta Valley.

Day 1 – Val di Rhêmes – Benevolo hut

Grade F S2 BS	Starting altitude 1800m	
Aspects N, E and W	Ascent 500m	Descent 0m

It is not uncommon to find the road just beyond Rhêmes-Notre-Dame blocked by snow. If this is the case, you can either park underground in the village, or on the side of the road just beyond the village. If the road is clear, you can often get to a large parking area at Thumel about 5km further up the valley. Skinning this section of the route is no great hardship though and warms you up nicely. There are also plenty of open spaces in which to practise a transceiver search.

At Thumel the valley road ends, and you follow a narrow path which weaves its way alongside the narrow valley and out into an open area. A bridge over the river leads to the south side of the valley. Depending on snow conditions and temperatures, you might want to follow the south (north-facing) side of the valley where the temperatures are often cooler. Staying on the north side is often OK, but the slopes above the valley are readily warmed by the sun and can create an avalanche hazard. The best route to take is very much dependent on snow and weather conditions. Further along the valley another bridge crosses the river and it is now best to be on the south side of the valley. Easy, more open slopes lead gently up to the Benevolo hut (2287m).

Options

Several short tour options exist above the hut, which can give a bit of fun for the afternoon. Consider the following:

Truc di Tsanteleina
Head south from the hut, on the west side of the stream. Continue around into a valley that runs back north-west and up to the summit.

Punta della Paletta
Not a short afternoon option, but it is easy to turn around at any point, especially if the snow is suffering from too much heat.

Gran Paradiso National Park

Fun snow on the descent of Punta Calabre.

Day 2 (day tour) – Punta Calabre

| Grade PD S2 BS | Aspect N and E | Ascent 1195m | Descent 1195m |

The Punta Calabre is a wonderful peak and gives a long but steady ascent over interesting and glaciated terrain.

Stay on the west side of the stream, Dora di Rhêmes, and head around the Truc di Tsanteleina into a small valley. The slopes at the north-west end of this valley lead up to a large plateau below the very impressive Granta Parei. Moraine banks below this massive wall lead to the Ghiacciaio di Tsanteleina at about 2850m.

Consider ski leashes for glacier travel here, and roping up if visibility is anything less than perfect. Crevasses do exist on this glacier and on its continuation up the Ghiacciaio di Soches. This large open glacier leads past the impressive Punta Tsanteleina to Punta Calabre (3445m). It is not unusual to feel the altitude before you arrive here, so going steady for the final hour or so is wise. The views into France are stunning, but be wary of cornices on the summit.

The descent can follow the same route, or any variations that you have seen on the way up. The northerly aspect of this tour often keeps the snow in good condition. A variation that heads west of point 2670m, leads to some steep slopes and gullies that lead more directly back to the hut. Expect slopes of up to 40° if you go this way.

Alternatives

Several alternative day tours exist from the Benevolo hut (see next page).

Gran Paradiso National Park

The wonderful Chivasso hut.

Punta Galisia
Long and steady, this tour heads south from the hut on to the steady Ghiacciaio di Fond and easily up to the peak at 3346m.

Gran Vaudala
The tour marked on some maps heads along the east side of the Dora di Rhêmes stream, but this puts you directly above a steep gorge. My preference is to stay on the west side and descend a little to cross the stream on the south side of the gorge. From here lovely slopes lead south-east across the Grand Croux to the Gran Vaudala (3272m). A wonderful outing!

Day 3 – Rifugio Benevolo – Rifugio Chivasso

| Grade PD-AD S3 BS | Aspects NW and NE | Ascent 1015m | Descent 570m |

This crossing is one of the most adventurous of this tour. Partly because it doesn't see a lot of traffic, and partly because you need your wits about you to find the best way down from the Colle Basei. Good weather and visibility are recommended for this day.

Head south from the hut to beyond the obvious gorge in the Dora di Rhêmes before crossing to the east side of the stream. Steady slopes lead gently south and east towards the ridge near the Colle Basei. The prominent shark's fin shape of Punta Basei gives you a landmark on the ridge to head for, but aim for the col to its north. Care is required to keep on gently-angled slopes, and in the upper reaches the best line

Gran Paradiso National Park

Windy conditions approaching the Colle di Punta Foura.

might actually lead you to a point on the ridge nearer the Colle di Nivoletta. That is fine, but you will need to head for the Colle Basei before starting your descent. From here you can see the Rifugio Chivasso.

Snow cover usually dictates your exact line of descent on to the Ghiacciaio Basei. Often you need to traverse a little to the north before cutting back below a rock band, then more easily down onto the glacier. Once on the glacier the skiing is fun, and you head for the left-hand end of the flat section where the glacier finishes and the terrain becomes noticeably steeper. This is at about 2950m.

A broad ramp leads down to the left of a very steep cliff and allows you to find a route that traverses back underneath the cliff to a flat area near a small col and point 2910m. North of this location, a couloir, which increases in angle as you descend, leads pleasantly to a large open bowl. Exit this bowl in a south-easterly direction to a point where it becomes obvious that you need to put skins on for the short climb up to the Chivasso hut at 2600m.

This hut is a very special place, mainly due to the guardian who currently runs it. Alessandro has such a peaceful manner about him, that you have no choice but to relax, enjoy the slow pace of life and delight in being made welcome in this truly wonderful hut. It also holds one of the finest mountain book libraries in the Alps.

At the time of writing the Chivasso hut is closed for winter 2018-19. We hope this is just a temporary situation so please check when planning your tour. If the Chivasso is closed you can descend to Pont and have a night in the valley. On the following day (day 4) you can ascend to the Vittorio Emanuele II hut, climb Gran Paradiso on day 5 and on day 6 climb the Colle del Grand Etret before heading for the valley.

Gran Paradiso National Park

Day 4 – Rifugio Chivasso to Pont

| Grade PD S2 BS | Aspects NW and NE | Ascent 700m | Descent 1100m |

It's downhill at first, but not for long. You can head either east or west of the Laghi di Nivolet to a height of about 2460m. From here the glide will have finished and it's time for skins and a lovely ascent to the Col de Punta Foura. This can take a couple of hours, but is beautiful.

From the col, you need to head south-east for 500m or so, aiming for a flat section above an obvious steepening, which hides a rock band barring access to the Vallon d'Etret. This point is at about 2950m. Often you can side slip through this rock band on a good cover of snow, but sometimes you might need to crampon down it, or even abseil if required. Once below this section, you head easily around, then down, onto the upper Glacier d'Etret.

Depending on the snow conditions below here you might have to hunt around to find the nicest skiing. One side can be crusty, the other powder. As you descend further into the Vallon d'Etret spring snow is soon found and you can have a lot of fun skiing close to the stream bed. The lower-lying woods are usually fun to ski through, after which you pick up a ski de fond track that leads to Pont. Only late in the season will you have to walk this section.

The Hotel Gran Paradiso is a wonderful place to stay. It's very friendly, comfortable and usually quiet during the week. A local walk in the afternoon can lead to fantastic sightings of bouquetin, chamois, marmot and possibly fox.

An alternative to staying in Pont is to go more directly from the Glacier d'Etret to the Vittorio Emanuele II hut. This involves leaving the valley at about 2730m and heading in a north-easterly direction. You cross various ridges and open glacier slopes to reach a point at 2940m on the north-west ridge of Ciaforon before heading downhill and northwards to the hut. A good option if the weather is looking poor for later in the week, or if you have been held up by poor weather so far.

Day 5 – Pont – Vittorio Emanuele II hut

| Grade PD S2 BS | Aspect W | Ascent 750m | Descent 0m |

This seems like an easy ascent on paper, but it can be surprising how difficult a summer footpath can become in winter. Hard packed snow or ice sometimes requires ski crampons or boot crampons for the initial, steep section of this journey. The line of the summer footpath is followed and before long you come out of the woods and onto easier-angled slopes that lead to the hut. The balcony is a great place to hang out to enjoy some late morning sun and realise that the day is far from over. A trip to Colle du Moncorve or up La Tresenta can give a fine afternoon outing. The snow on the Glacier de Moncorve is often wonderful.

If you came to the Vittorio Emanuele hut yesterday directly from the Chivasso hut, then it is likely that you will want to climb Gran Paradiso today. See tomorrow's description for details.

Gran Paradiso National Park

The summit rocks of the Gran Paradiso and the exposed section.

Day 6 – Gran Paradiso

Grade PD S2 BS   **Aspects** W, N and SW   **Ascent** 1350m   **Descent** 2060m

One of the nicest aspects of ski touring in the Gran Paradiso National Park is that the huts often do breakfast over a period of time that allows for an early or more relaxed start. Keep an eye on the weather so that you give yourself enough time for this ascent. It is worth considering an early start if you plan on descending to the valley today. The Gran Paradiso is high and it is worth allowing some time for a struggle with the altitude.

Leave the hut heading north initially, then east into a broad valley that leads to the Glacier du Gran Paradiso. An ascending traverse to the south allows you to find a way up a long slope, which differs in angle in places. The lower and upper sections are the steepest. Eventually you join a ridge at a junction with the route from the Chabod hut at about 3600m. Care is required on this section in poor visibility, especially in descent, as there are very steep cliffs a short distance away to the south.

The glaciated ridgeline above is followed to an obvious flat area below a short steep section leading to the upper glacier to the north. If the winter has been very windy, this section can be bare of snow and therefore very icy. Steel boot crampons, as opposed to the aluminium crampons often carried by ski tourers, can make all the difference in these conditions. Above the steepening, a short skin brings you to just below or onto the snowy col before the summit rocks. Skis off, crampons on and join the queue! (The summit can often be very crowded as there are not many places for teams to pass going in opposite directions.)

The route now follows a mix of snow and rock on the west side of the ridge until you actually need to get onto the ridge itself. A short exposed section protected by bolts leads to the summit block. This section can only accommodate one team at a time, so care and patience is required. An efficient team will have a leader equipped with a few karabiners to clip their rope into the bolts. Once over the exposed section, the rest of the team can follow by unclipping and re-clipping the bolts to protect all team members and keep things flowing. A bolt below the Madonna is useful for protecting the final few metres beyond the exposed section to the top. The summit is a wonderful viewpoint. Take care on your descent and time it so that you don't get in a tangle with other teams on their way up. The exact reverse of the ascent process works well and you'll soon be back at your skis.

The ski down pretty much follows the same line of ascent, unless you saw any worthwhile alternatives on your way up. As you get lower, the snow conditions will change. Sometimes the steeper south-facing aspects can give good spring snow as long as they haven't softened too much.

A well-earned and proper Italian coffee at the hut fires you up for the return to the valley. The line of the summer path is OK for this, but sometimes, if there is good snow cover, you can head south-west from the hut and follow one of the steeper gullies down into the Vallon de Seyvoz. The best line follows a steep gully that joins the main valley on the south side of the woods as they are marked on the map. This isn't always easy to find so ask the hut guardian for directions.

Alternative finish

If you happened to come from the Chivasso hut to the Vittorio Emanuele II hut instead of spending a night in Pont, then it is likely that you climbed the Gran Paradiso yesterday. If this is the case, then it is wise to descend to the Chabod hut and spend a final night there. In this case, you will need to descend the Glacier du Laveciau from the snow ridge at 3600m. Following a line in the valley bottom is safest, but there are very large crevasses in this valley, so care is required not to ski too closely together. Once below 3110m make your way northwards heading for the hut on the plateau at 2750m. Day tour options from the Chabod hut for the final day include the Col del Grand Neyron (3410m). This can be done as an 'aller-retour' trip, and from the col you retrace your steps back down the valley past the hut and on to the Valsavarenche. If conditions are favourable, it is possible to cross the col and head down the north side into the Vallon du Timorion and on to the Valsavaranche at Eaux Rousses.

If you chose to spend a second night back at the Vittorio Emanuele II hut, then La Tresenta is a good day tour option.

Once back in the Valsavarenche, public transport or taxis can be used to get back to your start point.

About Andy Teasdale

www.themountainphotographycompany.com
www.andyteasdaleguiding.com

See page 70.

Di Gilbert on the way into the Miage Basin. Photo – Mike Austin.

Miage

By Andy Perkins

Tour overview

Chamonix is a great place to ski. The problem is that everyone else thinks so too, and so the mountains can get mobbed. However, just like the roadside picnic theory (walk 10 minutes and lose 90% of the people), if you investigate the surrounding areas basking in the reflected glory of the Grands Montets (readers may detect a note of irony here) you will find some even better skiing. What??? Better than the Grands Montets? "Sacré bleu! Zut alors. Ce n'est pas possible. Incroyable ..."

Just one of these areas is the Montjoie valley, with the lovely resort of Les Contamines at its end and, watching over this charming Haute Savoyard village, the ridgeline of the Dômes de Miage. This tour warms up in the ski resort of Les Contamines before heading up to the Refuge des Conscrits for a star tour. Tours like this, based in one hut for multiple nights, are a great way to reduce pack weight for most of the week, and to cope easily with the vagaries of snow and weather by simply waiting out the storms so you're in position for that all-important powder day. The Conscrits is one of the best CAF huts in existence, with modern comfortable dorms, good food and a stunning south-facing view. The tours from here are varied and all in a high mountain ambience. In particular, you get a great view of the wild Italian side of Mont Blanc from the Dômes de Miage. "Allons-y!"

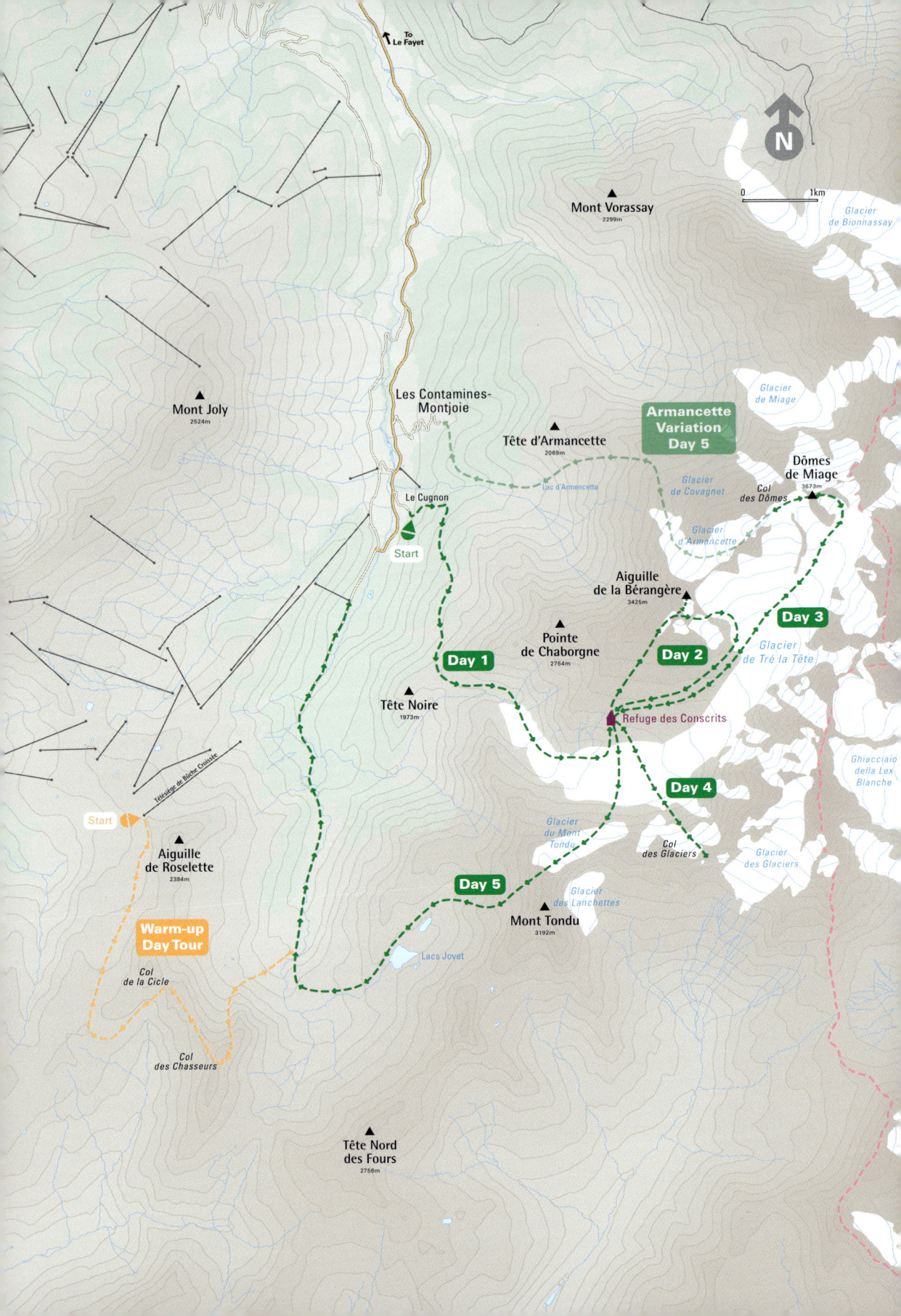

Miage

Grade
AD S3-S4 BSA
After the big day getting in to the hut (1500m), most vertical intervals are less than 1000m. Skiing wise, Col des Chasseurs is the toughest section. Mont Tondu to Lac Jovets has some 30–35° in it. There's some mountaineering on the Chasseurs.

Season
Mid March to end of April

Map
IGN 1:25000 St Gervais 3531 ET
IGN 1:25000 Megève 3531 OT

Kit
Full ski mountaineering kit, including glacier travel kit, ice axe, crampons, cuddly toy etc.

Weather forecast
www.chamonix-meteo.com
www.meteoblue.com
www.yr.no

Avalanche forecast
www.meteofrance.com
Click on the Montagne tab, then Bulletins neige et avalanches. Go to Haute Savoie and then select the Mont Blanc massif.
And if you think that's complicated, try dealing with a utility company helpline in France!

Hut information
www.refugedesconscrits.ffcam.fr/

Useful information
Les Contamines uplift – www.lescontamines.net/

Alternative guidebook
Toponeige Mont Blanc by Lionel Tassan, Pierre Tardivel published by Volopress 2008. Written in French, with good photos.
Ski de Randonnée – Haute Savoie – Mont Blanc by François Labande. Published by Olizane (also in French).

Alan Scowcroft enjoys some spring snow on the descent from the Col des Chasseurs.

Warm-up (day tour) – Col des Chasseurs

Grade AD S3-S4 BSA	**Starting altitude** 2150m	
Aspect all	**Ascent** 450m	**Descent** 1200m

I always like to have a warm-up day on my tours. Remembering how to ski (curly bits to the front, shiny bits on the snow) is useful, as is a transceiver exercise. A warm-up day also gives us an opportunity to check out snow conditions and, a special bonus with this tour, to get great views into the area where we'll be based for the following five days.

Les Contamines has several fabulous day tours, some of which are described in *Ski Touring* by Bruce Goodlad (Pesda Press 2nd edition 2018). Of these, the Col des Chasseurs is the toughest and most serious. If you have any doubts about your ability or the snow stability, warm up on the Col de la Fenêtre or the Col de la Cicle. I've selected the Col des Chasseurs as a warm-up, on the basis that if you can handle this competently then the rest of this touring week should be within your abilities.

Park up at Notre Dame de la Gorge, get smiled at by the lovely personnel at the cash desks and buy a touring ticket. This gets you up the Télécabine de la Gorge, then the Télécabine du Signal and finally the Télésiège Bûche Croisée from where the tour kicks off. Ski down and left to the west of the Aiguille de Roselette, put skins on and traverse south along a broad bench to a col at 2283m before heading back north-east to the Col de la Cicle. Put skis on packs, crampons on boots and axe in hand and head south up the ridge. A short boot followed by some scrambling leads to a flattening where you can put skis back on. The skinning from here can be technical and steep in some places, so you need to be on your game.

On arrival at the Col des Chasseurs, you need to have a careful think. Are you sure it's stable? If you're not, turn back – it's not worth it. So – if you're sure – drop in carefully and then ski whichever line feels best. Sometimes you can have that exquisite instant change from powder to spring within a few seconds. As the slope flattens, head right towards the Chalet de la Balme and then follow the road north from here past Nant Borrant. Just below here, the old Roman road is narrow, and can feature either water ice or snowshoe parties. High-speed encounters with either of these rarely end well, so keep your skiing under control.

At the end of the road, check out the baroque chapel before the few hundred metres back to the car park.

Day 1 – Ascent to the Refuge des Conscrits

Grade PD S2 BSA	Starting altitude 1150m	
Aspects W and S	Ascent 1500m	Descent 0m

This is an uphill day. All day. Get used to it.

Note: in periods of increased avalanche risk, conditions on the approach to the Tré la Tête hut can be really exposed. There is a track that can be followed from Nant Borrant which is a safer approach to the Tré la Tête hut but is longer. The Mauvais Pas is also exposed and there are no alternatives. Call the hut guardian for the latest information and advice if you're unsure.

From the hamlet of Le Cugnon, put skis on packs and walk up the path leading south and up the pine-forested hillside. After approximately 1km, turn left and zigzag steeply uphill to the south of the Nant des Tours. Where the path emerges from the trees at 1700m, turn south again and diagonally right past the Maison Forestière (a big name for a small shack) and then across open hillside to reach the Refuge de Tré la Tête. This last section can be exposed and if you're in any doubt you should have taken the variant via Nant Borrant mentioned above. If the Tré la Tête is open, have a reinforcing brew and a rest. Otherwise just get your flask out. You have the key section to do and you want to be fresh.

Skin up directly behind the Tré la Tête for a short way before traversing across and down into the Mauvais Pas. Again, this area is a terrain trap with serious consequences in case of avalanche. You should be sure of stability and turn back if conditions are warm, as the massive slopes above are south facing.

As the gorge widens above, gain the glacier and head up it, firstly in the middle. Move looker's left as you approach the Séracs de Tré la Grande at 2300m. These are altering rapidly with climate change, and map to ground interpretation may be tricky. Just after passing the seracs at about 2400m, you will need to turn left. The Conscrits hut guardian often puts a marker post there. Check by phone beforehand. Zigzag steeply up the slope to the Conscrits hut and a welcome brew.

Miage

Jon Bracey approaching the Col Infranchissable with Mont Blanc and the Bosses Ridge in the background.

Day 2 (day tour) – Aiguille de la Bérangère

| **Grade** PD S2 BS | **Aspects** S and SE | **Ascent** 830m | **Descent** 830m |

This is very much a warm-up day for the high mountain environment. You can get to see what's going on with the snowpack a few hundred metres higher than your day in Les Contamines. Look for recent avalanche activity, maybe dig a pit and do some stability tests?

Leave directly behind the hut, it is quite steep at first and might require ski crampons. As the slope eases, head north-east up gently-undulating terrain towards the Aiguille de la Bérangère. Pull gently right as you ascend, following the natural line. Towards the top, depending on snow cover, you may well have to make a ski depot and scramble with crampons to the summit. You'll get great views looking across to the Dômes de Miage and the Armancette Glacier, a famous and demanding descent back to Les Contamines. It can be accessed either from the Bérangère or the beautiful sinuous ridge of the Dômes. For this tour, however, retrace your steps and ski down to the col between the Bérangère and the Pointe des Conscrits. Drop in carefully here. If you have any doubts then simply ski back to the Conscrits hut following your up track. But if conditions allow, the descent under the north face of the Pointe des Conscrits often holds good, cold snow. Then ski down the right bank of the Glacier de Tré la Tête to the marker post for the ascent to the Conscrits hut.

Day 3 (day tour) – Dômes de Miage

Grade PD-AD S2 BSA   **Aspects** S and SE   **Ascent** 1100m   **Descent** 1100m

There are two ways to start this great ski mountaineering day, depending on conditions and ability of the party:
1. Option 1 is to ski directly down to the glacier from the hut. You already know how steep this is, and in the morning this is often hard and is therefore a no fall zone. Once on the glacier, skin easily up its true right bank.
2. Alternatively leave the hut as per the previous day, and as soon as the slope eases about 100m above the hut, start to traverse right, rising gently. You will very likely be on ski crampons for much of the way and it's not the easiest skin. Rejoin the glacier at approximately 2800m. Head up the Glacier de Tré la Tête. Note that there is an area of crevasses around 3000m as you ease over a convexity and you might think about skinning roped up here. It's worth going to the Col Infranchissable from here to get some great views of the wild, southern flank of Mont Blanc.

From here, retrace your steps almost horizontally back towards point 3336m. Depending on the configuration of the slope, choose the easiest line just underneath the spur dropping south-east from point 3673m and head towards the Col des Dômes. At the col, turn south-west and follow the ridge to the summit of point 3633m. From here there are great views along the ridge, and you may wish to skin or bootpack to the top of point 3666m as well. Depending on conditions, you have two descent options. The most obvious is to retrace your steps but, if conditions allow, ski just south of the south-east ridge of point 3633m. It is steep here and the start has seracs below, so you should be sure of both your ability and / or conditions. Follow the best line to rejoin the Glacier de Tré la Tête just west of point 3169m. From here, ski back to the Conscrits hut, normally via the upper of the two ascent lines described.

On the Dômes de Miage. Photo – Tim Blakemore.

Day 4 (day tour) – The Col des Glaciers

Grade AD S3-S4 BSA   **Aspect** NNW   **Ascent** 700m   **Descent** 700m

This day, in the right conditions, gives one of the best skis you will ever have – an even slope at 30 to 35° for 500m in full view of the hut. Make those tracks look good!

Leave the hut and ski directly down to the glacier. This is often a no fall zone.

Head across the glacier, passing looker's left of La Bosse and skin with increasing steepness upwards the Col des Glaciers. The terrain here is very definitely in the avalanche zone of 30 to 45°, and there are also some crevasses, so you need to have made a good assessment of the risk. Once on the col, have a butty and a brew and then ski back down. Like many things in life, the simplest things are often the best. Return to the hut and admire your tracks with a beer. See also the variant at the end of the chapter.

Miage

Day 5 – Lacs de Jovet from the Pain de Sucre

| Grade AD S3 BS | Aspect NE and W | Ascent 800m | Descent 1890m |

This south-west face is a big ski, and needs stable conditions. It is complex terrain that requires good visibility as well. Head directly down from the Conscrits hut to the glacier and cross the Glacier de Tré la Tête to hit the left bank just west of La Bosse. Skin up and then right with the occasional steep section to reach a wide runnel on the right bank of the Glacier de Mont Tondu. Follow this south-west passing below the Col de Mont Tondu to hit the north ridge of the Pain de Sucre de Mont Tondu. This is quite steep and may require ski crampons. Enjoy the summit view, then get ready for the descent. Ski down the north-west ridge to the col, and then drop off left down sustained steep terrain and 150m of couloir until it opens out and eases at around 2700m. Head gently left across a broad snowfield to an exit down another gully through a rocky barrier at about 2500m. Once through this, trend down and right before gradually turning left at 2200m to follow the valley down to the Lacs de Jovets. Pass these and follow their drainage valley to the Chalets de Jovet. Cross the river coming from the Col du Bonhomme and follow the track of the GR5 down to the chalets at La Balme which you will have seen on your warm-up tours in Les Contamines. Follow the road as per Warm-up Day to Notre Dame de la Gorge.

Skinning on the Tré la Tête Glacier with the Pain du Sucre in the background. Photo – Tim Blakemore.

Possible variants or alternatives

Warm-up Day
Warm up on the Col de la Fenêtre or the Col de la Cicle if you have any doubts about snow stability on the Col des Chasseurs.

Day 4
Instead of a return trip, you can make the Col des Glaciers into a circuit. This is quite a long day and requires good assessment of the snow stability and a necessity to hit the ascent to the Col des Glaciers early enough to avoid sun effects. Ski down to the glacier and head up the ascent towards Mont Tondu described in Day 5. Instead of the Pain de Sucre, head to the Col de Mont Tondu. On the south side of this col there are some cables leading down and skier's left. Once you're down these, head across left to the Robert Blanc hut. It's alleged that the wine cellar here in the summer is particularly fine. Unfortunately in winter it's shut and there is no winter room as it's private. Head south-east and round the base of the south ridge of Pointe des Lanchettes. Skins on and head north-east up the right bank of the Glacier des Glaciers. Pull left and finish by climbing steeply, usually with a bootpack, to gain the Col des Glaciers. You had better be sure the descent is stable as you're well committed here, with a long and tedious retreat if you decide to back off.

Day 5 – Dômes de Miage, Armancette Variation (by Bruce Goodlad)

Grade AD S3 BSA	Aspect W	Ascent 1100m	Descent 2410m

The traverse of the Dômes de Miage and descent of the Glacier d'Armancette is one of the finest ski mountaineering days in the Alps and a great way to exit the Miage basin. The day starts as per Andy's description of Day 3. From the Col des Dômes put skis on your pack and traverse the beautiful snow crest to the highest point at 3670m. It's ski mode now, the first turns off the summit heading north-west can feel pretty committing in anything but good snow, in hard snow the terrain can feel steep and exposed. Keep skiing down until you are level with a rock band at about 3050m.

Now make a traverse skier's right (north) to cross the top of a ridge and drop into a faint gully besides the rocks. It is really tempting to carry on as the pitch is perfect and offers great skiing, but it is extremely difficult, if not impossible, to get through the rock band below. You may need to side step and shuffle a bit to make the traverse. Now follow the faint gully down beside some rocks heading north-west again. Keep skier's right as you follow some great skiing under the rocks of the Pic de Covagnet, then down a gully heading for the Lac d'Armancette.

This may be the end of the skiing but, depending on the time of year, you may be able to join patches of snow to get much lower. Follow a forestry track through the wood passing the Chalet d'Armancette then onto the hamlet of Les Frasse. If you have pre-placed a vehicle here you are done, alternatively you will have to walk down to Les Contamines.

About Andy Perkins

www.andypmountainguide.com

Andy Perkins has been an IFMGA guide since 2001. He originally entered the guiding profession via climbing and mountaineering, and now spends more time ski touring than anything else. Based in Chamonix, he travels the length of the Alpine chain from the Hautes Alpes to the Tirol in search of ski adventure. He has a policy of going to new areas with clients every year on sight (to use climbing parlance) to keep expanding his repertoire and maintain a sharp, fresh approach rather than dropping into old familiar routines.

This exploration has expanded in recent years to include the Arctic in general and ski sailing in particular. "The snow quality, the Arctic light and the wild scenery combine to give a really special ski experience, especially if you're skiing down to the beach," he says. Recent trips have included Finnmark in northern Norway and the north-west tip of Iceland. The west coast of Greenland is next on the list.

He worked for the climbing brand Troll in a previous life, where he dealt with everything from rope access and rescue to the design of garish trousers. He has a PhD in Textile Industries.

Andy was a vice president of the British Mountaineering Council. He is a member of the British Mountain Guides and its French equivalent, the Syndicat National des Guides de Montagne. Andy has a reputation for coaching as well as guiding, so clients can expect to improve their skiing during their tours with him.

Andy lives in Chamonix with his wife Lise, and in his spare time he climbs rock and eats cake.

Dawn on the approach to the Arête Royal. Photo – Tim Blakemore.

Mont Blanc Ascent

By Mark Charlton

Tour overview

Mont Blanc, the highest mountain of Western Europe, a grand objective and challenge. This is definitely a ski trip that involves very real and committing mountaineering. A two-day trip that involves 2500m of ascent and a potential descent of 3530m, snow conditions permitting!

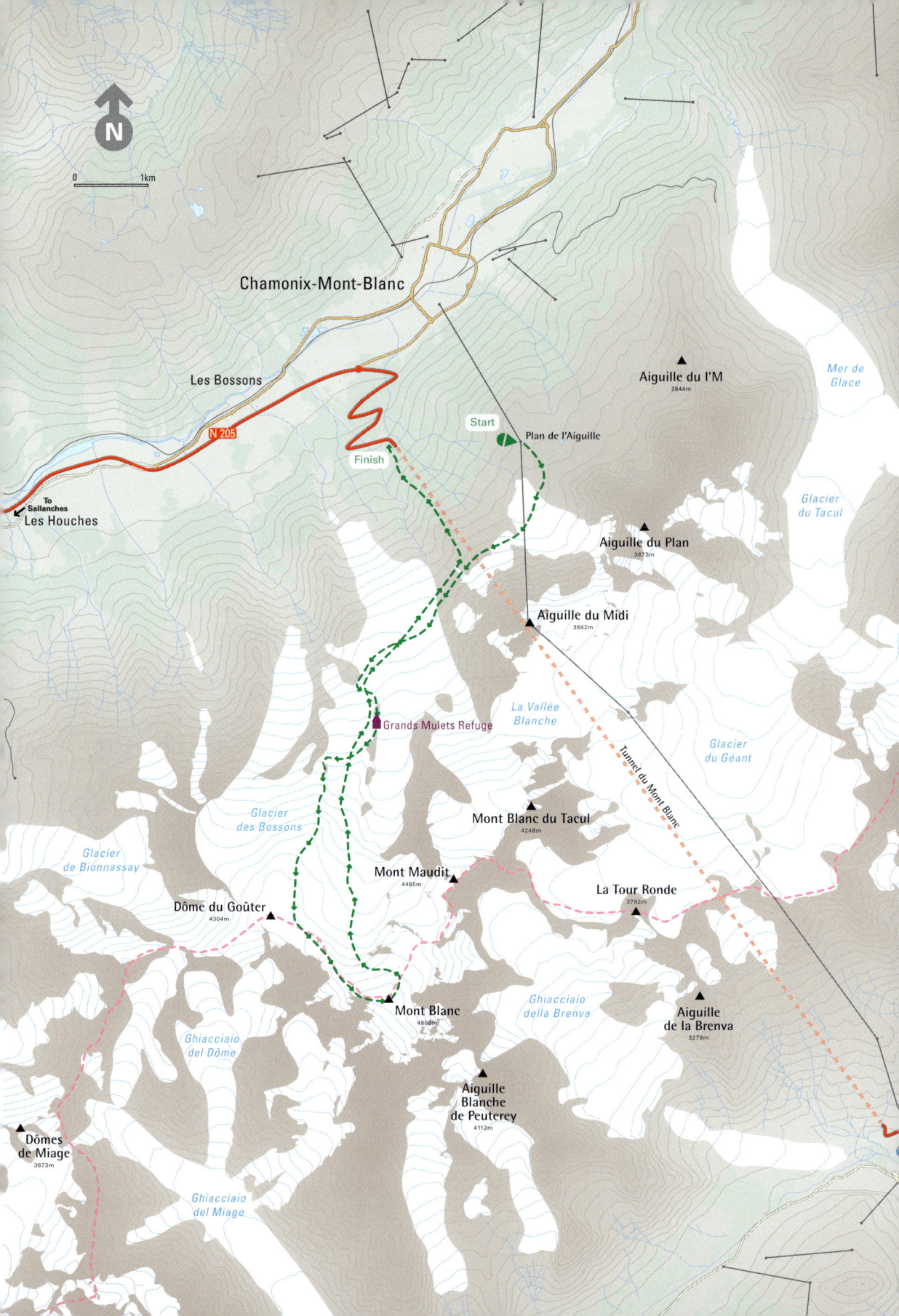

Mont Blanc Ascent

Grade
AD BSA S3

Season
End of March to mid June

Map
IGN St Gervais-Les-Bains 3531 ET

Kit
Classic ski touring kit, including ice axe, glacier travel / crevasse rescue kit and warm clothes.

Weather forecast
www.meteofrance.com
www.weatherchamonix.com

Avalanche forecast
www.meteofrance.com – Bulletins Montagnes – Alps du Nord – Haute Savoie-Mont Blanc

Hut information
Refuge des Grands Mulets – www.refugedesgrandsmulets.ffcam.fr

Useful information
Tourist office – www.chamonix.com
Lift Aiguille du Midi / Plan de l'Aiguille – www.montblancnaturalresort.com

Alternative guide book
Mont Blanc and the Aiguilles Rouges: A guide for skiers, Anselme Baud
Mont Blanc Ski Tours, Eric Delaperrière, Franck Gentilini (Vamos)

Mont Blanc Ascent

Skiing through the Junction on the approach to the Grands Mulets hut. Photo – Tim Blakemore.

Day 1 – Grands Mulets hut

Grade AD S2 BSA	**Starting altitude** 2310m	
Aspect N	**Ascent** 750m	**Descent** 0m

Take the first stage of the Aiguille du Midi Téléphérique to the Plan de l'Aiguille station. It is usual to buy a return ticket, but if snow conditions allow a descent to the Tunnel du Mont Blanc, then a single is all that is needed!

From the Plan de l'Aiguille station, make your way through the moraines and moraine walls to the Glacier des Pèlerins, generally a southerly direction.

Conditions here change yearly and often, even on a daily basis. Remember where the snow is lying for the return journey the following day.

Gain height in a south-westerly direction, climbing more moraine walls until the final and largest one is breached. Quite often skis need to be carried to make efficient progress through these.

Eventually, a large snow patch is reached directly below the north side of the Aiguille du Midi. This is traversed west to a descent to the edge of the Glacier des Bossons at the Plan Glacier (2550m). Stone fall is possible here if it is warm.

Continue on the glacier south-west, gaining a little height till you reach the Junction. This is where the two glaciers, flowing either side of the rocks of the Grands Mulets, meet. This area is always crevassed, sometimes badly, and it's always a challenge to find a way through. Once through this area, follow the slope up to the west side of the Grands Mulets to reach the refuge on the crest (3057m).

It is well worth the effort of leaving early to arrive at the refuge in good time. The position of the hut's deck / balcony allows a good vantage point to study the first part of tomorrow's ascent. As this part of the route will be done in the dark, having a good view of it in daylight will serve you well.

Mont Blanc Ascent

Impressive glacial scenery on the descent from Mont Blanc. Photo – Tim Blakemore.

Day 2 – Mont Blanc

| **Grade** AD | **Aspect** N | **Ascent** 1760m | **Descent** 3458m |

The 'old' way up Mont Blanc from the Grands Mulets hut follows the glacial valley due south of here below the seracs of the Petit and Grand Plateau. This area is best avoided, as the seracs are quite active. You will pass under these in the descent, only for a minimal amount of time, but care will still be needed.

Breakfast is early, possibly the earliest you will have had, unless a kebab on the way back from a nightclub counts!

Cross the glacier in a WSW direction, rising up to the foot of the Arête Royal. Here, at some point, you will need to attach skis on the rucksack, crampons on boots, and most of all, need your ice axe in hand.

Follow the blunt arête near its crest (keeping a sharp lookout for icy sections), till a point close to Pointe Bravais, where skis can be put back on.

All of these transitions need care as they are in crevasse areas.

South to the Col du Dôme, then up to the Vallot emergency shelter. This slope can often be ascended on skis, but be prepared to crampon if icy.

From the Vallot hut, the Bosses ridge is a crampon ascent. Usually your skis are left here. If you are contemplating a ski from the north face of the summit, then carry skis on your rucksack.

To attempt a north face descent, it would have needed to be studied on the way up. The usual route, conditions permitting, would be via the Petits Mulets (west side) and then by the Anc. Passage superior, east of point 4309m to the Grand Plateau. Conditions need to be good for this section.

If returning to the Vallot and picking skis up there, ski down to the Col du Dôme and then east into the Grand Plateau.

Mont Blanc Ascent

On the summit of Mont Blanc. Photo – Tim Blakemore.

From the Grand Plateau, the descent is pretty much due north back to the Grands Mulets hut. Return following the line of ascent back to the Plan de l'Aiguille station.

If snow conditions allow, you can descend to the Mont Blanc Tunnel entrance. Once the ascent from the Glacier des Bossons has been made, head down to the old téléphérique station at 2414m.

Descend in a northerly direction, eventually coming to the tree line, then work your way through these as best you can, arriving eventually at the tunnel entrance area.

A car left here makes the return to Chamonix easier, although hitchhiking usually works pretty well too.

About Mark Charlton

www.bmg.org.uk/guide/?mark-andrew-charlton#bio

See page 60.

On the mountaineering section of the Col de Beugeant. Photo – Tim Blakemore.

Chamonix Day Tours

By Jonny Baird

Area overview

Chamonix is an iconic destination for skiers and climbers from around the world. The majesty of the peaks and the easy access to high glaciated terrain is unique; there are very few places in the world where you can be drinking coffee at 1000m in the valley then be transported to 3800m in 20 minutes. Chamonix is not all about the Aiguille du Midi and high-glaciated terrain however, and there is a huge variety of ski touring to suit all levels of ability and aspiration. Some of the classic glaciated tours and descents are covered in the guidebook section of *Ski Touring* by Bruce Goodlad. In this chapter I would like to share some of my favourite day tours, most of which use lifts to gain height so the skiing to skinning ratio is very good. The Pointe Ronde gives a longer ascent and a start from the road as a bit of an alternative. If the weather is too difficult to try any of these tours, have a look at some of the tours in the surrounding area that can be found in *Ski Touring*.

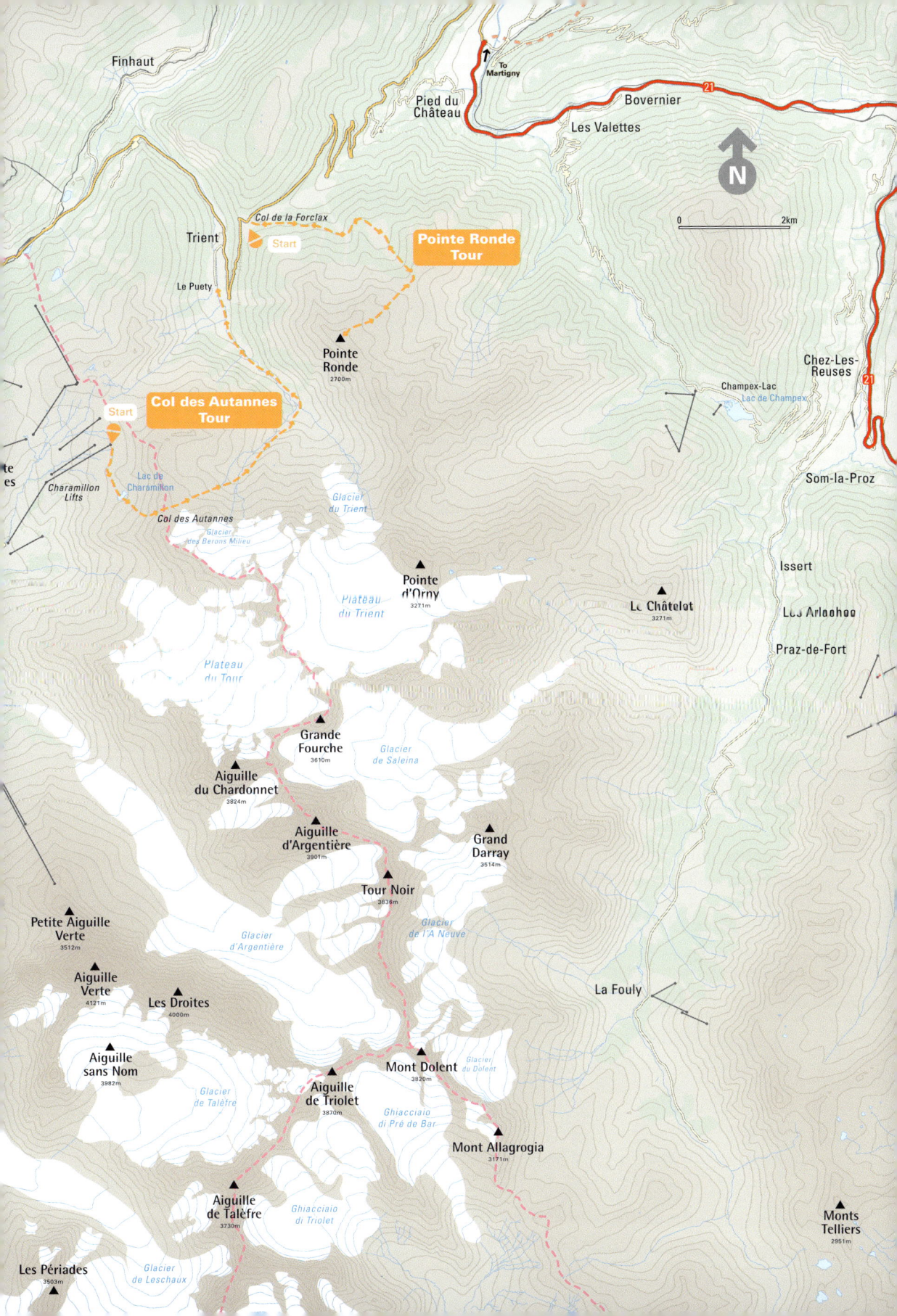

Chamonix Day Tours

Grade
Various – see individual tour descriptions.

Season
December to May

Maps
Various – see individual tour descriptions. For sections in Switzerland (Pointe Ronde) see www.map.geo.admin.ch for free map printing (A4 sheets).

Kit
Classic ski touring kit – ice axe and crampons are only needed where indicated in the tour description. Glacier travel and crevasse rescue kit are not required. There is as a small glacier on the Col de Belvédère but this is more like a permanent snow field these days. So glacier travel kit is generally not carried.

Weather forecast
www.chamonix-meteo.com/chamonix-mont-blanc/weather/forecast/morning/5_days_weather_forecast.php
www.meteofrance.com/previsions-meteo-montagne/chamonix-mont-blanc/74400
www.meteoswiss.admin.ch

Avalanche forecast
www.meteofrance.com/previsions-meteo-montagne/bulletin-avalanches/mont-blanc/OPP03
The Swiss forecast overlaps the Mont Blanc Massif so it is also worth having a look at www.slf.ch

Useful information
www.chamonix.com/chamonix-mont-blanc,0,en.html – Chamonix tourist information website.
www.chamonix.net/ – lifts, accommodation, weather and general information.
www.chamoniarde.com/?lang=en – Office de Haute Montagne, good site for mountain conditions.
www.camptocamp.org – up-to-date information on ski touring conditions.

Alternative guide books
Mont Blanc Ski Tours – Eric Delaperriere & Franck Gentilini
Les Plus Belles Traces du Mont Blanc – Christophe et Jean-François Hagenmuller (French language)
Ski de Randonnée – Haute Savoie – Mont Blanc by François Labande (French language)

Chamonix Day Tours

Stuart Galbraith on his way to the Aiguillette des Houches. Photo – Andy Perkins.

Day Tour 1 – Traverse of Aiguillette des Houches (2285m)

Grade PD S3 BS-TBS	**Starting altitude** 2524m	
Aspects W, SW, S and SE	**Ascent** 220m	**Descent** 1025m
Season December to March	**Maps** IGN Samoëns 3530 ET, IGN St-Gervais 3531 RT	

A fantastic round trip, ideally with a car drop in place at Le Bettey (1352m).

Due to the principal aspects of the skiing being W, SW, S and SE, the best conditions for the tour would either be midwinter with fresh snow and sustained cold temperatures, or later in the winter with a spring snowpack. Although a short tour with few difficulties, good navigation would be needed in bad visibility due to a number of crags, cliffs and terrain traps.

To start the tour, buy a one way ticket on the cable car to le Brévent (2525m), leave the piste and ski the W to SW slopes through the combe at 2212m going above the Creux aux Marmottes. Keep skiing west until you reach point 2062m (marked on map). Here put your skins on and skin south-west past the Chalets de Carlaveyron, through rolling terrain above Lac de l'Aiguillette, and then south to the Aiguillette des Houches (2285m).

Ski south off the ridge line, steeply at first (35°), but the angle eases quickly and the slope widens. This part may be scraped out a bit or missing snow and the summer path might be visible.

Enjoy the open slopes S to SE until the Chalets de Chailloux (1922m), then from here ski down the summer path (may be scraped and icy) past Le Plan de la Cry to Le Bettey.

Possible variants or alternatives

In poor visibility or suspect snow conditions it may be preferable to start and finish the tour from Le Bettey, thus enabling better assessment of the snow conditions without being committed.

A further alternative in stable conditions is to leave the summit, then after a few turns ski north-west into a couloir; the entrance can feel pretty steep and the skiing is consistently 30 to 35°. The couloir is quite broad but shady enough to hold cold snow for a long time after the last snow fall. At 1660m you can pick up a path that leads slightly uphill to a ridge then it is downhill on a track to Le Bettey. A slight alternative is to keep skiing for another 100m and put your skins on to climb to the ridge.

Day tour 2 – Pointe Ronde (2700m)

Grade PD TBS S3	Starting altitude 1527m	
Aspect N	Ascent 1230m	Descent 1230m
Season December to April		
Map Carte de Randonnées à Ski Martigny 282 S, Swisstopo 1324 Barberine, Swisstopo Sembrancher 1325		

A fantastic tour, with some good north-facing skiing and great views over the Rhone valley. This tour is slightly different from the others selected, as it starts over the border in Switzerland and skins from a road, so it is a good option if you are finding the lifts a bit busy or want a purer ski touring experience.

Park at the Col de la Forclaz (1527m) in the Swiss Valais which is about 7km from the French border. Put skins on and head in an easterly direction descending slightly before picking up the line of the TMB (Tour de Mont Blanc) summer path which traverses the steep forest in an easterly direction. The path crosses steep, open couloirs and therefore has potential avalanche danger, so careful assessment of conditions is needed. It can also be hard and icy due to descending skiers, so ski crampons or even boot crampons could be desirable. Continue along the path until you are below La Giète (1884m) where terrain opens up. From the flat area at La Giète (2259m), skin up north-west facing slopes to the col at 2259m on slopes which gradually steepen with a handful of kick turns. From the col skin up a fairly gentle north-east facing broad ridge with small bowls in it, eventually narrowing slightly towards the summit which is a fine viewpoint into the Swiss Valais and surrounding areas.

Generally the same route is followed in descent, but there is a wide variety of terrain to play with and get the best snow. The slopes from the summit are skied in a north-easterly direction back to the col with lots of options in the bowls and slopes of the broad ridge. From the Col to La Giète there are plenty of options both in and out of the trees for good skiing and fresh tracks in a north-westerly direction.

From La Giète follow the path back to the car, or ski the meadows down to the parking at La Caffe 1225m (and a café!) then hitch a ride up the road back to your car.

Possible variants or alternatives

The tour can be started from La Caffe (1225m) and follows a fairly direct summer path to join the TMB path before La Giète.

Day tour 3 – Traverse of Col du Belvédère 2780m

Grade D S5 for 100m, S4 then S3 TBSA		Starting altitude 2430m
Aspects E, S, SE and N	Ascent 700m	Descent 1450m
Season December to May	Map IGN Chamonix Massif du Mont-Blanc 3630 OT	

A great journey usually involving some mountaineering and ropework skills, and a fantastic north-west and north-facing descent. Although it is in an area that attracts a lot of ski tourers, the descent is often quiet with vast scope for fresh tracks.

Passing Lac Blanc on the way to the Col du Belvédère. Photo – Andy Perkins.

Take an ice axe, crampons, harness, abseil device and two 50m ropes to make the abseil. The tour starts in Les Praz de Chamonix where you take the cable car to Flégère followed by the Index chairlift and finally the Florin button tow (teleski). From here, ski a high descending traverse in a south-easterly direction before crossing the south-east ridge of the Aiguille Crochues at a small shoulder at about 2280m. It is slightly exposed and an alternative is to ski lower, easier-angled ground to 2100m and add some skinning.

From where you put your skins on ascend in a north-easterly then northerly direction to Lac Blanc, then traverse the east side of the lake before climbing in a north-westerly direction to the col with the occasional steepening requiring some kick turns.

There is an anchor at the col which can be used to safeguard the initial descent which at 45° is often scraped out and narrow – it is 45 for 150m but widens out lower down. You may wish to abseil / lower further than the first 50m if snow cover is lean, so be prepared to make your own anchors if needed and check all fixed anchors. Dependent on snow cover and quality it is often easier to keep the skis on when abseiling.

When on the Bérard Glacier the angle eases, and from here enjoy skiing the superb north-west facing slopes on the right bank of the glacier. At 2000m traverse to the left bank of the glacier before descending to the main Bérard Valley and down to Le Buet.

Possible variants or alternatives

When there is a spring snowpack and sunny weather, a good alternative is to ski the same way back down towards Lac Blanc, making sure of getting the timing right to let the sun soften the slopes up for good spring snow.

Day tour 4 – Col de Beugeant (2807m)

Grade AD S3 TBSA **Starting altitude** 2430m
Aspects S and N **Ascent** 820m **Descent** 1570m
Season December to May
Map IGN Chamonix Massif du Mont-Blanc 3630 OT, Ski Carte Martigny 282S

A fantastic, varied ski tour where a reasonable knowledge of mountaineering techniques is needed, involving mixed rock / snow terrain and a potential abseil.

Take standard ski touring kit plus a rope, some karabiners, ice axe, crampons and an abseil device.

The tour starts in Les Praz de Chamonix where you take the cable car to Flégère followed by the Index chairlift and finally the Floria button tow (téléski). From here, ski a high descending traverse in a south-easterly direction before crossing the south-east ridge of the Aiguille Crochues at a small shoulder at about 2280m. It is slightly exposed and an alternative is to ski to lower, easier-angled ground to 2100m and adding some skinning, as per the Col du Belvédère.

From where you put your skins on, ascend in a north-easterly then northerly direction to Lac Blanc; from here skin in a northerly direction passing the Tête sur les Lacs on the right and keep skinning up into the Combe Beugeant above. At around 2750m there is a ledge on your left; be prepared to wear crampons when you traverse up and along the rock / mixed ledge. It has some fixed gear but take some slings and a couple of wires as well.

From the col dependent on the snow cover you may have to abseil, often 30m but be prepared for longer. Once your skis are on, ski north-east facing slopes, traverse west at about 2550m under the Aiguille de la Tête Plate, then ski north-east and north facing bowls and slopes into the main Bérard Valley and Le Buet.

Skiing fantastic powder on the way down from the Col de Beugeant. Photo – Andy Perkins.

Possible variants or alternatives

From the bottom of the abseil traverse hard right in a north-westerly direction below the Aiguille des Chamois towards the Col de l'Encrenaz (2579m), a very small amount of bootpacking may be needed to gain the col. From here ski the E / NE facing combe, then at about 2000m ski towards the left bank to avoid some cliffs at the Tête de Praz Torrent. Ski NE-facing slopes, then easier angled north-facing slopes to arrive at the road below the Col des Montets. From here it is possible to walk to Le Buet or Argentière.

A more direct descent to the Bérard valley is possible by traversing towards the Col de l'Encrenaz then skiing north-west then north facing slopes to the valley floor on steeper terrain. This needs good snow cover to give good skiing!

One of Bruce's favourite variations is to combine the Col de Beugeant and the Col de l'Encrenaz. After the initial few turns down the Glacier de Beugeant head north-east to the Col de l'Encrenaz. You might need to hike up a few metres to get over the col, then ski ENE down the Combe de l'Encrenaz.

Chamonix Day Tours

Climbing towards the Col des Autannes. Photo – Andy Perkins.

At 2200 metres start trending north to avoid a cliff band, keep trending north to the Tête de Praz Torrent then ski north-east, skiing down a broad firebreak – depending on snow cover this can be a bit of a bush bash. When you reach the road, ski down the side of the road to Le Buet and the train back to Les Praz.

Day tour 5 – Col des Autannes (2777m)

Grade PD+ S3 TBSA
Aspects W, NE and N
Season January to April
Starting altitude 2193m
Ascent 580m
Descent 1444m
Map Carte de Randonnées à Ski Martigny 282 S, IGN Chamonix - Massif du Mont Blanc 3630 OT

A great tour where you benefit from a lot of skiing from minimal ascent. Careful assessment of the avalanche conditions is needed due to the nature of the terrain especially near the exit to Trient.

From the village of Le Tour take the télécabine then the Charamillon-Balme chairlift.

Ski a descending traverse in a southerly direction passing below the Tête de Charamillon before skinning to Lac de Charamillon, then skin and boot up west-facing slopes to the Col des Autannes. Depending on the snow, crampons may be needed.

From the col, ski E / NE facing slopes under the Glacier de Bron; there is a lot of terrain to play with. The combe becomes a valley which, when lower down at 2055m, it is best to ski rightwards to the Chalets du Milieu. From here descend to the Prise de Bisse and pick up a track on the left bank which can be followed to Le Peuty. At the time of writing the bus service from Trient to Vallorcine has stopped, so either a car drop or a taxi is desirable.

Possible variants or alternatives

If the slopes in ascent are suspect, a safer ascent would be to climb the ridge from the Col de Balme and over the Grandes Autannes; this is fairly easy mixed ground.

Via a small col south of the Croix de Bron, the Glacier des Grands and the Pointes des Grands can be reached.

The Col du Passon is also a fantastic day tour in its own right. It is mentioned in the Haute Route chapter, you just turn left instead of right at the col and head for La Tour.

About Jonny Baird

www.jonathan-baird.com

Jonny's love of the hills and wide open spaces originated where he grew up on the west coast of Scotland, and spent his time hillwalking and then climbing. After moving to Fort William he rock climbed regularly in Glen Nevis, Glen Coe and the rest of the Highlands. Winters were spent focusing on the great ice climbs of Ben Nevis and discovering the magic of winter climbing in the Highlands.

He progressed to the Alps where he loved the perfect granite, the big classic north faces and the ephemeral ice climbs. Chamonix was the perfect place where he could climb all year and enjoy his developing passion for skiing in winter. Jonny has also climbed and skied in Norway, Canada, Greenland, New Zealand, the Tien Shan, Peru, Morocco, Australia, Antarctica and the US.

A good friend, who was training as a mountain guide, encouraged and inspired Jonny to start his training. During the second half of the training he moved to the French Alps permanently. He has been guiding now for 15 years and lives with his family in Passy, close to the Chamonix Valley, and within easy reach of Switzerland and the Val d'Aosta in Italy.

Jonny really enjoys doing ski tours or climbs he has not done before, as well as established classics. He is keen to share this with you and teach you new skills, both locally and further afield, as well as maximise your potential and have fun!

He is a member of the British Mountain Guides BMG and the Syndicat National des Guides de Montagne SNGM.

John Naismith descending the Pigne d'Arolla. Photo – Bruce Goodlad.

Chamonix-Zermatt Haute Route

By Graham Frost

Tour overview

Linking Chamonix and Zermatt on skis is probably the most famous ski-tour in the world – more usually known as the Haute Route – and its fame is well-deserved. Yes, it can be busy and huts can be crowded, but completing the journey through the high mountains of the Alps is an unforgettable experience, and high on the tick-list for most ski tourers.

There are lots of variations, some using lifts and public transport to make a five-day trip. The route described here covers the whole distance on skis in seven to eight days, rarely dropping below 2500m, with a lot of glacier travel and some mountaineering to cross the steeper cols. Success needs an elusive combination of fitness, determination, stable conditions, good weather and careful planning, but is well worth the effort!

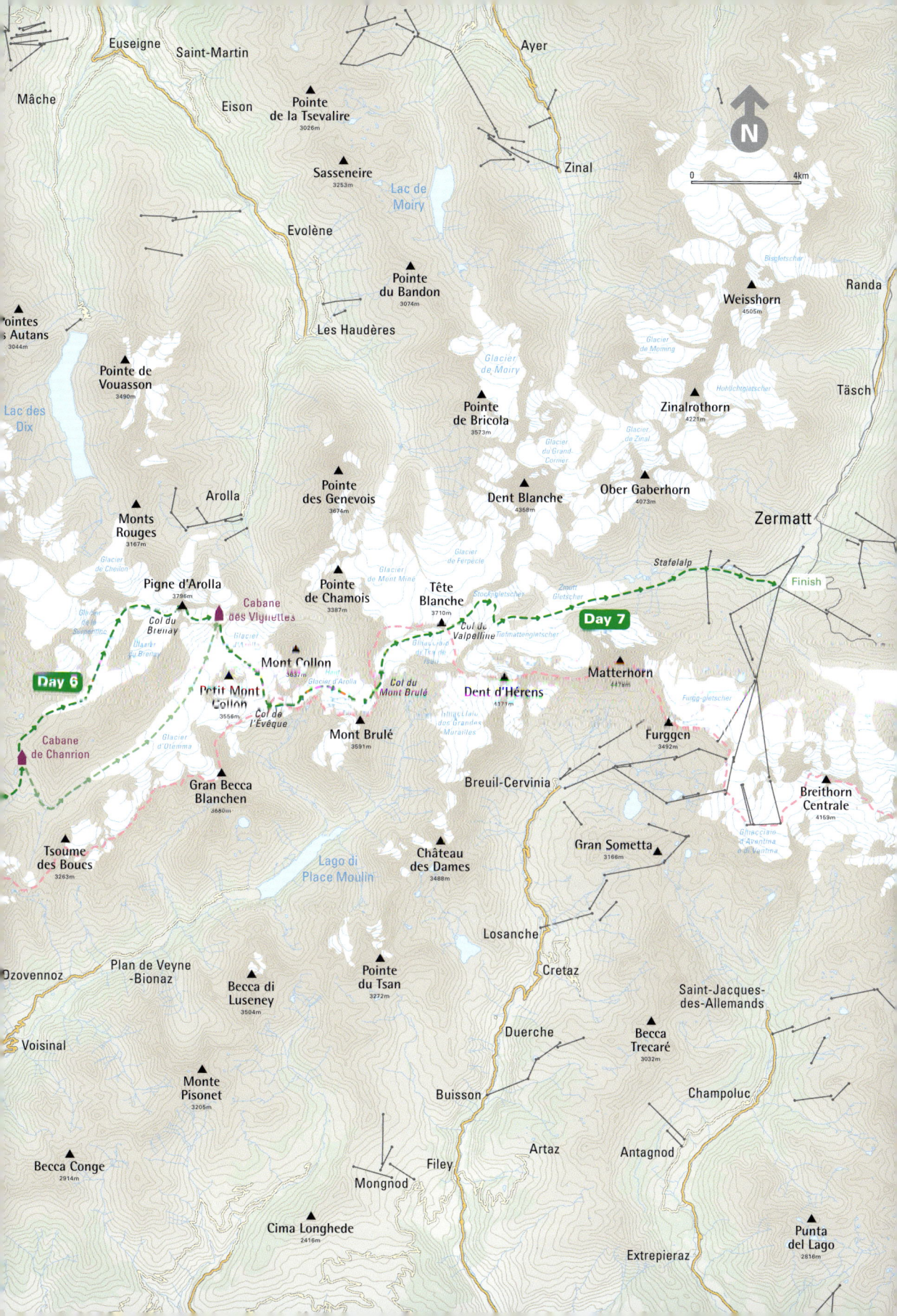

Chamonix-Zermatt Haute Route

Grade
AD S3 BSA

Season
February (using winter rooms); huts usually open from early March to early May.

Maps
Swiss 1:50000 Martigny 282 S , Swiss 1:50000 Arolla 283 S, Swiss 1:25000 Orsières 1345, Swiss 1:25000 Gd St Bernard 1365, Swiss 1:25000 Chanrion 1346, Swiss 1:25000 Matterhorn 1367
It is worth having the 1:25000 sheets as some of the days are difficult to follow on the 1:50000.
www.map.geo.admin.ch for free map printing (A4 sheets)

Kit
Full ski touring kit; axe, crampons and glacier travel kit. Consider extra rope for Col du Chardonnet (see text). Stove and food if using bivvy huts.

Weather forecast
www.meteosuisse.admin.ch
www.meteoblue.ch

Avalanche forecast
www.slf.ch

Hut information
Refuge d'Argentière – www.refugedargentiere.ffcam.fr/ – +33 (0)4 50 53 16 92
Bivouac des Dorées – www.cas-dent-de-lys.ch
Cabane du Trient – www.cas-diablerets.ch/trient.htm – +41 (0)27 783 14 38
Auberge des Glaciers – www.aubergedesglaciers.ch/ – +41 (0)27 783 11 71
Hospice du Grand St Bernard – www.gsbernard.com/fr/ – +41 (0)27 787 11 53
Plan du Jeu Refuge – www.cabaneplandujeu.ch/ – +41 (0)79 428 01 75
Cabane du Vélan – www.velan.ch/ – +41 (0)27 787 13 13
Cabane de Valsorey – www.valsorey.ch – +41 (0)27 787 11 22
Cabane de Chanrion – www.chanrion.ch/ – +41 (0)27 778 12 09
Cabane des Vignettes – www.cabanedesvignettes.ch/ – +41 (0)27 283 13 22

Useful information
Taxi return to Chamonix is cheaper (for 4+ people) and much quicker than public transport.
www.taxi-des-combins.ch/
www.taxifollonier.ch/

Chamonix-Zermatt Haute Route

Matteo Maino climbs to the Col du Passon. Photo – Bruce Goodlad.

Day 1 – Argentière - Bivouac des Dorées

Grade PD S2 BS	Starting altitude 3295m	
Aspect E and W	Ascent 780m	Descent 1366m

This is the most direct route (Argentière - Grands Montets lift - Argentière Glacier - Col de Chardonnet - Bivouac des Dorées), but you'll need food and a stove for the bivvy hut (see options below).

Use the lifts in the morning (be early to avoid queues!) and ski down to the glacier – often a tough bump-run! Cross the glacier and start the climb to the Col de Chardonnet. Steep at first and sometimes best in crampons. The angle eases higher up.

The east side of the col is steep for 80m, rarely skiable and often busy. Most climb down in crampons. There's often a fixed rope of variable quality. Beware the bergschrund!

Next, a gentle ski down the left bank of the glacier leads to a short re-ascent to the hut.

Options

Sleep at the Argentière hut for an early start. Some teams push through to La Fouly in a day from there, but may find very poor snow late in the day!

Sleep at Cabane du Trient – more distance but avoids the bivvy hut.

Via Col du Passon to Trient hut avoids the queue at the Col de Chardonnet.

Day 2 – Bivouac des Dorées – Col de la Grand Lui – La Fouly

Grade AD S3 BSA **Aspects** N and S **Ascent** 750m **Descent** 1826m

From the hut (from Trient hut via Fenêtre de Saleina or Col des Plines) cross the Saleina Glacier southwards and start the climb to the Col de la Grand Lui. (Spot the route from the hut – see photo below.) This is crevassed and ends with a steep climb carrying skis to the col at point 3419m. Be sure it's the right col! (Wrongly marked on old French maps, Swiss maps are correct.) If you've timed it right for the snow conditions, enjoy the 1900m descent to La Fouly! Head south-east then east (left) at first to pass below the A Neuve hut.

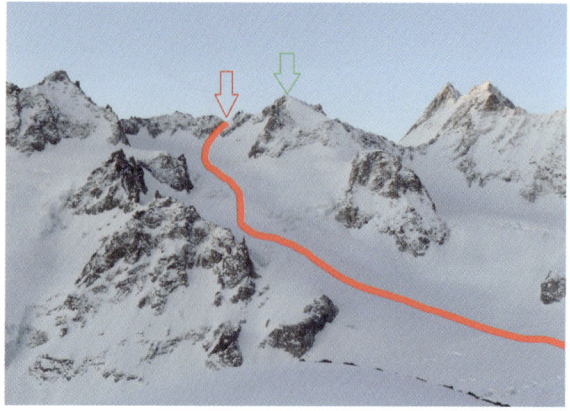

Route to the Grand Lui.

Day 3 – La Fouly – Ferret – Lacs de Fenêtre – Col d'en Haut – Grand St Bernard

Grade PD-AD **Aspects** all **Ascent** 1190m **Descent** 253m

Low altitude but a serious day needing stable snow conditions. Avalanches seriously threaten much of the climb out of La Fouly! If you are concerned about snow conditions, using Switzerland's excellent public transport service can keep you moving towards Zermatt.

Start early, heading south on the road through Ferret, then Les Ars and Plan de la Chaux (2041m), and then steeply on serious terrain to the Lacs de Fenêtre (2456m) following roughly the summer path. Continue to the Fenêtre d'en Haut (2722m) on the Italian border. A short ski descent finds the summer road at a tunnel entrance (2400m). Follow the road up east (left) to the Col du Grand St Bernard.

The Hospice is a great place to stay, but skiing north down the road back into Switzerland and staying at the Plan du Jeu (2073m) hut is quick and gains some time on the next day.

Day 4 – Bourg St Bernard – Cabane de Valsorey or Cabane de Vélan

Grade AD S3 BSA **Aspects** W, N and S
Ascent 1354m to the Cabane de Vélan (add 750m of ascent if you continue to the Valsorey)
Descent 1147m

No glaciers, but a technical day with some steep ground and several changeovers.

If you stayed at the Hospice ski down the road to the car park at Bourg St Bernard; if you stayed at the Plan du Jeu hut then you are in position already. Start easily following the old draglift above the car park at the tunnel entrance in Bourg St Bernard. Above point 2273m a steep moraine leads up east with plenty of kick-turns! Follow it to point 2795m. The Col de Prox (2779m) is now visible to the north.

Climb this, sometimes on foot, then continue north and north-east to a col at 2922m (south-east of the Montorge summit – Swiss ski maps show other lines). Ski down north-east with a choice of aspects to around 2300m. The route to Valsorey leads into the obvious narrow gorge, and another 700m of ascent on sunny slopes. Instead, turn south for the Vélan hut – a shorter climb and often a much quieter hut, although it leaves more to do tomorrow!

Day 5 – Valsorey – Cabane de Chanrion

Grade AD S3 TBSA **Aspects** SW, S and E
Ascent 1810m from the Vélan hut (1060m from the Valsorey) **Descent** 1196m

A tough day (Valsorey - Plateau du Couloir - Col du Sonadon - Glacier du Mont Durand - Cabane de Chanrion) with ski, mountaineering and navigation challenges! Committing and serious in poor weather.

From the Vélan hut, make an early start! A quick ski down (check the route the day before) joins the track to Valsorey, 600m above. You have missed the crowds and will often be alone.

Starting from Valsorey can be busy – everyone goes the same way. On skis at first, change to crampons (3300m) for the climb to the Plateau du Couloir. This becomes steep (50° below the col) with significant avalanche risk after bad weather, and can be very cold early morning.

Back on skis for a quick descent south-east then east (surprisingly steep for a 'plateau'!) before skinning to Col du Sonadon (3504m). Ski south-east on the Glacier du Mont Durand, turning sharply south around 3300m to avoid a big serac / cliff band. Continue on the right bank of the glacier to 2700m, then traverse out right (east, skins on, or lots of side-stepping!) to find point 2697m. This is tricky in poor weather, steep ground below. Continue east onto easier ground, turning north before a final climb to the Chanrion hut!

Route to Valsorey hut and Plateau du Couloir.

Chamonix-Zermatt Haute Route

Enjoying the view from the Tête de Valpelline.

Day 6 – Chanrion – Cabane des Vignettes

| Grade PD S2 BS | Aspects SW, S, SE and E | Ascent 1440m | Descent 630m |

A long, remote day (Chanrion hut - Serpentine Glacier - Pigne d'Arolla - Cabane des Vignettes) with the highpoint of the Haute Route on the Pigne d'Arolla. (See option below.)

Head north then north-east from Chanrion to gain the lower Brenay Glacier, then turn north (2900m) to the Serpentine Glacier. (The Brenay Glacier direct is becoming difficult with glacier recession.) The ascent is long but gentle to the Col de la Serpentine (3542m). Turn east and join the trail from the Dix hut, climbing steeply to the Col du Brenay (sometimes on foot, crampons, big crevasse at the top!). From here, the Pigne d'Arolla summit is in sight, 45 minutes away, the highest point on the tour.

From the summit, ski wide open slopes ESE (crevasses). Turn south onto a steepening at 3300m. A large cairn marks the way to Cabane des Vignettes, but there are easier lines further down right.

Option

For tired teams or poor weather, an easier day is to return south below the hut into the gorge leading to the Otemma Glacier. A long but scenic ascent gains the Col de Charmotane (3024m). Turn north and climb a short steep slope (avalanche risk), then to the Col des Vignettes and the hut. About 900m of ascent.

Chamonix-Zermatt Haute Route

Day 7 – Vignettes hut – Zermatt

Grade PD-AD S2 TBSA   **Aspects** all   **Ascent** 1300m   **Descent** 2530m

The 'grand finale'! A long day over three cols, with a 2000m descent below the Matterhorn to Zermatt. Leave promptly ahead of the crowds, and keep an eye on the time – allow about 2 hours for each col.

Return to the Col des Vignettes and turn south, making a short, steep descent to the Col de Charmotane (often icy and intimidating). Skins on for the gentle climb to Col de l'Evêque.

Ski east, staying right to avoid crevasses (tricky in poor visibility), then easily north-east down open slopes turning east around 2900m onto the Haut Glacier d'Arolla. (Easy escape to Arolla from here if weather or fitness are in doubt.) Skins on for a rising traverse to the foot of the Col du Mont Brulé (hard to spot if untracked – don't go to the Col de Tsa de Tsan!). Either skin very steeply, or more usually, crampon to the top (3213m). The final col is now in sight!

A short descent working left gains the glacier and the gentle but very foreshortened climb to the Col de Valpelline (3554m). The col is the end of the uphill, and has stunning views of the Matterhorn. The option of skiing the Stockjigletscher is spectacular but very serious. There are huge crevasses from 3500m to 3100m, and the descent needs good visibility. Instead, head north-east at first through the steepening crevassed area, turning sharply south around 3140m when the angle eases. Ski steeper slopes south (serac risk to the right), then turn back east at 3000m, keeping the rocks of the Stockji on your left. Below point 2735m work east across the Zmutt Gletscher and follow the right bank below the Matterhorn, all the way out to Stafel. In firm snow this is fast traversing, but in fresh snow or late in the day it is a long and tiring traverse, and very difficult for snowboarders!

Around point 2183m, join the road where a 10-minute walk leads up to the Stafelalp Restaurant and the Zermatt pistes. Ski the blue run to Furi (lift down late season) and down to Zermatt for a well-earned beer!

About Graham Frost

www.frostguiding.co.uk

Graham is a British Mountain Guide holding the IFMGA qualification. He lives in Evolène in French-speaking Switzerland (just down the valley from Arolla) where he runs Frost Guiding offering year-round courses and guiding on skis, mountaineering and rock climbing.

Grand Combin seen from the Vélan hut with the approach to the Valsorey behind the moraine. Photo – Bruce Goodlad.

Sunset from the Vélan hut.

Mont Vélan

By Bruce Goodlad

Tour overview

Most of the tours in this book are multi-day hut-to-hut adventures or a selection of day tours, but I would like to propose a stand-alone mountain in this chapter. Mont Vélan is my favourite overnight ski tour in the Alps, and it has every element that makes up a great tour.

    We start the climb from the car, so no lifts and everything that goes with them. You skin or maybe walk, depending on the conditions, up a beautiful valley. You stay in a really cool hut in a spectacular location, then climb a great route that involves easy skinning, a technical col with climbing chains, and a possible abseil. Then you climb a spectacular crevassed glacier to an incredible viewpoint with the Alps laid out below you. The ski descent takes an intricate line down a glacier, followed by a steep couloir, and another glacier; then a gorge leads you back to your ascent track. Every time I climb Mont Vélan on skis I have a smile on my face for days afterwards – it's got to be one of the classics of the Alps.

Mont Vélan

Grade
AD BSA S3

Season
Mid March to early / mid May

Map
The map for Mont Vélan is particularly awkward being right on the divide between multiple sheets. For the mountain above the hut the best sheet is the 1:25000 Mont Vélan 1366, and for the approach the 1:50000 ski map Martigny 282 S is best. It is worth printing one off from www.map.geo.admin.ch so that you can get the mountain in the middle of the sheet.

Kit
Classic ski touring kit for glacier skiing, plus ice axe and crampons. It would also be worth bringing a few extra karabiners for the climb over the Col de la Gouille.

Weather forecast
www.meteoswiss.admin.ch/

Avalanche forecast
www.slf.ch

Hut information
Cabane du Vélan – www.velan.ch info@velan.ch – +41 (0)27 787 13 13

Useful information
Accommodation ideas before you head into the mountains – www.vicheres.ch/

Alternative guide books
Ski de Randonnée Bas-Valais by Georges Sanga, Swiss Alpine Club
Les Classiques de Randonnée à Ski by Georges Sanga, Swiss Alpine Club (French language)

Mont Vélan

Day 1 – Bourg-Saint-Pierre – Cabane du Vélan

Grade PD S2 BS	Starting altiude 1827m	
Aspect SW, W and N	Ascent 800m	Descent 0m

The start of the tour depends on how much snow is left on the ground. Drive to Bourg-Saint-Pierre; don't turn off into the village but stay on the main road heading for the Grand Saint Bernard tunnel. Just after a garage / petrol station, and before you pass all the buildings, turn left onto a single-track road (the turn-off is signposted to the Vélan and Valsorey huts). Drive up the road, quite steep with a few hairpins. You may be stopped by the snow, in which case park where you can at the side of the road. If the road is clear of snow it is not worth driving beyond the hairpin at 1762m.

It's time to start skinning or walking, the guardian can usually tell you what altitude you can ski from. You can continue up the road then turn right (southwest) next to a building at 1834m, or cut the corner on a small path. The ascent follows the north side of the valley, any path junctions are signposted to the hut. At 2258m the valley opens out and you should be able to see the hut to the south at 2642m. You need to climb the moraine in front of you. In cold conditions there is usually a skinning track heading up the face, but in warmer spring conditions it is worth climbing the left-hand side to get onto the moraine crest as early as possible, to reduce your exposure to wet snow avalanches. In the spring I will always try and start from the car no later than 0900, to make sure I am on top of this ridge before the sun gets too strong and increases the avalanche hazard. When you are on the ridge, follow this and the easier ground above to the hut.

Liz O'Connor approaching the Vélan hut.

Day 2 – Mont Vélan

Grade AD S3 TBSA	Aspects N, NE and W	Ascent 1200m	Descent 2180m

It is worth getting out the door pretty early to make sure the lower slopes are still skiable on the way down, and not too soft. You also want to be ahead of the crowds on the crossing of the Col de la Gouille, as you can waste a lot of time if you get caught up with other people. You can start skinning from the door or the terrace at the side of the hut. Head up the Glacier du Tseudet, trend to the left (north side) to keep away from any potential serac fall from the above. You need to head left anyway to get around a steep crevassed section as you head for the Col de la Gouille. This looks quite intimidating from below but it all fits together when you start climbing. As you look up at the col, the climbing starts down and left. There is usually a good track leading to the point where you need to take skis off and strap them to your pack (leave skins on), and put your crampons on.

Put poles away as well and get your ice axe out. The route over the col has a series of chains that can be used for security. Unless you are really comfortable moving on this type of terrain I would suggest roping up, and as a minimum move together with a karabiner clipped into the chains and the rope clipped into the karabiner, creating a running belay. The chains lead up and right to reach the col. On the other side, follow the chains down and across right to reach the Glacier de Valsorey. If you feel the terrain is too steep you can abseil here, there are a series of anchors on the rock wall to your right (looking out). When you get onto the easy-angled snow it is worth moving out of the way (to your right) before sorting your skis out in case anyone knocks any rock or snow down on you from above.

Have a drink and a snack, then start skinning up the glacier. The easiest line skirts under a rock buttress at about 3350m with a crevassed area on your left. As you gain height there is an area of crevasses at about 3400m, the track sometimes goes around these on the south side or threads through them. (This will depend on the conditions from year to year. In 2016 it was easiest to thread the middle, as the left-hand track forced some exposed kick turns.) Above the crevasse band the glacier eases for a while until a final steepening leads to the summit plateau. This last steepening always poses some tactical challenges as the slope is about 40°, which is about the maximum that can be reasonably ascended on skins. If there is a good track you can carry on skinning, but as this is also the descent route the track usually gets destroyed by descending skiers. I usually put my skis on my pack and crampons back on, then climb this slope. If you keep to the left you will be out of the way of any descending skiers. Where the slope eases, put your skis back on and skin to the summit. The actual summit is not well defined but you can select the highest point.

The descent starts by skiing down the slope you have just climbed. The best skiing line is often through the crevasses we discussed above, and on the line of ascent until about 3200m, then trending north-east. You are heading for a couloir that cuts through the rocks / cliffs. In bad visibility this could be difficult to find and can be a bit intimidating as the ground rolls away as you approach the top of the couloir. It is easier to see into the couloir as you approach from skier's left, at the top, close to the rocks. The couloir is about 40° and gives great skiing; it leads you onto the lower section of the Glacier de Valsorey. Ski down the glacier and continue across the flat section. There are now two possibilities and you need to ask the guardian about conditions to be able to choose. If the gorge ahead of you (just under the word 'Les Grands Plans' on the map) is skiable, it gives the easiest and most logical descent. If this has melted out or is unskiable for any reason, you need to climb and shuffle round the moraine ridge on your left (west) to gain your ascent track. Either route puts you on your ascent track at about 2250m, which is followed back to the car.

Crossing the Col de la Gouille.

Mike Austin descending the steep upper section on Mont Vélan.

Mont Vélan

Possible variants or alternatives

In rare circumstances it may not be possible to ski down the couloir as described. On one occasion I was there just after the hut had closed for the season, and an avalanche had removed all of the snow from the couloir. In such a situation you can re-ascend the chains and ski back down the Glacier du Tseudet, then make a short climb back to the hut and ski down the moraine; or ski down and join the route as described above. When we were forced to do this by conditions, we had an amazing ski down on perfect spring snow.

Matteo enjoying some great spring snow on Mont Vélan.

About Bruce Goodlad

www.mountainadventurecompany.com

Bruce was born and brought up in the west of Scotland. The Scottish mountains gave him a classic apprenticeship in climbing and mountaineering and the Scouts gave him a taste of skiing, but it wasn't until he was struggling knee-deep in soft snow down a glacier after a winter route in Chamonix that he realised he needed to learn to ski. After studying for a geography degree at Glasgow University, Bruce spent the following year as a trainee instructor at Glenmore Lodge on the 'Night Watch Scheme'. It was during this year under the tolerant tutelage of 'Lodge' instructors that he actually learnt how to ski and discovered ski touring.

What started as means of transport to access winter climbs in the Alps has become a life-long passion that has taken Bruce all over the world, ski touring and guiding in Antarctica, Greenland, Norway, Iceland, the Alps, Argentina, Japan, Armenia, Sweden, Canada, the USA and Russia. He is always looking for the next new place to explore and share with his clients.

Bruce has made this passion for the mountains into a career, qualifying as an IFMGA guide in 2001. Since 2008 Bruce has been involved in the training of mountain guides and served as the Technical Director for the British Mountain Guides from 2012 to 2016. Much of his focus during that period was the development of the avalanche education and ski guiding for trainee guides.

He also partners Mike Austin in the avalanche education business (www.avalanchegeeks.com), which delivers structured avalanche education in Scotland and the Alps.

Bruce now lives full time in the Alps with his wife and two children; he is the author of two previous books also by Pesda Press; *Alpine Mountaineering* and *Ski Touring*.

Classic touring in the West Oberland.

West Oberland Ski Haute Route

By Terry Ralphs

Tour overview

The West Oberland Ski Haute Route traverses the Alpine range between the villages of Les Diablerets and Kandersteg. It is a delightfully scenic ski tour offering fantastic ski descents in a quiet corner of Switzerland. The tour is not as glaciated, or the mountains as dramatic, as those around the 4000m peaks, but it has its own charm and is a good warm-up tour for those considering the Chamonix-Zermatt Haute Route. This ski tour does, however, contain some exposed passages and can be difficult to navigate in poor weather.

The route traverses over the summits of Les Diablerets, Arpelistock, Wildhorn, Schnidehore and Wildstrubel, which are all around 3200m high, with the huts lying between 2000m and 2500m. A summit can be taken every day between the huts, which cannot be said for all Alpine tours. The ski descents from these summits are on open slopes with most having more than 1000m in vertical descent. If you are lucky with the conditions, the final ski into Kandersteg can give over 1500m of vertical descent!

As you weave your way across the west Bernese Oberland chain, the route boasts magnificent views of the Valaisanne peaks to the south and the Bernese peaks in the east. Steep dramatic limestone cliffs, through which the route snakes its way on largely open slopes, define the landscape. The limestone strata and rock folding on the Wildhorn is particularly impressive. It must be said, however, that this combination of limestone cliffs and open slopes does make for very tricky route finding in poor visibility.

Wildlife such as ibex, chamois, fox, arctic hares and eagles can be spied en route, as well as the famous bearded vultures, which nest near the Gemmi Pass.

West Oberland Ski Haute Route

The huts are comfortable, with indoor toilets and drying rooms, and some have showers. They offer traditional Swiss German hospitality. The Gelten, Wildstrubel and Lämmeren huts have been recently renovated to a high modern standard. The Lämmeren hut is one of the busiest in the Alps but the other huts are very quiet and a delight to stay in.

In case of bad weather, which can make this tour very difficult to navigate, you may consider the many excellent day ski tours available in the region around Les Diablerets. Another option would be to go directly to the Lämmeren hut from the Gemmi Pass, as the peaks around the Lämmeren are less serious and more user-friendly in poor conditions.

The route starts in the village of Les Diablerets, which is easily accessed by train from Geneva airport and has plenty of accommodation to suit your budget. Kandersteg is the classic finishing point where the onward / return journey can be undertaken easily using public transport. Both Les Diablerets and Kandersteg have train stations.

Grade
AD S3 TBS

Season
The huts are open from the first week in March to the first week in May, but it is possible to do this tour as early as February and as late as mid May, although you will have to use winter rooms in the huts, except for the Lämmeren hut which is open from early February.

Maps
1:50000 St-Maurice 272 S, 1:50000 Wildstrubel 263 S, 1:50000 Montana 273 S, 1:25000 Lenk 1266, 1:25000 St Leonard 1286, 1:25000 Gemmi 1267, and for full cover the 1:25000 Adelboden 1247 and 1:25000 Les Diablerets 1285

You can find a 1:50000 online map at www.map.geo.admin.ch choose 'Snowsport' under 'Change topic' to reveal the ski route overlay.

Kit
This ski tour does traverse glaciers, although crevasses are rare, so the usual ski touring equipment is needed including ice axe, crampons, harness and crevasse rescue equipment. The route does cross steep enough slopes to warrant taking ski crampons, especially in spring conditions.

Weather forecast
www.meteosuisse.ch

Avalanche forecast
www.slf.ch

Hut information
Cabane de Prarochet (44 places)
www.ski-club-saviese.ch/prarochet.htm – prarochet@gmail.com +41(0)27 395 27 27
Gelten hut (83 places) showers available
www.geltenhuette.ch – huettenchef@gmx.ch – +41 (0)33 744 54 23
Cabane des Audannes (46 places)
www.audannes.ch – gardien@audannes.ch – +41 (0)79 310 90 60
Wildhorn hut (96 places)
www.wildhornhuette.ch – wildhornhuette@bluewin.ch – +41(0) 33 733 23 82

West Oberland Ski Haute Route

Wildstrubel hut (68 places)
www.wildstrubelhuette.ch – info@wildstrubelhuette.ch – +41 (0) 33 744 33 39
Lämmeren hut (96 places) showers available
www.laemmerenhuette.ch – info@laemmerenhuette.ch – +41 (0)27 470 25 15
Hotel Wildstrubel Gemmipass. Hotel facilities. It is a useful alternative to the Lämmeren hut if it's full.
www.gemmi.ch – +41 (0) 27 470 12 01

Useful information
Swiss travel information – www.sbb.ch/en/home.html
Les Diablerets tourist information – www.villars-diablerets.ch/en
Glacier 3000 ski resort – www.glacier3000.ch/en/
Gemmibahn, Leukerbad – www.gemmi.ch/
Swiss Alpine Club – www.sac-cas.ch/en.html

Alternative guide books
Ski Randonnée Alpes Fribourgeoise et Vaudoise by Ralph Schnegg, Daniel Anker, Swiss Alpine Club (in French)
Skitouren Berner Alpen West Ralph Schnegg, Daniel Anker, Swiss Alpine Club (in German)

Day 1 – Traverse of the Arpelistock (3036m) – Gelten hut (2002m) from the Sex Rouge

Grade AD S2 BS-BSA	Starting altitude 2010m	
Aspects E, S, N and NE	Ascent 830m	Descent 1700m

There is a free navette bus from Les Diablerets to the Col du Pillon. From there, take the Glacier 3000 lift to the Sex Rouge (2940m). Follow the piste towards the Combe d'Audon passing the Dome T-bar on the right. Just before the col leading to the Combe d'Audon, leave the piste and ski down the Glacier de Tsanfleuron. Follow the valley below the glacier and when the terrain opens out and flattens you may need to skate and side step to gain the Col du Sanetsch (2252m, 45mins). Put on skins and take the striking Arête de l'Arpille to the summit of the Arpelistock. Follow the crest of this ridge, which can be done on foot if snow cover is poor, to a flat area at 2700m (1hr 45mins). There is a key passage here as the ridge above becomes steep and rocky, so veer right (east) to traverse a slope for 300m to gain a flat area leading to open slopes to the right of the ridge which can be skinned up. At 2900m the summit slope steepens. In good conditions, you may be able to skin all the way to the summit, but in lean conditions it is better to carry your skis on your rucksack. If there is no snow here care is needed to find the correct line as it is slabby and a bit exposed (1hr 45mins). (5hrs from Sex Rouge, 800m vertical ascent.)

The summit of the Arpelistock (3036m) which is on the border between Valais and Bern, has great views of the Wildhorn (tomorrow's route). It is important to ski down in a NNE direction initially to avoid the exposed edge on the left, then more northerly before dropping in to the valley to gain the col at 2685m. Take care in poor visibility. From the col, the valley splits into two. Either route takes you to the hut, but it is more logical to take the Furggetäli (north-most valley) on the way down and the Rottal on the ascent to the Wildhorn (following day). From the valley bottom, a short ten-minute skin or steep walk takes you to the Gelten hut (2002m), (1hr, 1040m descent). Hot showers and a warm welcome from Ueli and Marianne await.
Ski routes 615c, 607b and 607a as marked on the Swiss ski touring map.

West Oberland Ski Haute Route

Skiing down from the Arpelistock.

Day 2 – Traverse of the Wildhorn (3248m) – Wildhorn hut (2303m)

| Grade AD S2 BS | Aspects all | Ascent 1300m | Descent 1000m |

This is one of the harder days on the tour. If it is warm, then an early start is essential, so that you can traverse the steep east-facing slopes under Mont Pucel while they are still frozen.

Walk back down the summer path from the terrace passing the water fountain, then skin a short way up the valley before turning hard right and making a rising traverse on the terrace between small cliffs which face the hut (when looking south-east from the hut). It would be advisable to check out this traverse line the day before. This leads to an impressive plateau at the base of the Rottal, which is dominated by a huge limestone cliff. Continue up the left side of this valley in a south-westerly direction until 2350m where you start to head southwards towards the Gältehore. At 2450m veer left (north-east) to traverse on the terrace which is above the impressive cliff. Make a rising traverse (west then south) to the Col du Brochet (3hrs). Pass the col on the north side and keep climbing up a slope to the shoulder (at 2900m) on the left (east) side of the col, then descend a few metres over the rib and traverse the large, and slightly exposed, slopes below the Wildhorn to gain a col on the south side of Mont Pucel at 3000m. Keep spiralling up and to the left (north-east) around Mont Pucel until you are on the south-east side on a bench above a steep slope.

This is now the key passage. I find it easier to take the skins off here and make a short ski descent and a high traverse (northwards) just clipping the bottom of the east-facing cliffs of Mont Pucel. If you keep the traverse high, you should find a slightly less steep slope in front of you, on which to put the skins back on. It is possible, of course, to keep the skins on for this traverse, but it will feel much more exposed, especially if icy.

West Oberland Ski Haute Route

Enjoying a great descent from the Wildhorn.

Alternative route

The Cabane des Audannes (not always guardianed) provides a shorter day and refuge in case of poor conditions. If you descend from this key passage on Mont Pucel (ski route 637h) you will arrive at the Cabane des Audannes. You can then continue the tour over the Col des Eaux Froides (ski route 636b) to join the normal route on the Wildhorn from the Wildhorn hut (ski route 637a).

However, it is much better to continue to the Wildhorn hut if possible, by climbing the vague valley above and break out right to gain the Wildhorn Glacier. Once on the glacier the slopes become easy-angled and you can make a beeline to the summit. As you approach the summit ahead, go slightly past it on the north-east side and then climb the steeper slopes back on yourself to gain the summit. A short, exposed walk (without skis) leads to the summit cross (5hrs to 6hrs, 1300m ascent).

The Wildhorn is a heliski peak, which endorses the quality of the descent. Fortunately, the landing zone is on the subsidiary peak to the south.

From the summit descend the steep easterly slope back to the Wildhorn Glacier. From here head north to the Téné Glacier, taking care to give the cliff line to the left a wide berth while not to drifting too far to the right. At 2950m head west (left) to gain a col which gives a passage through the cliffs to the Tungel Glacier. Keep heading north to traverse the Tungel Glacier until you see the Chilchli. You can ski either side of this rocky peak but it is more direct and less steep on the right (north) side. If you take the easier option it is better to traverse under the north face of the Chilchli so that you avoid the steep slopes where the snout of the glacier used to be. Gain a col which divides the Chilchli from the Niesehore and continue on easy-angled slopes to the hut which is at 2303m. The hut is hidden in a wind scoop so can be difficult to find in bad visibility (1hr, 945m descent).

Ski routes 605a, 637c, 637a.

West Oberland Ski Haute Route

Sunset from the Wildstrubel hut.

Day 3 – Traverse of the Schnidehore (2937m) – Wildstrubel hut (2791m)

Grade PD S2 BS   **Aspects** N, SE and S   **Ascent** 1100m   **Descent** 600m

The Schnidehore is not the highest of the peaks on this tour but it should not be underestimated, especially in poor visibility. You will need to retrace your tracks to the Tungel Glacier and then head directly to the Schnidejoch (1hr 30mins, 2756m). From this pass go left (north) up the rib and make a high traverse across a slope to gain flatter ground and the fore summit. Traverse just below the ridge on the east-facing slopes to gain the summit (2hrs, 635m vertical ascent), it might be easier to ski across rather than skin. This exposed summit gives fine views of the Wildhorn and Wildstrubel.

Head eastwards down the valley being careful to find the correct continuation at 2790m which is to the east. At just above 2500m in this valley there is a key passage between cliffs. Be careful to find the correct way here; this is normally down a short, steep north-facing slope between the cliffs. Below 2500m carefully (if warm) traverse the south-east facing slopes to gain the flat terrain of the Plan des Roses and then the Alpage de Rawil (40mins, 540m descent).

It is also possible to get here by bypassing the Schnidehore by skiing down the valley from the Schnidejoch to Lac Ténéhet and traversing north to the Alpage de Rawil (ski route 640a).

Continue north-east to the flat area to the east of the Rawil Pass. From here take the steep valley eastwards breaking out left (north) at 2800m to gain the Wildstrubel hut (2789m) (5hrs, 1050m overall ascent). There is a military installation on the Wisshore and a cable car from Iffigenalp (military use only) passes just in front of the hut. Enjoy the cake and coffee!

Ski routes 641a, 641c.

West Oberland Ski Haute Route

Day 4 – Traverse of the Wildstrubel (3244m) – Lämmeren Hut (2501m)

Grade AD S2/3 TBS **Aspects** S, E and SE **Ascent** 780m **Descent** 930m

There are two ways to start this day; the first is to climb to the col which is south-west of the hut to access the Glacier de la Plaine Morte (30mins), but if conditions are good it is much better to climb just above the military installation on the Wisshore (45mins, 200m ascent) as this gives a great ski onto the Plaine Morte. It is possible to escape the tour by deviating south to the Crans Montana ski resort. The Glacier de la Plaine Morte can have a ski de fond track on it, but it is better to take a direct line to the small lake (marked on the map) under the south rib of the Wildstrubel.

You can attack this rib directly, but I find it better to take a wide berth on the east side as it is less steep, avoids kick turns, and it takes the same time. If you take the wide berth route you need to traverse onto the rib just north of point 2910m. In good conditions, it is possible to climb this steep rib on skis making exposed kick turns, but it is not much slower, and a lot safer, to carry your skis (boot crampons can be useful) to the Wildstrubel summit (3hrs, 500m). In poor visibility, it requires good navigation to descend from this summit. Make a short, steep descent north-eastwards to the col just east of point 3157m. It is possible to make a long ski traverse to just below the middle summit (Mittelgipfel, 3243.5m), but it is more logical to skin to the middle summit as you then have a fall line ski down the Wildstrubel Glacier. The Wildstrubel Glacier is not badly crevassed but it is probably the only glacier on the tour where crevasse danger might be an issue. The safest line down the glacier is on the skier's left of point 2999m (on 1:26000 map, route 734a). As you ski past the valley on the left which leads to the Steghorn, keep right and ski into the narrow valley below. If you are in good time then the Steghorn is a great peak to take in on your way (2hrs 30mins extra, 600m ascent). At 2500m you can traverse under the cliff on the left (north) to gain the terrace on which the hut is situated. Don't worry if you miss the traverse as a few more downhill turns take you to a flat area (1hr, 800m descent). A short 20 minute skin north-eastwards leads to the popular Lämmeren hut.
Ski routes 733a, 733d, 734a.

Day 5 – Descent of the Üschenetal via the Rote Totz (2829m) – Kandersteg (1200m)

Grade PD S2 BS **Aspects** SW and N **Ascent** 350m **Descent** 1590m

A short skin to the Rote Totz (2848m, 1hr 30mins, 350m vertical ascent) gives access to the north-facing Üschenetal, which descends to Kandersteg. This is a fitting finale to the West Oberland Haute Route and an amazing ski in powder conditions. The descent is straightforward enough until 2400m, where it is essential to find the traverse which leads right (eastwards) towards the Wyssi Flue as the valley cliffs out. A large, steep slope awaits, although traversing further right gives a slightly less steep ski, and this slope leads to the inner Üschenetal. In warm conditions the big slopes on the east face of the valley can avalanche all the way down to the valley floor, so don't be too late passing between the Inner Üschene (1700m) and Usser Üschene (1500m). You may need to walk down the road to Sunnbüel (Kandersteg) if the snow runs out (2hrs, 1590m descent). There is a bus connection between Sunnbüel and Kandersteg (train station).
Ski route 738b, 738d.

West Oberland Ski Haute Route

Skiing great snow from the summit of the Wildstrubel.

Possible variants or alternatives

Day 1 (day tour) – Summit of Les Diablerets (3210m) – Cabane de Prarochet (2555m)

It is possible to extend this tour by having a warm-up day ski touring to the summit of Les Diablerets (route 615a on the Swiss ski map), and combining this with some of the brilliant off-piste that Glacier 3000 offers. To reach the summit of Les Diablerets take the Dome T-bar; from its top there are two options:

1. Skin along the ridge until you get to the steep ground above the col (2986m). You will need to carefully down-climb (old fixed rope in place) to the col. From the col, ski or skin down to the Glacier les Diablerets and continue skiing westwards to the summit (which is the peak on the right (north) (2hrs, 290m ascent).
2. From the top of the Dome T-Bar descend southwards to reach a bench (at 2850m, 30m vertical descent) which leads across to the Glacier Les Diablerets. This is technically easier, but more prone to avalanche risk as the slopes run out over big cliffs and a small sluff on the south-facing steep slopes could knock you over the edge.

If conditions are good, skinning along the ridge (first option) and skiing back over the bench (second option) provides a more interesting route.

There is a transceiver training centre at the bottom of the Ice Express chair lift, which you may find useful. If you plan to stay at the Cabane de Prarochet is important to contact the guardians as they may not be there.

Ski route 615a.

There are several other variants to end this tour depending snow cover and conditions; here are three possibilities:

Day 5 – Schwarzhorn (3105m) and Les Faverges – Aminona (1514m)
This is a brilliant south-facing ski in spring snow conditions. From the Lämmeren hut, ski down to the flat area to the south-west of the hut north-east of point 2449m. Take the terrace below the Schneehore and keep traversing to the east side of the Lämmeren Gletscher. A small steep slope gives access to the easy-angled upper Lämmeren Gletscher. It is possible to ski straight from the col at 3005m (2hrs), but more fun to continue to the summit of the Schwarzhorn at 3105m (20mins – 2 hrs 20mins from Lämmeren Hut, 655m ascent), care needed for cornices near the summit. Timing is important here to make sure you get the snow just softening in the top section of the descent but not to be too warm low down as this valley is avalanche prone on its large east and south facing slopes. Ski south and south-west into the valley marked as Les Outannes at its most westerly point to the east of Mont Bonvin before making a 180° switch back down a small valley before turning south once more. Then head to the Cave du Sex by following the summer footpath past a small dam on the stream. If you are lucky the piste will be still open but if not improvise to Aminona. During the time when the Montana lifts are running there should be a free navettebus to take you to the funicular to Sion. (2hrs, 1590m descent.)
Ski routes 728a, 728b.

Day 5 – Grossstrubel (3243m) and Ammertetali – Simmefäll (1105m) or Engstligenalp (1965m).
The Grossstrubel is the most northern summit on the Wildstrubel summit ridge, which is accessed by traversing along the ridge from the middle summit. You can reach this on your way from the Wildstrubel hut (on Day 4) or by reclimbing the Wildstrubel from the Lämmeren hut. The skiing in the Ammertetäll is steep, committing and in a remote environment. From the summit of Grossstrubel return to the col at 3098m and from there commit to the north-west facing slopes of the Ammerte Gletscher. Keep to the skier's right and make a steep traverse towards the Früestücksplatz.

At the Früestücksplatz it is possible to traverse over the Ammertegrat to descend to Engstligenalp (hotel and lifts), which means you can return to the Lämmeren hut via Chindbettipass and the Rote Totz Lücke.

Otherwise ski back to the left (west) and continue down to Lenk (2hrs, 2140m descent!). You will need a bus or taxi to reach Lenk train station from Simmefäll.
Ski routes 734b, 735a (Engstligenalp), 735c (Simmefäll).

Day 5 – Daubenhorn (2942m) and Gemmibahn (2314m)
The Gemmibahn is the safest and easiest way to exit the mountains from the Lämmeren hut. Follow the cairns and marker south-west at first until you can turn safely to the left (north-west). There is a tricky, steep passage (2315m) leading to the flat area of the Lämmerenboden; please be mindful of ski tourers on the approach to the hut and try not to damage the uphill track on your way down. If conditions are good then the Daubenhorn (3hrs from the Lämmeren hut, 640m ascent) is a great ski peak to do on the way. To reach the summit cross of the Daubenhorn requires an exposed but easy scramble (rope useful). You will need to skin back up to the Gemmi Pass (1hr 15mins from the Lämmeren hut without climbing the Daubenhorn).
Ski routes 725a, 12b.

West Oberland Ski Haute Route

A continuation to the Central Oberland

It is possible to carry on this ski tour from Kandersteg to Lauterbrunnen. From Lauterbrunnen you can then take the train to the Jungfraujoch to continue along the Central Bernese Oberland ... and then the East Oberland.

From Kandersteg there are two options to get to the Mutthorn hut:

1. Climb up the Gasteretal to the Mutthorn hut (15km and 1600m of vertical ascent, 8 to 10hrs). Although a long way it is a very impressive and remote journey. Stay at the Mutthorn hut (not guardianed in the winter / spring) to get an early start on the descent to Lauterbrunnen.
2. Take the train to Goppenstein and bus to Kippel. Take the first lift on the Lauchernalp ski resort to the Hockenhorn and traverse eastwards to the Petersgrat and point 3202m (2hrs). From here you can ski down to the Mutthorn hut and continue down to Lauterbrunnen.

Ski route 335f / 64b.

The descent to Stechelberg / Lauterbrunnen from the Mutthorn hut is very long (2km vertical) so an early start is recommended.

Ski route 64c.

You can then link into the Bernese Oberland tour proposed by Al Powell.

About Terry Ralphs

www.alpin-ism.com

Terry is a British Mountain Guide who lives in the village of Leysin, Switzerland.

He started his career in the mountains on the assistant instructor scheme at Plas y Brenin in North Wales, going on to work as a climbing and trekking guide in the Himalayas, later qualifying as an IFMGA mountain guide in 1994.

Terry has been involved in training guides since the year 2000. He was the British Mountain Guides Training Officer from 2008 to 2012, during which time he helped to form a guides training school for the Kyrgyz Mountain Guides Association.

He has climbed, skied and guided throughout the world in countries such as Nepal, India, Pakistan, Russia, North America, Kyrgyzstan, Norway, and in the European Alps.

He is a director of the International School of Mountaineering (www.alpin-ism.com) which specialises in ski mountaineering and Alpine climbing courses and has worked as a full-time ski guide since 1995.

Seb Ancianiec enjoying the south face of Kranzberg.

Bernese Oberland Tour

By Al Powell

Tour overview

The Bernese Oberland, in Switzerland, is generally regarded as the premier high-altitude ski touring region in the Alps. Large-scale glacier scenery, extensive views and big ski peaks are the attractions here. Huts are modern and comfortable, but also at high altitude, with all skiing taking place between 3000 and 4000m – so you need to be fit and acclimatise quickly in order to ski here. If in doubt it may be wise to do a couple of easy days prior to the proposed tour, to help you acclimatise if you are coming from low altitude.

Because the glacier systems and crevasse fields in the region are so extensive, this is an area where it's much more common to skin roped in parts of some ascents. Likewise, roped skiing may be necessary – especially in poor visibility – so you need to be familiar with these techniques, as well as crevasse rescue skills.

Although it's possible to travel safely between many of the huts in less than ideal conditions, the Oberland is also no place to ski or be caught out in bad weather, as all of the days are on crevassed glaciers and escape routes are long and serious. If you are caught you may just have to sit tight until conditions and weather improve.

Bernese Oberland Tour

Grade
PD BS S2-S3

Season
April to early May

Maps
Swisstopo 1:50000 Jungfrau 264 S
Swisstopo 1:25000 Finsteraarhorn 1249
You can find a 1:50000 online map at www.map.geo.admin.ch choose 'Snowsport' under 'Change topic' to reveal the ski route overlay.

Kit
Classic ski touring kit including an ice axe, crampons and glacier travel / crevasse rescue kit.

Weather forecast
www.meteosuisse.ch

Avalanche forecast
www.slf.ch

Hut information
Konkordia hut – www.konkordiahuette.ch – +41 (0)33 855 13 94
Finsteraarhorn hut – www.finsteraarhornhuette.ch – +41 (0)33 855 29 55
Hollandia hut – www.hollandiahuette.ch – +41 (0)27 030 11 35

Useful information
www.grindelwald.ch – Grindelwald tourist information

Alternative guide books
Les Classiques de Randonnées à Ski de Suisse – Club Alpine Suisse

Bernese Oberland Tour

Day 1 – Trugberg – Konkordia hut

Grade PD S2-3 TBS	Starting altitude 3453m	
Aspects S and E	Ascent 680m	Descent 1320m

Trugberg makes for a good first day as, depending on conditions, either the south or north faces can be skied en route to the Konkordia hut, whose (in)famous steps make for a tough finish to the day. Start in Grindelwald and take the (expensive!) mountain railway up to Kleine Scheidegg and then up through the Eiger to the Jungfraujoch at 3500m. To escape the station, follow signs to the 'Mönchsjochhütte' and once outside skin 1.5km along the marked piste on the left (heading N) to the Mönchsjoch hut. Ski off the back, 3km down the right side of the Ewigschneefeld, keeping a respectful distance away from the seracs. Just beyond the seracs (around 3350m), skin east directly up the slope (some crevasses) to a rocky shoulder at 3700m. If time allows, you can now skin / boot pack further up the ridge to a viewpoint on Trugberg at about 3850m. Return to the shoulder at 3700m and if it's early enough and conditions are good, traverse right (S3, 30–35°) onto the south face of Trugberg and enjoy a wonderful spring snow descent – first trending leftwards below the ridge, then straight down (S3) to join the Konkordiaplatz at 2750m. From here, schuss south-east for 2km heading for the foot of the steps leading up to the Konkordia hut. Skin the last 400m to reach the steps, leave your skis under a boulder to save you carrying them up the ladders, then slog up to the hut!

Alternatives

Trugberg north-east flank. From the shoulder at 3700m on Trugberg, ski ENE; at first down the broad ridge, then left of the rocks (sometimes powder) back to the Ewigschneefeld. Cross to the far side and ski down the left side of the icefall to Konkordiaplatz.

In poor weather, the safest way to reach the Konkordia hut from the Jungfraujoch is: from the tunnel exit, head down and right (E) for 400m (some crevasses, but often a pisted track) onto the Jungfraufirn, then turn left and head south-east down the easy-angled glacier for 6km to Konkordiaplatz.

Day 2 (day tour) – Kranzberg

Grade AD S2-3 TBS	Aspect S	Ascent 1100m	Descent 1100m

The plan for today is to climb Kranzberg, one of the classic ski peaks of the Oberland. Head down the steps and schuss out onto the glacier, before skinning east across Konkordiaplatz to the steep east-facing slope at the foot of Kranzberg. This slope is over 35° and often awkward, so try and minimise kick turns. Above here, climb easily up the glacier to a bowl at 3300m, where you cut diagonally leftwards to a snowy shoulder on the ridge on the left at 3400m. Round this shoulder and climb up the bowl beyond, to finally reach the east ridge of Kranzberg. Leave skis here and climb the last 300m on foot to the summit.

Ski down the same way as you came up, until just above the final steep east-facing slope above Konkordiaplatz. Here, it's better to go right for 100m and pick up a small south-facing gully / rib which leads more safely down to the glacier. Finally, schuss and skin back to the foot of the Konkordia hut steps for another joyful lap!

Bernese Oberland Tour

The legendary Klemen Gricar IFMGA leading a team up Wyssnollen.

Alternative descent off Kranzberg

If you are heading on to the Hollandia hut, it's possible to ski the first upper bowl of Kranzberg, then instead of cutting left around the shoulder, continue straight down (crevasses) onto the Kranzbergfirn, thus saving a few kilometres of skinning up the Aletschfirn.

Day 3 – Wyssnollen – Finsteraarhorn hut

| Grade PD S2 BS | Aspects SW and E | Ascent 1367m | Descent 1180m |

Another good day's skiing, heading east to the Finsteraarhorn hut, taking in Wyssnollen en route. From the foot of the Konkordia hut steps, skin east up the Grueneygfirn to the Grünhornlücke (3280m). (Note: The final slope here is sub 30°, but it's overlooked by a steep south-facing slope above, which can sometimes avalanche across the route during or after heavy snowfall.)

Ski off the col, heading rightwards underneath Wyssnollen until about 2900m on the main Fieschergletscher. Here, turn right and skin up Wyssnollen from the east side. The summit is easily gained on skis and gives another great descent, before a final skin north across the Fieschergletscher to the broad, snowy gully below the Finsteraarhorn hut. (Note: This final section up to the hut is usually fine, but if you see large creep line cracks in the slope above, e.g. after a period of hot weather, or near the end of the season, then treat the slope as suspect and use the summer path up the rocks on the right instead – I've seen this slope avalanche twice in such conditions!)

Bernese Oberland Tour

Fresh powder on the Grosses Wannenhorn.

Day 4 (day tour) – Grosses Wannenhorn

Grade PD S2 BS   **Aspects** N and NE   **Ascent** 1100m   **Descent** 1100m

The Wannenhorn is a great ski peak and a big day out, skinning up to 3900m in order to enjoy some excellent views and a long, perfect-angled glacier descent. Start by schussing 2.5km down and across the Fieschergletscher to its south side at the foot of a rocky spur (point 2901m). From here, begin the long skin up the Wannenhorn initially up the centre, then the right side of the glacier bay, before finally traversing left onto the snow ridge near point 3602m. Follow the snow ridge for a short while, heading for steeper slopes on the right (30°), then continue up the broad, shallower-angled snow ridge above. Most parties visit the nearer south summit on the left. Ski back down the same way as far as point 3602m. Below here, if there is powder on the glacier, then stay on the right-hand side as much as possible, whereas for spring snow pitches, traverse left across to the bounding ridge on the far side – the flanks of this face east and receive more sun. Finally, skin back up across the Fieschergletscher back to the Finsteraarhorn hut.

Alternative

For good skiers and experienced ski mountaineers, the Finsteraarhorn itself gives an excellent, steeper day out. Skin up sustained slopes directly behind the hut (35°, often icy, good kick turning skills are essential), then cross the ridge on the left near point 3616m and continue up to the Hugisattel Point (4088m). Leave skis here and climb the north-west ridge of the Finsteraarhorn (Alpine climbing grade PD) – many teams just skin up to the Hugisattel to enjoy the descent, which is one of the best in the range.

Bernese Oberland Tour

Stephen Wass donning skins outside the Hollandia hut.

Day 5 – Grünhornlücke – Hollandia hut

Grade PD S2 BS   **Aspects** NE and SW   **Ascent** 800m   **Descent** 805m

A mountain travel and repositioning day, in order to get in place for a great exit to the range. Leave the Finsteraarhorn hut and skin back westwards, in order to re cross the Grünhornlücke. Enjoy the west side of this, as it's the only descent of the day, before donning skins again and beginning the long march up the Aletschfirn to the Hollandia hut, which lies on a rocky promontory overlooking the Lötschenlücke on its north side. This section feels endless on a hot afternoon, but close-up views of the huge north face of the Aletschhorn opposite offer some distraction.

Day 6 – Äbeni Flue – Lötschental

Grade PD S2 BS   **Aspects** SE, W and SW   **Ascent** 706m   **Descent** 2170m

A fitting finale to the week, with Äbeni Flue marking the highest point reached on the tour, followed by the famous final 2200m descent down into the Lötschental.

Skin north-west from the Hollandia hut, following an easy-angled glacier shelf, then after 2km go north, heading for the left-hand sky ridge of Äbeni Flue. Climb a steepening slope to join the ridge, then turn right and skin up to the snowy summit (it's also possible to follow the right-hand ridge instead). From the summit, ski back down the glacier, passing beneath the Hollandia hut to the Lötschenlücke. Cross the Lötschenlücke and ski south-west down the Langgletscher into the Lötschental. Schuss and pole down the lower part of the valley to the village of Blatten, where you can catch a postbus to the train station at Goppenstein and hence back to Grindelwald. (If there is insufficient snow to ski all the way to Blatten, a shuttle bus usually operates between Fafleralp and Blatten – ask hut guardian for details.)

Other suggestions in the area

If you only have five days available, there are a number of excellent ways to exit the range by heading south-east from the Finsteraarhorn hut (Nufenenpass 265S map required. Either stop at the Oberaarjoch hut, or get an earlier breakfast from the Finsteraarhorn hut).

Arguably, the best of these is the descent of the Bächital from the Vorder Galmihorn. From the Finsteraarhorn hut, ski 3km down the Fieschergletscher, then skin east up the Galmigletscher, passing the rock rognon at 2800m on its south (right) side. Now climb south-east up the north-facing slope (30°) on the right to the col at point 3382m. Finally, turn right and skin up the Vorder Galmihorn (3517m – excellent viewpoint).

Return to col 3382m and drop down right into the SW-facing Bächital (steepest sections at 30°), descending 2200m down to the train station at Reckingen. It's often necessary to walk the final part of the descent to the main Rhône valley. Other alternatives are to pass through the Galmilucke and ski down to Münster – this is safer (a couple of short sections at 30°), but tricky navigation in poor visibility.

Escape routes

From the Konkordia hut
Skin back up the Jungfraufirn to the Jungfraujoch – **Note:** any bad weather is likely to get worse as you gain height up the glacier.

Ski down the Aletsch Glacier to Märjelensee, From here you can either skin over the ridge east of the Eggishorn, or walk through a 1km long tunnel (entrance 200m south of the Gletscherstube – sometimes tricky to find) and ski out to Fiescheralp. You can also ski out to Bettmeralp or Riederalp further down the glacier.

From the Finsteraarhorn hut
Ski down the Fiescher Glacier to Fieschertal – nowadays this is a complicated route and may not always be possible – speak to the guardian for latest information.

About Al Powell

www.alpine-guides.com

See page 54.

Tête Blanche summit with views of the Matterhorn and Dent d'Hérens.

Arolla Day Tours

By Graham Frost

Area overview

Arolla is already firmly on the ski touring map with the world-famous Chamonix-Zermatt Haute Route crossing the head of the valley, and the Patrouille des Glaciers, the world's biggest ski mountaineering race, coming through Arolla every two years. The village of Arolla – and indeed the whole Val d'Hérens – has a different feel to most ski resorts. It's quiet, almost deserted out of season, and not to everyone's taste – there's not much après-ski! – but skiing here is a refreshing change from the hustle of the bigger stations.

The day tours described here try to give a varied introduction to the area – there's something for everyone, from short lift-access touring to tough days with long ascents in glaciated terrain. All six tours are possible as day tours, but some could be split with an overnight in a hut, or combined into multi-day tours. Some of the descents and variants described will take you into rarely skied terrain where it's unlikely you'll meet another team.

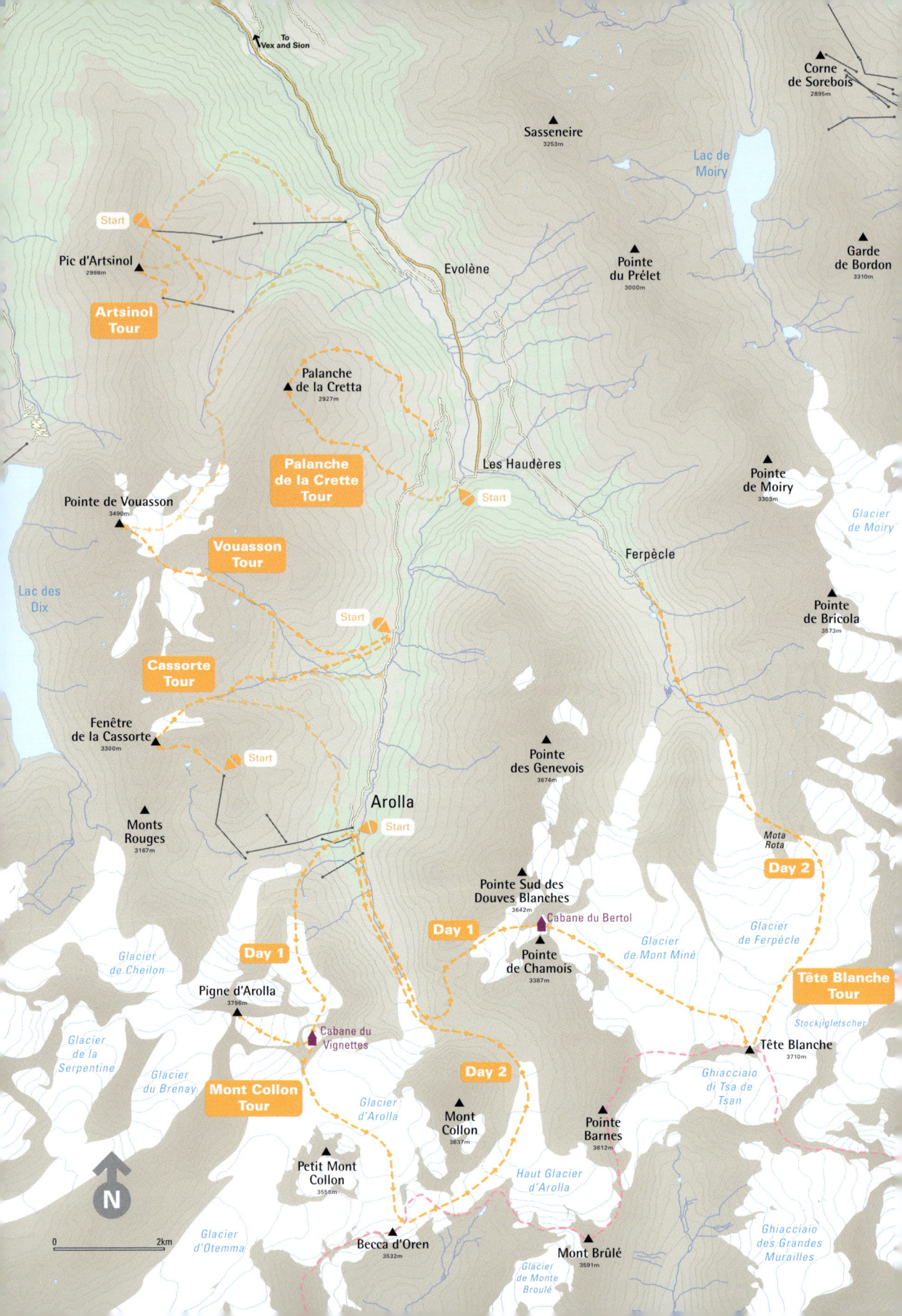

Arolla Day Tours

Grade
Various – see individual tour descriptions.

Season
See individual tours

Maps
1:50000 Arolla 283 S All tours are on this map.
1:25000 Evolène 1327, Rosablanche 1326, Chanrion 1346, Matterhorn 1347
www.map.geo.admin.ch for free map printing (A4 sheets)

Kit
Classic ski touring kit – ice axe and crampons, and / or glacier travel crevasse rescue kit are only needed where indicated in the tour description.

Weather forecast
www.meteosuisse.admin.ch/

Avalanche forecast
www.slf.ch/

Hut information
Aiguilles Rouges hut – www.aiguillesrouges.ch – +41 (0)27 283 16 49
Bertol hut – www.bertol.ch – +41 (0)27 283 19 20
Vignettes hut – www.cabanedesvignottes.ch – +41 (0)27 203 13 22

Useful information
Public transport www.sbb.ch/ and www.postauto.ch
Train from Geneva Airport to Sion, bus from Sion to Arolla (or Evolène / les Haudères).
A car is useful but all the tours can be accessed by public transport. If driving, snow tyres or chains are essential and the road beyond les Haudères can be difficult if snowy.

Shops
Good ski shop, bank, chemist, cash machines and Coop supermarket in Evolène, plus smaller shops in Les Haudères and Arolla.

Alternative guide books
Ski de Randonnée Bas-Valais by Georges Sanga (in French)

Arolla Day Tours

Just below Vouasson heading for the bridge at point 1872m.

Day tour 1 – Pic d'Artsinol

Grade PD S2-S3	**Starting altitude** 2630m	**Aspects** all except W
Ascent 390m (1600m without lift)	**Descent** 1600m	**Season** January to March

Tucked away on the hillside opposite the village lies the quirky Evolène ski area, home to the slowest chairlift in the Alps, and some great off-piste terrain. High above sits Pic d'Artsinol (2998m). This is a great viewpoint and a good start to a week's touring with a fine descent.
Start at the Evolène ski area car park.

It's a long climb on skis from Evolène, either from Lanna through the ski area, or through the pretty Arbey hamlet and on through Vouasson. It's (much!) easier to buy a single ticket on the lifts (chair + two drags) to 2632m. If you're lucky, the Arpilles drag will be running – ski across and ride the lift to 2600m. If not, ski the track to GR 600 404, 106 759 and start skinning … find the top of the Arpilles drag then head NNE to the ridge then follow it WNW to the summit.

Descents
1. Back the way you came is easiest, and least steep.
2. Drop east from the summit into a hanging valley and down to la Nouva.
3. Look north-east into the steep gullies leading to the top of the drag lift.
4. Explore the big west face down to the Dixence valley – but you'll need a cunning plan for the return trip!

The first three descents all lead into the ski area so you can head home down the piste or off-piste through the trees. Better still, ski to Vouasson and cross the bridge at point 1872m, then along the track to Arbey and down to Lanna.

Arolla Day Tours

Day tour 2 – Palanche de la Cretta

Grade PD S2 BS	**Starting altitude** 1800	**Aspects** ESE, E and N
Ascent 1127m	**Descent** 1127m (1500m to les Haudères)	**Season** December to April

The Palanche de la Cretta is an Arolla classic with easy access, no glaciers, great views and plenty of options for the descent, making this a great introduction to the area. Unfortunately it can be busy, and there's often a big track up the sunny alpages above the Arolla road. Careful route choice avoids anything over 30° on the normal route. Other descents need stable conditions and are very prone to wind slab.

Begin at the la Coutaz request bus stop, plenty of car parking (GR 604 076, 102 834).

Start up the track from the bus stop, zigzagging up through typically Swiss 'mayens' (Alpine pastures) which provide ideal spots for a break! Above, the slopes open up but the summit stays hidden until the last minute.

It is worth noting that Palanche may be spelt differently on different versions of the map. It is Palanche on the 1:50,000

Descents

The easiest descent is back the way you came – nice, open skiing in fresh snow or spring conditions, but often sun-affected. Skier's right into the streambed gives shadier (but steeper) slopes. With good snow cover you can cross over the road and continue all the way to les Haudères – over 1500m of descent!

With stable snow, the slopes north-east of the summit give steeper skiing. Walk NNW down the ridge (rarely enough snow to ski) then make steep turns north-east into the valley and continue via La Vuilla (point 2 401m), Moyons de la Niva and la Giette, where you might see a herd of yaks! Regain the road – and wonder how to get back to the car.

The WNW face gives an adventurous, wild ski. The 700m descent into la Luessa is steep and very prone to cross-loading by westerly winds – rarely skied, it needs very stable conditions and is best checked out from the Evolène ski area first!

Day tour 3 – La Cassorte, Arolla

Grade AD S3-S4 BSA	**Starting altitude** 2874m	**Aspect** S, N and NE
Ascent 400m (1300m without the lift)	**Descent** 1500m	**Season** December to April

The Cassorte is a small summit above the Arolla ski area with a steep col leading through to the Ignes valley. It works well on its own as a shortish day, or combined with a morning in the lift area, or as an approach to the Aiguilles Rouges hut.

There is some steep skiing to get into the Ignes valley. The first section is often descended on foot. Then comes a 40° pitch very prone to wind slab.

In addition to normal ski touring kit (ski crampons often useful), bring rope, harness, crampons and axe for the col.

Start in the Arolla ski area car park. From the top of the area's highest drag lift there's often an obvious skin track. It's often easier to carry skis the last 50m to the col (from here it's a short scramble to the actual summit).

Climbing the Cassorte Gully.

Arolla Day Tours

The other side is steep and rarely has enough snow to be enjoyable on skis – most people downclimb in crampons. A large block provides a belay (bolt added in 2015).

From the saddle (3180m) a steep (40°) slope leads down east. Beware wind slab! Below, wide open slopes give great skiing with a choice of aspects. Traversing high on the right at 2700m leads back to the ski area (the line of the summer footpath), but it's better to head well left into the valley north of point 2643m (beware the large cliffs of Les Ignes below here) where shady slopes lead past the Cascade des Ignes to a flattening at 2200m. Traverse out left to Lac Bleu and ski down the path to the bar at la Gouille (or continue direct down the stream to Satarma – often quality 'combat' skiing!)

Return to Arolla by infrequent bus or a pre-placed car.

Day tour 4 – La Pointe de Vouasson

Grade PD S2 BS (S3–4 on northerly descents)   **Starting altitude** 1800m   **Aspects** S, E and N
Ascent 1590m (1010m to Aiguilles Rouges hut + 612m to summit)
Descent 1590m to la Gouille, 2080m to Lanna (Evolène)   **Season** February to April

La Pointe de Vouasson is the striking peak opposite the Evolène ski area. An easy walk in summer, it becomes a fine ski summit. Vouasson translates loosely as 'viewpoint' in the local Evolènard dialect and the name is well deserved. Sadly, the summit is now on the route of a bi-yearly ski race so it's getting busier, but the length of ascent still means it's rarely crowded. As a day tour you'll need an early start and a fit team, but the Aiguilles Rouges hut is well-placed for an overnight stop, splitting the climb. (La Cassorte tour could make a good approach for a two-day trip – see previous route.)
Start at la Gouille (bus stop, car parking) GR 603 999, 100 282.
You will need glacier safety kit, as well as standard ski touring kit.

Nearly there! The top of the long climb to the Pointe de Vouasson.

From la Gouille head steeply up to Lac Bleu (2092m). Turn east then steeply up right (NW) on open, sunny slopes passing Remointse du Sex Blanc (2417m); the Aiguilles Rouges hut is visible from here. Continue to point 2824m. Turn left for the hut, or continue to the col east of Pointe de Darbonneire (not the Col Sud de Darbonneire!). The summit is visible across the glacier.

Descents

1. Back the way you came – good in fresh snow or spring snow. If the lower slopes are bare or sun-affected head south at 2600m into the shady slopes below les Ignes – the end of La Cassorte tour.
2. The Glacier de Vouasson – a fantastic, challenging descent, complex route-finding and quite crevassed around 3200m (good views from the Pic d'Artsinol).

Pass east of the central rock point (3294m) then aim for point 2864m. At 2900m work east and find a way through a small cliff band (2850m), then down into the valley bottom. (Alternatively, from 2900m head north on steepening ground (35 to 40°) down the glacier tongue – an exciting ski on first acquaintance and not for the faint-hearted!)

Follow the stream bed and either skin up left (N) into the Evolène ski area at the foot of the Arpilles drag, or battle on direct down le Merdesson (fun in good snow, but aptly named in poor snow!) to the bridge at 1872m and an easy track out to Arbey.

Day tour 5 – Cabane de Bertol and Ferpècle Glacier

Grade: AD 3.2 TBS
Aspects: SW and N
Descent: 1000m to Ferpècle
Starting altitude 2000m
Ascent 1830m (1330m to Cabane de Bertol, 500m Tête Blanche)
Season March to early May

This is a long day – a night at the Bertol hut makes it more relaxing! Leave the hut after the Haute Route teams, and the mountains will be deserted. Superb views of the Dent Blanche, Matterhorn and Dent d'Hérens before a long and spectacular north-facing descent on crevassed ground – not to be underestimated!

Start at Arolla ski car park.

Take glacier kit as well as standard ski touring kit (overnight kit if staying in the hut). Plan for the return trip from Forclaz (see descent options)!

The Bertol approach is long – start up the Bas Glacier d'Arolla before climbing steeply up left below Mont Collon (threatened by serac fall – stay well left on awkward ground, ski crampons often useful). Turn north to Plans de Bertol (2664m) then ENE to Col de Bertol (4 hours). Stash skis here if staying in the hut. If not, make a traversing descent right down to the Mont Miné Glacier. (It's possible to turn north and ski the left bank of the glacier from here.) Then make the long but gentle climb to Tête Blanche, a spectacular viewpoint (2 hours).

Descents

There are several options:
1. Back via Bertol hut is easiest, and best if in doubt or the weather is turning.
2. The left bank of the Mont Miné Glacier is a wild and wonderful descent, very crevassed below point 3023m, and very unlikely-looking seen from below!
3. A great option is to ski north-east along the ridge past Col d'Hérens, then stay high (maybe skins on and go up the Wandfluehorn) until you can head down passing well east of the Mota Rota (3232m). This is all very crevassed and it's easy to turn north too soon. Once under the Mota Rota turn west,

then north-west, to reach wide, easy slopes. Don't relax yet! The lower glacier is changing fast and the exit, direct down the riverbed, is complicated. Eventually, reach the bridge at 1959m then hope the snow lasts down the road! You'll have to walk some of the way to La Forclaz, where there's a café and bus stop – but it's worth pre-placing a car or arranging a lift.

Day tour 6 – Tour of Mont Collon

Grade PD S2 BS	**Starting altitude** 2000m	**Aspects** all
Ascent 1170m to Vignettes, +350m to Col de l'Évêque (the first Arolla draglift saves 450m)		
Descent 1520m	**Season** March to early May	

This is a long day in high-mountain glaciated scenery with fine views of Mont Collon, the peak dominating Arolla. There will usually be a track as it's the main Chamonix-Zermatt trail, but starting from Arolla avoids the crowds. Easy skiing, but the day is spent at altitude and needs good weather. Staying at the Vignettes hut makes a good two-day trip, allowing a fast team to ski the Pigne in the morning then follow this tour back to Arolla.

Start at the Arolla ski lift.

Take glacier kit, as well as standard ski touring kit.

Skin up the piste in Arolla then south-west into a moraine valley around 2160m (or take the first drag, ski down the piste to around point 2291m and turn south to the same point). Work steeply up onto the moraine (ski crampons useful) then more easily past point 2519m to the Glacier de Pièce. Stay left (E) on the glacier to avoid serac fall from the Pigne d'Arolla, then back right (SW) to the Col de Vignettes (3 to 4 hours).

Skins off for a quick traverse south and steep descent onto the Col de Charmotane. (This is the start of the classic last day of the Haute Route, but is much nicer in daylight!) Skins on again for a gentle but longer-than-it-looks climb to Col de L'Évêque (3377m, 2 hours).

Descend east, (crevassed between 3300 and 3300m) then easily north-east on open slopes to the Haut Glacier d'Arolla, often a nice ski! Onwards down the glacier with fine views, turning west below Mont Collon. A flat section leads to the final drop into the Bas Glacier d'Arolla (2500m). This is threatened by seracs from Mont Collon – ski quickly through to the long run-out back to Arolla.

About Graham Frost

www.frostguiding.co.uk/

See page 125.

Skinning up the Barrhorn with the Bishorn and Weisshorn behind. Photo – Hannah Burrows Smith.

Val d'Anniviers Tour

By Rob Collister

Tour overview

Running south from Sierre, a small industrial town in the Rhône valley on the main line from Geneva to Brig, the Val d'Anniviers is the last of the Alpine valleys to be French rather than German-speaking as you travel east. At its head lie some of the finest and most famous peaks in the Alps: Dent Blanche, Obergabelhorn, Zinalrothorn, and Weisshorn. Strictly speaking, some of this tour unfolds in the Turtmanntal, a smaller parallel valley to the east, but the road up it is usually blocked by snow until late spring, so that access in winter tends to be from the Val d'Anniviers. Local guides have invented and promoted two circular tours, the Haute Route Imperiale and the Tour du Ciel, which cover some of the same ground as this tour, but they start and finish in Zermatt or St Niklaus in the neighbouring Mattertal.

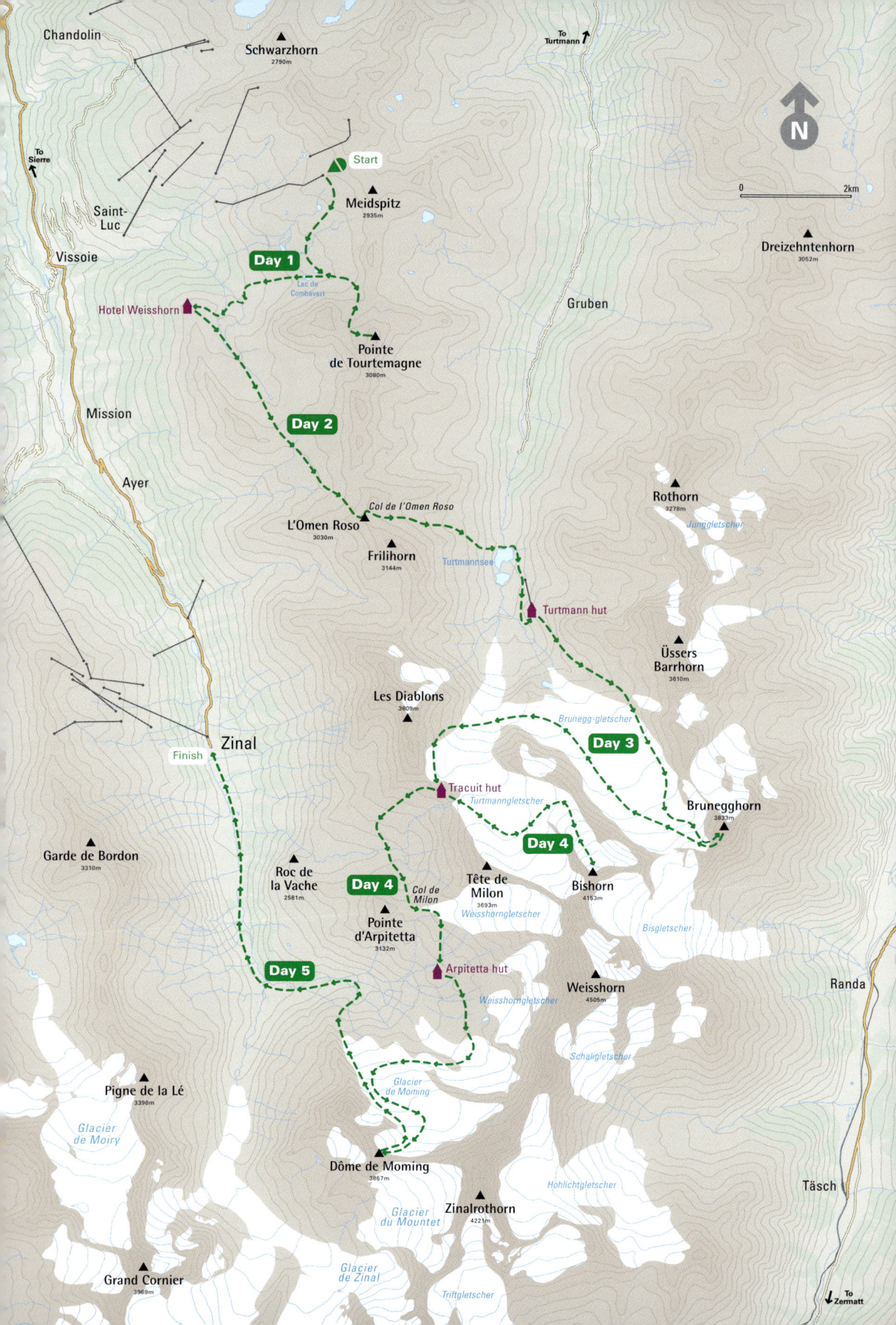

Val d'Anniviers Tour

Grade
AD S3 TBS

Season
March to April

Factors to take account of are: the late opening of the Turtmann hut towards the end of March (not an insuperable problem as you can always use the winter room); and the closing of the St Luc lift system in the middle of April.

Map
Swiss 1:50000 Ski Series (blue cover) Montana 273 S, Visp 274 S, Arolla 283 S, Mischabel 284 S

The whole tour is shown on sheet 5006 Matterhorn / Mischabel (green cover) but without ski routes marked or ski information on the back.

You can find a 1:50000 online map at www.map.geo.admin.ch choose 'Snowsport' under 'Change topic' to reveal the ski route overlay.

Kit
As for any high glaciated tour: rope, harness, crevasse rescue kit, ice axe, crampons, transceiver, shovel and probe.

Weather forecast
www.meteoswiss.com

Avalanche forecast
www.slf.ch

Hut information
All the huts in this area prefer to take bookings over the phone during the season. Bookings via the SAC online booking system are not always successful!
Cabane Bella Tola – +41 (0)27 475 1537
Hotel Weisshorn – +41 (0)27 475 1106
Turtmann hut – +41 (0)27 932 1455
Cabane de Tracuit – +41 (0)27 475 1500
Cabane d'Arpitetta – +41 (0)27 475 4028

Useful information
Tourist information offices:
Sierre railway station – +41 (0)27 455 8535 – www.sierretourisme.ch
Val d'Anniviers – www.sierre-anniviers.ch

Alternative guide book
Les Plus Belles Randonnées a Ski (Swiss Alpine Club) published in French, German and Italian.

Val d'Anniviers Tour

Skiing down from the Blanc de Moming. Photo – Hannah Burrows Smith.

Warm-up day – Val d'Anniviers

A warm-up day to find your ski legs and start acclimatising always makes sense before a tour if you are fresh from the UK. The Val d'Anniviers is renowned for its off-piste skiing and now that Grimentz and Zinal are linked by cable car there is no necessity to choose between the two. In poor visibility the trees at Chandolin are worth considering, while if you want a short day-tour as well as some skiing, Grimentz will be your best bet.

You could stay in Grimentz, Zinal or St Luc as they are all connected by bus, St Luc might be best to give you a quick start on the morning of Day 2.

Day 1 – Pointe de Tourtemagne (Turtmannspitze) (3080m) – Hotel Weisshorn

Grade PD S2 BS	Aspects S, N and W	Ascent 900m	Descent 980m

Try to be on the first funicular up the hill from St Luc and make your way to the top of the Pas de Boeuf lift. Follow the piste until it is possible to make a long, rather convoluted, descending traverse towards the imposing north face of Le Toûno. Somewhere north of the Lac de Combavert put on skins and start a steady uphill pull, first east and then south, to reach a basin beneath the north-west flank of the Pointe de Tourtemagne. Slopes of 35° or more lead to the west ridge and thence, usually on foot, to the summit.

If you are already fit and acclimatised and object to paying for a day pass to use the lifts, you can always skin up beside the piste from the roadhead at Le Prilett (where there is also a handy gite). This adds about 700 metres of ascent making a relatively short climb into a long one, but it has the advantage that you can start much earlier.

Descend by the same route as far as the Lac de Combavert then continue westward down to Le Chiesso at 2198m. From here follow the cat-track uphill to the Hotel Weisshorn, a distinctive landmark from the valley though not visible from this side. It is very expensive but worth it for the convenience next day. The alternative, at half the price, is the Cabane Bella Tola among the pistes of St Luc, which adds well over an hour to the journey time and tends to be noisy by day and stuffy by night. A third option if you are feeling fit is to start from Le Prilett and skin 500m up the piste to Le Chiesso. With either of these alternatives there is no need to go all the way up to the hotel in the morning.

Day 2 – L'Omen Roso (3031m) – Turtmann hut

Grade AD S3 TBS   **Aspects** all   **Ascent** 1130m   **Descent** 950m

A bigger day than it appears on the map, where efficiency with skins and a sense of urgency will pay dividends later on.

Leave the Hotel Weisshorn, ideally at 5am if you can negotiate breakfast that early, and skin south-east across an undulating plateau for 3km to a saddle at 2621m. Continue in the same direction descending slightly, across a broad shallow basin for another kilometre. Pick a way up steeper slopes onto the west ridge of L'Omen Roso and so to point 3032m.

Descend the north ridge a short distance to a small col marked as the Col de l'Omen Roso on the 1:25000 map. This is often corniced, but the way into the hanging valley of Frilitälli is usually easier than it first appears. A tremendous descent down into the Turtmanntal follows, provided you can be on the steep (35°) slope at the bottom by mid-morning. Any later and it becomes narrowing, not to say dangerous, as it faces south-east and will have been getting the full bore of the sun for some hours already. The 350m pull up to the Turtmann hut is a less than welcome sting in the tail.

Day 3 – Brunegghorn (3833m) – Tracuit hut

Grade AD S2-3 TBS   **Aspects** SW, NW and N   **Ascent** 1300m   **Descent** 1040m

This is a big day with a total of 1750m of ascent if the summit is reached, but it is easy enough to shorten it if needed.

From the Turtmann hut a horizontal traverse across a steep slope leads to a couloir known as the Barrloch. It is not impossible to skin up this couloir, but it is definitely easier to boot up, and it is also much easier to put crampons on at the bottom rather than being forced to near the top. The initial traverse can be awkward on skins when icy or covered with avalanche debris, and it is then easier to ski down and across, losing at least 100 metres in height, to reach a lower, easier-angled couloir splitting the rock band (not shown on older maps). Above the Barrloch, trend right to cross a moraine wall and follow a valley to about 3000m. Traverse onto the Brunegg Glacier and follow this south-east without difficulty to its head, making for the saddle between point 3671m and the summit. Steep skinning leads to the top (beware cornices!).

In descent, ski across to the true left side of the glacier and follow it down to the junction with the Turtmann Glacier at 2800m. The 450m ascent to the Tracuit hut in the heat of the afternoon is, as the Kiwis say, "a bit of a grunt", but once at the hut the view makes it all worthwhile. The hut itself is new, an unattractive box from the outside, but spacious and airy inside with an incomparable outlook over the whole western Alps.

Val d'Anniviers Tour

Descending the Brunegghorn. Photo – Hannah Burrows Smith

Day 4 – Bishorn (4153m) – Arpitetta hut

Grade PD S2 BS   **Aspects** NW, SW, S and N   **Ascent** 1340m   **Descent** 920m

If one is brutally honest, the Bishorn is not much more than an incident on the north ridge of the Weisshorn and not an overly exciting mountain. Nevertheless, it is a 4000er (hence the size of the new Tracuit hut!) and the highest point on this tour. Although not a long climb from the hut, you cannot afford to be too relaxed as you may well be slowed down by the altitude, and there is still the journey across to the Arpitetta hut later in the day to consider.

From the Tracuit hut trend south-east up the true left side of the Turtmann Glacier to about 3400m where you cross the glacier, skirting round beneath a spur running north-west from the Bishorn to reach a broad glacial shelf leading up to the summit. This is often disappointingly wind-blasted and covered with sastrugi, which is unpleasant for both skinning and skiing; nor should the crevasse hazard on these upper slopes be underestimated. There are actually two summits of virtually the same height. The western is the one most often visited in spring and, while in good conditions it can be both ascended and descended on skis, the last 30m is more usually climbed with an ice axe and crampons.

Descend by the same route back to the Tracuit hut. Tempting though it is to stop for lunch and a beer there is a good case to be made for pressing straight on before the snow below the hut gets any softer and momentum is lost. Chains help to scramble down some rocks on the south side of the Col de Tracuit and the initial slope below can feel steep and awkward when it has been heavily skied. Around 2800m, start a traverse across to the Col de Milon (2976m) which requires some down-climbing on the far side. Continue across the hillside beneath the huge west face of the Weisshorn on a descending traverse to reach the Arpitetta hut, a much smaller and simpler affair than the Tracuit, hidden from view until almost the last minute.

Val d'Anniviers Tour

Cabane d'Arpitetta. Photo – Hannah Burrows Smith.

Day 6 – Pointe de Moming (3657m) – Zinal

Grade AD S2-3 TBS   **Aspects** W, NW and N   **Ascent** 950m   **Descent** 2070m

Once again an early start will ensure reasonable conditions at the end of the day. The traverse from the hut across the Glacier de Moming towards Le Besso requires route-finding acumen and good visibility if there is no track in place. Once across, hug the true left bank to reach a plateau at 3260m where you can climb steeply back south-east to reach the top.

In descent, follow the left bank of the glacier all the way down to reach the river draining out of the Weisshorn Glacier. From here a combination of trees, bushes, avalanche debris and streams can provide a final challenge for tired legs, requiring what is best described as 'combat skiing', not to mention a sense of humour. Once down into the main valley a good track leads, with a certain amount of poling and skating, to a ski du fond area and a car park on the outskirts of Zinal. With 2000m of skiing under your belt you have every right to stride into town like conquering heroes!

Incredible scenery skiing down from the Blanc du Moming.
Photo – Hannah Burrows Smith.

Val d'Anniviers Tour

Possible variants or alternatives

Day 3
In the event of bad weather it will be much easier to reach the Turtmanntal by way of the Meidpass, reached from the Pas de Boeuf lift. However, the road up the valley to the hut is not without hazard in very warm conditions or during heavy snowfall.

Day 4
An ascent of the Barrhorn (3610m) instead of the Brunegghorn (3833m) would give a shorter, but still quite demanding, day with rather more in the way of interesting skiing. The only real advantage of the Brunegghorn is in terms of acclimatisation for the Bishorn 4153m the following day.

About Rob Collister

Rob retired recently after a lifetime working in mountains. He first guided the Haute Route on skis in 1977, the year that British guides were accepted into the International Association of Mountain Guides' Associations (IFMGA). Subsequently, he was President of British Mountain Guides from 1990 to 1993 and did much to raise the level of avalanche and ski training for aspirants.

Based in North Wales throughout his career (apart from a year in New Zealand), he has travelled worldwide on foot and ski, always displaying a preference for 'the way less travelled'. He was something of a pioneer among British guides in leading adventurous ski expeditions outside Europe in the eighties and nineties. Nowadays he is much more conscious of his carbon footprint and usually travels to the Alps by train. An honorary member of the Eagle Ski Club (a club devoted to ski touring), he hopes to continue leading tours, unremunerated, for the club and for groups of friends for a few more years yet.

He has written four books, the most recent of which, *Days to Remember*, was published by Vertebrate in 2016.

Skinning above the Refuge Mantova with the Gnifetti hut behind.

Monte Rosa Summits Tour

By Olly Allen

Tour overview

The Monte Rosa massif straddles the Swiss / Italian border above Zermatt and constitutes the end of the Western Alps. There are more than 38 peaks above 4000m, so an impressive sight from any direction. The vertical descent on skis from some of the peaks is huge which makes this area popular with ski tourers. It also has some of the wildest glaciers in the Alps. It is no surprise that the Monte Rosa area is a ski mountaineering favourite. The resorts nestled below the peaks; Zermatt, Cervinia, Gressoney and Alagna are also a big draw for off-piste skiers.

This ski tour weaves its way along the Swiss / Italian border taking in many 4000m peaks. Most of the terrain covered is above 3500m so good touring conditions can be found in late May. High altitude, steep terrain and long ascents make this a demanding advanced-level tour where good ski mountaineering skills are essential.

It is worth taking a longer rope (or joining two together) as there are large crevasses, and some of the steeper 'mountaineering' sections may be icy in ascent or descent. Parties need to be comfortable cramponing on narrow ridges (e.g. Castor) and on 45° slopes both in ascent and descent. Depending on conditions, parties might need to abseil off Il Naso using an 'Abolakov' or ski belay. Take care on the first couple of days and factor in acclimatisation, as all the huts and terrain are above 3300m. This tour becomes really serious in poor weather.

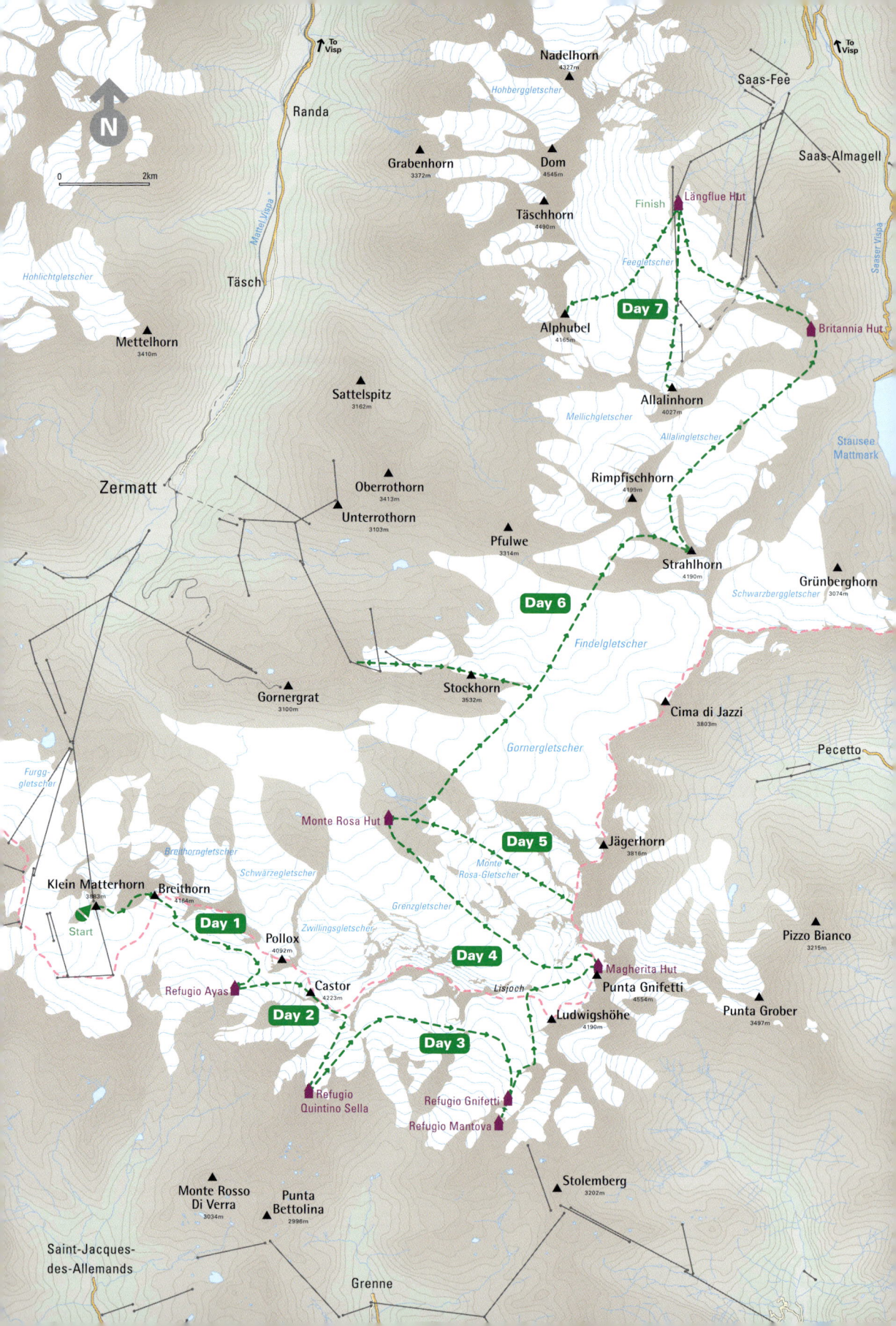

Monte Rosa Summits Tour

Surely there is no more dramatic sight in the Alps than the distinctive shape of the Matterhorn! At 4478m it may not be the highest mountain in the Alps, but it is easily the most recognised.

Zermatt itself is a charming Alpine village. It is car-free and reached only by a 15 minute cog-wheel train from the valley station of Täsch. As you would expect given its location, it is one of Europe's main centres of alpinism and is a bustling town in both winter and summer.

Having sung the virtues of Zermatt, some parties may find it more relaxing to start the tour in the Gressoney valley as it's easily accessed from the airports in Turin or Milan ... and has infinitely better coffee.

Grade
AD- S3 TBSA

Season
Early April to late May

Map
Swiss Skitourenkarte 1:50000 Mischabel 284 S (All the tour is on this map. Note there is an extra map section on the back of the Swiss map for the Italian side.)
You can find a 1:30000 online map at www.map.geo.admin.ch choose 'Snowsport' under 'Change topic' to reveal the ski route overlay.

Kit
Classic ski touring kit including an ice axe, crampons and glacier travel / crevasse rescue kit. It's worth having steel crampons and a decent ice axe just in case some sections are icy.

Weather forecast
www.meteosuisse.ch – the mobile app is excellent and has an English option.

Avalanche forecast
www.slf.ch – the mobile app is excellent and has an English option.

Hut information
Rifugio Ayas (Rifugio Lambronecca) - www.guidechampoluc.com – info@rifugio-lambronecca.com – +39 (0)125 308 083
Rifugio Quintino Sella – www.rifugioquintinosella.com – +39 (0)125366113 – info@rifugioquintinosella.com
Rifugio Mantova – www.rifugiomantova.it – info@rifugiomantova.it – +39 (0)16378150
Rifugio Gnifetti or Rifugio Margherita – www.refugimonterosa.it – info@rifugimonterosa.it
Orestes hut (useful in poor weather as it's easily accessed from the Gressoney lift system) – www.oresteshuette.eu – info@oresteshuette.eu – +39 (0)125 1925484
Monte Rosa hut – www.section-monte-rosa.ch – huettemonterosa@gmail.com – +41 (0)27 9672115
Britannia hut – www.britannia.ch – +41 (0) 27 9572288
Längflue hut – info@ferienart.ch – +41 (0) 27 9572132

Useful information
www.zermatt.ch – Zermatt tourist office
www.visitmonterosa.com – Gressoney, Champoluc and Alagna information for lifts
www.lovevda.it – Val d'Aosta regional tourist information for hut contacts

Monte Rosa Summits Tour

Day 1 – Zermatt – Ayas

Grade PD S2 TBS	**Starting altitude** 3883m	
Aspects E, S and SW	**Ascent** 700m	**Descent** 700m

From Zermatt catch the cable car up to the Klein Matterhorn (3883m) and try not to ponder the Swiss Franc / Sterling conversion rate. You soon leave the busy pistes and head up the first 4000m peak of the trip. The Breithorn (4076m) is a 2.5 hour skin from the lift to the west summit. This is perfect acclimatisation and affords views across the whole Monte Rosa range. It is possible to traverse easily using crampons to the central and east summit (4159m). A ski descent is made between the east and west Breithorn summits. Ski south from the col, then an easterly traverse and short skin deposits you below the south-east ridge of Pollux (4092m).

Pollux is usually climbed via the south-east ridge. Leave skis at the base and follow the ridge wearing crampons. There is one technical section where you need to pull quite steeply on some fixed ropes and you may like to use a rope for protection; above the rocks there is a fantastic snow crest that leads to the summit. Descend the same way.

This section can be bypassed by climbing and descending the west face. In good conditions this can be skied, but be aware it is 50° at its steepest point and a fall would be very serious.

From the toe of Pollux it's an easy, glaciated descent to the Rifugio Ayas (3400m). This hut is run by the local guides bureau, has great food and is well known for its after dinner drinking antics.

Day 2 – Ayas – Castor – Quintino Sella

Grade AD S3-4 TBSA	**Aspects** SW, SE and S	**Ascent** 760m	**Descent** 700m

An early 'Alpine start' is needed for good conditions to skin from the Rifugio Ayas to the summit of Castor (4228m) via the west face. Toward the summit ridge you will have to rope up, use crampons and carry skis. Traverse the very narrow summit ridge of Castor (4223m) and try to take in the views on the summit while concentrating on your feet! Continue balancing down from the summit to the Felikjoch (4087m).

The steep descent from the Felikjoch to the Rifugio Quintino Sella (3585m) is memorable, with spectacular remote glaciated scenery. Take care on the first few turns from the col as it is over 40° and can be icy. The hut is welcoming but basic, with all water made from snow melt or helicoptered in.

Day 3 – Passo del Naso

Grade AD S3 TBSA	**Aspect** S	**Ascent** 520m	**Descent** 600m

From the Rifugio Quintino Sella make an ascending easterly traverse across Felikgletscher to point 3744m and then onto Passo del Naso (4100m). Passo del Naso on the toe of Liskamm can be icy and steep on ascent so crampons may be needed. A steep sideslip or abseil descends the SE slope to the heavily-crevassed Lys Glacier. It is also possible to ascend 80m above Passo del Naso to Point Naso and ski the steep, easterly couloir to the Lys Glacier.

Monte Rosa Summits Tour

The summit ridge on Castor.

The descent down past the Gnifetti hut (3625m) and on to the recently renovated Rifugio Mantova hut (3498m) is wild – watch out for big crevasses! The Mantova is a very comfortable hut with a spectacular dining room overlooking the Lys Glacier. The Gnifetti hut has excellent food, but more traditional accommodation.

Days 2 / 3 Poor weather alternatives

Days 2 and 3 can be made more manageable in poor weather by taking lower alternatives as follows. From the Val d'Ayas hut ski down to the Refuge Mezzalama (3002m) and on to the alpage of Véraz (2382m). There are two options here:
1. Traverse north-easterly up towards the Rifugio Quintino Sella, north of points 2853m and 3029m. This route gets fairly steep towards the top and takes an easterly turn towards the hut at 3100m where there can be crevasses.
2. Continue down from Véraz to the village of St-Jacques (1689m) and take the Champoluc lift to the Colle Bettaforca (2672m). This point can be accessed without using lifts from just below Véraz; then continue on up to the Sella hut. The winter route swings out east at about 3350m onto the steep snow slopes below the hut. If the avalanche risk is high it is possible to follow the rocky ridge up to the refugio via an easy via ferrata.

In really bad weather avoid the Refugio Sella and continue on through the Gressoney lift system to the Rifugio Gnifetti.

Please note the Monterosa lift system has intermittent opening times in May and early June. A 4x4 taxi is available from near Véraz down to St-Jacques and on to the Bettaforca if there is poor snow cover (ask in the Ayas hut).

Monte Rosa Summits Tour

The summit of the Parrotspitze with Liskamm behind.

Day 4 – Signalkuppe – Monte Rosa hut

Grade AD S2 TBS   **Aspect** S and NW   **Ascent** 1100m   **Descent** 1672m

Today reaches the highest point of the ski tour with an ascent of Signalkuppe (4554m).

On leaving the Mantova hut head north passing east of the Gnifetti hut heading for the Lisjoch, on the way you can bag the classic ski peaks of Ludvigshöhe (4341m) and Piramid Vincent (4215m). It is worth stopping at the Margherita hut (4554m) on the summit of Signalkuppe. Named after the queen of Italy it is the highest hut in the Alps and serves the highest pizza in the Alps.

From here we descend the spectacularly-crevassed Grenz Glacier to the new Monte Rosa hut. This is one of the most spectacular ski descents in the Alps passing under the imposing north face of Liskamm. The new space age Monte Rosa hut (2795m) is covered in solar panels making it completely energy efficient. It provides modern, comfortable rooms although it is rather busy. Please note the descent to the Monte Rosa hut down the Grenz Glacier should only be undertaken in reasonable visibility as navigation is complicated through heavily crevassed areas. If you can't see, the only real option is to ski back down the way you came, then to start looking at logistical options to cross back into Italy. Being caught out on the Grenz Glacier in bad weather is incredibly serious and the Margherita hut only has a winter room open in the ski touring season.

Monte Rosa Summits Tour

Day 5 (day tour) – Monte Rosa hut – Dufoursattel

Grade AD S2 BS   **Aspect** NW   **Ascent** 1615m   **Descent** 1615m

An early start is needed to ascend to the Dufoursattel (Silbersattel) (4515m). This spectacular col lies between the gigantic summits of Nordend (4609m) and the Dufourspitze (4634m). This is a long, but not overly steep, ascent. Looking west there are incredible views of the Matterhorn, and a long ski descent back for a second night in the Monte Rosa hut.

It's possible to summit Dufourspitze but this involves fairly technical PD+ ground where good mountaineering skills are needed. The normal line of ascent is via the rocky, mixed west ridge which takes just over an hour. You can either descend back down the west ridge or quickly down some fixed ropes to the Silbersattel. (At the time of writing these ropes were not in place so check conditions at the hut.)

Day 6 – Monte Rosa hut – Zermatt

Grade PD S2 BS   **Aspects** W and N
Ascent 1075m   **Descent** 650m to Hohtälli, 2275m if you can ski to Zermatt

From the Monte Rosa hut traverse east and scramble (fixed rope) across a rocky ridge to the Gorner Glacier. Cross the Gorner Glacier to the Stockhornpass. From here go up either the Stockhorn (3532m) or Cima di Jazzi (3803m), which affords spectacular views of the Zermatt and Macugnaga valley. A descent back to the Gornergrat Railway via the Stockhorn is the best option in spring.

A good option to extend this tour over successive days is to incorporate ascents of some peaks in the Saas valley. This may include the Strahlhorn (4190m), Alphubel (4206m) or Allalinhorn (4027m), follow the alternative below.

On the way to Zermatt from the Monte Rosa hut.

Day 6 Alternative Monte Rosa hut – Strahlhorn

Grade PD S2 BS   **Aspects** W, NW and N
Ascent 1128m to Britannia hut, 1762m to Längflue   **Descent** 1685m to Britannia hut, 2265m to Längflue

From the Monte Rosa hut traverse east and scramble (fixed rope) across a rocky ridge to the Gorner Glacier. Cross the Gorner Glacier to the Stockhornpass. Head north past the Strahlchnubel and on to the Adlerpass (3789m). Ascend the pass on crampons and then follow the broad south-east ridge to the summit of the Strahlhorn (4190m). The descent from the summit is a classic all the way to below the Britannia hut. You can either stay here or continue on down to Saas Fee via the piste. If you have the legs left, continue to the Längflue hut ready for a final big day.

Monte Rosa Summits Tour

Day 7 – A final summit

Grade AD S3 TBS
Ascent 1360m
Aspects N and E
Descent 1360m to Längflue, 2360m to Saas Fee

After staying in the Britannia hut or better still the Längflue hut (2869m) (always open as it's at the top of the Längflue lift), the final ascent of Alphubel or Allalinhorn can be made. The ascent of Allalinhorn is pretty easy, following the pistes with a few minutes cramponing to get to the summit.

The Alphubel is a more adventurous option and ascends the steep east flank. This glacial slope can be crevassed and icy in poor conditions. Crampons may be needed for the steep section around 3800m. It would be advisable to check at the Längflue hut whether a track is in and possible. The descent back down the line of ascent from the summit is epic all the way to Saas Fee.

About Olly Allen

www.mountaintracks.co.uk
olly@mountaintracks.co.uk

Over the past 25 years Olly has skied and climbed all over the world; from chasing powder in Russia, to scaling rock in Yosemite and climbing vertical ice in Cogne, Italy. He holds the prestigious International Mountain Guides (IFMGA) carnet. Olly splits his time between Finhaut in Switzerland and the Peak District in the UK.

Olly has a traditional mountaineering, rock climbing and ice climbing background. This includes hundreds of routes throughout the UK and Europe with ascents of winter climbs up to VII, 7 on sight E6 and sport 8a+. Olly has climbed extensively throughout the French, Swiss and Italian Alps ascending many classic north faces such as the Eiger, Matterhorn and Grandes Jorasses. He is one of the most experienced ski guides in the business and has spent many seasons honing his off-piste skills. Ski touring is a major part of his winter, having competed in World Cup ski randonnée races as part of the British team and raced the Patrouille des Glaciers in 8 hours.

He has also worked on numerous films as safety and stunt coordinator, including Touching the Void, Blindsight, Alive, Mountains and Alien vs. Predator.

He is a director of the highly professional ski and mountaineering company 'Mountain Tracks', which provides guided adventure holidays.

A beautiful morning skinning above Passo di Rotondo.

Tour de Soleil

By Olly Allen

Tour overview

The Tour de Soleil is a classic hut-to-hut ski tour that follows an old smugglers' trail in a remote, but charming, corner of the Swiss Alps. The route criss-crosses the Swiss and Italian borders making use of the excellent huts in the area. If you are craving for some solitude and adventure then this is the tour for you. The terrain is not overly steep and there are numerous options for bagging peaks along the way. The Mittlebarg hut and the Cabane Piansecco are firm favourites, and will open especially for bookings.

We begin our tour in Binntal, a small valley near the remains of the Rhône Glacier. This area still remains hidden from the rest of Switzerland, giving it a wonderfully remote feel. A tunnel was built in 1965 to connect the lost valley to the town of Fiesch and civilisation.

A 16th century stone bridge leads into the village with cobblestone lanes, timber houses and traditional farms. In the centre of Binn there is the Hotel Offenhorn and a small chapel. The village burned to the ground in the 15th century and was rebuilt with the addition of the chapel. It has remained unchanged ever since. Binntal residents still retain a traditional way of life set in a region of exquisite natural beauty.

It's worth noting that this tour can be done in either direction and there are numerous variations to accommodate poor weather. Despite its remote, quiet ambience it is escapable by public transport served roads. The only place you don't want to get stuck is the Rifugio Claudio e Bruno, as it is not easy to navigate out of. The route is glaciated but pretty benign – crevasse rescue kit is needed, but go light.

Tour de Soleil

Andermatt is the obvious start and finish point and has the advantage of great off-piste skiing and day touring for warming up. However some parties will start in Fiesch or even the small hotel in Binn. Andermatt is a traditional Swiss-Alpine town with a wide range of facilities and now boasts a huge five star hotel and lots of great apres-ski bars. Despite this, the town retains its Swiss character and allows easy access to the Gemstock lift system. There are numerous ski shops which stock a good range of ski touring equipment and also supermarkets for hill food.

From the Gemstock summit lift we can access the Felsental and Guspis valleys by a short skin, thus getting us away from the crowds. From these valleys, day tours to Hospental and the Gotthard Pass are recommended.

Grade
PD S2-S3 TBS

Season
Mid March to late April

Map
Swiss ski maps 1:50000: Nufenenpass 265 S, Sustenpass 255 S

Kit
Classic ski touring kit including an ice axe, crampons and glacier travel / crevasse rescue kit.

Weather forecast
www.meteosuisse.ch – the mobile app is excellent and has an English option.

Avalanche forecast
www.slf.ch – the mobile app is excellent and has an English option.

Hut information
Mittlenberg hut – www.mittlenberg.ch – mittlenberg@bluewin.ch – +41 (0)27 971 45 48
Binntal hut (no guardian in winter) – www.cas-delemont.ch – +41 (0)77 415 28 47
Rifugio Claudio e Bruno – www.rifugi-omg-formazza.it – refugicladioebruno@yahoo.it – +39 342 351 3145
Capanna Corno-Gries – www.corno-gries.ch – info@corno-gries.ch – +41 (0) 91 869 1129
Capanna Piansecco – www.casbellinzona.ch – enrica.vella@bluewin.ch – +41 (0) 91 869 1214
Rotondo hut – www.rotondohuette.ch – info@rotondohuette.ch – +41 (0)41 887 1616

Useful information
www.andermatt.ch – Andermatt tourist office (they speak excellent English)
www.ticino.ch – Regional tourist information for hut contacts

Alternative guide books
Swiss Alpine Club *Ticino / Mesolcina / Calanca* by Massimo Gabazzi & Giovanni Cavallero in Italian, also available in German

Tour de Soleil

Leaving the Mittlenberghut.

Day 1 – Mittlenberg hut

Grade PD S2 BS	**Starting altitude** 1547m	
Aspect SW and S	**Ascent** 1050m	**Descent** 0m

From Andermatt travel by train, through the Furka tunnel, to Fiesch (journey time about 1 hour) and take a taxi for the short 20 minute ride to the 'lost village' of Binn (there is a bus but it's very infrequent). The tour actually starts a couple of miles up the road in Fäld, but the road can be closed if there is still snow lying. From Fäld ascend the old smugglers' trail on the north side of the river (trainers may be useful late in the season). The trail passes through a few little hamlets until you reach a wooden bridge (1.5 hours from Fäld). The track now crosses the bridge and then climbs up to the spot height at 2098m.

From here, a series of steep kick turns directly upwards accesses an easier-angled bench that traverses east below the cliffs where the Mittlenberg hut is perched. At the end of the bench another series of steep kick turns allows access to the back of the hut via easy-angled snow. The traditional Mittlenberg hut (2393m) is nestled between steep cliffs and affords great views of the Northern Valais (4 hours in total from Fäld). Pre-booking the hut is essential as it only has 25 bed spaces. If the Mittlenberg hut is full you could stay in the unguardianed, but well-equipped, Binntal hut (2265m) which is situated on the opposite side of the valley.

Tour de Soleil

Day 2 – Rifugio Claudio e Bruno

Grade PD S2 BS   **Aspects** all   **Ascent** 1020m   **Descent** 820m

On exiting the hut and retracing your previous day's steps for a few minutes, you are presented with a quandary; either an icy traverse on skins and ski crampons, or a short ski down and equally icy skin up. Fortunately this is only short and allows you to follow an easy-angled valley towards the Passo del Sabbione (2906m). From the pass there are two options to ascend the dramatic Ofenhorn (3236m) – this is a remote peak and together with the Blinnenhorn (3373m) is one of the higher peaks in the region:
1. The most direct route is to skin up the north slope that you can see from the Passo del Sabbione. This isn't as steep as it first appears and zigzags its way up to the right of the rocky ridge.
2. The second option is to contour from the col round to the toe of the east ridge and then up the east face, which is slightly longer but less steep. When descending from the summit the northerly descent is better.

From the Passo del Sabbione there are further options for the descent to the Rifugio Claudio e Bruno:
1. The quickest direct line is to ski down slopes to the Lago del Sabbione and traverse round just above the lake to below the hut.
2. The longer option is to climb back over the Passo del Sabbione then skin up to the Mittleberg Pass. If time allows you can ascend Punta del Sabbione (3182m) just above the pass. You are now in Italy and the descent down the Hohsandgletscher is breath-taking.

After a short skin you reach the Rifugio Claudio e Bruno (2708m) for a welcome rest and some delicious Italian food and wine! It's worth noting at this point that skinning directly up to the hut from above the lake is less steep, and safer, than the steep moraine ridge climbing directly off the glacier.

Day 3 – Corno-Gries hut / Rifugio Piansecco

Grade PD S2 BS   **Aspects** SE, E and N
Ascent 826m to Corno-Gries hut, 1316m to Piansecco   **Descent** 1255m, 2000m to Piansecco

Today's objective is the main summit of the tour, the Blinnenhorn (3374m). On exiting the hut you have two skinning options. However, the track that ascends the north-westerly valley is better (rather than the direct northerly which is steeper), and an hour or so of steep kick turning eventually allows you to reach the large flat area of Gran Sella del Gries (3112m). Then head west up the Griesgletscher until the slope steepens and crampons will be needed. It will take about 5 hours from the hut, but affords stunning views across to the Finsteraarhorn, the highest peak in the Bernese Oberland.

From the summit enjoy the superb and long descent down the Griesgletscher to Griessee reservoir. At the south-east corner of the lake a steep, awkward, but thankfully short, skin allows access to the Cornopass (2485m). From here it's a great descent via a coffee at the Corno-Gries hut (2338m), finally ending in the small, remote village of All'Acqua (1600m).

From the tiny hamlet of All'Acqua a steep skin up a wooded track reaches the very beautiful Swiss Rifugio Piansecco (1964m). In case of poor weather, escape from All'Aqua via public transport back to Andermatt is pretty straightforward.

Alternative

This day can be split if you use the Corno-Gries hut, which give you a more leisurely itinerary.

Tour de Soleil

Powder skiing on the Blinnenhorn.

Day 4 – Rotondo hut

| Grade PD S2 BS | Aspects all | Ascent 1290m | Descent 700m |

From the Rifugio Piansecco the ascent of Passo di Rotondo (2754m) is a lengthy four hours. It includes a couple of short steep sections where, in certain snow conditions, crampons would be advised. Pizzo Rotondo (3192m) can be ascended at this point by skinning up the broad south face, and then cramponing up a steep snowy gully to the top (descending this gully on skis is quite exciting!). Crossing the Passo di Rotondo leads to a small descent, followed by a skin accessing the Gerengletscher and then on to the spectacular Witenwasserenpass (2816m).

You now get a great descent down the Witenwasseren Glacier to the Rotondo hut (2570m). The Rotondo is a popular hut so don't expect solitude here.

Alternatives

If time (and strength) permits, the ascent of the Witenwasserenstock is also worth the effort, either from the Gerengletscher side via the Passo dei Sabbioni, or via the north-east ridge on the Rotondo side.

You could easily factor in an extra day here to ascend the Leckihorn (3068m) and the Chli Muttenhorn (2935m).

Tour de Soleil

Day 5 – Andermatt

Grade PD S2 BS   **Aspects** E, W and N   **Ascent** 800m   **Descent** 1250m

The final day ascends the classic Piz Lucendro (2962m). Descend from the hut to the head of the Witenwasseren valley just below Meschitollerberg (2368m). A three hour skin east lands us on the col next to the Giacciaio di Lucendro. Ski crampons or boot crampons may be needed for the final 100m ascent to the giant summit cross. From the summit you can trace the route all the way from the summit of the Ofenhorn on the first day, to the long glacier descending from the Blinnenhorn and the route from the previous day. With good visibility Mont Blanc can be seen in the far distance.

Then it's back on with the skis for the wonderful final descent down the west face and Witenwasseren to Realp to catch a train for the journey back to Andermatt.

In poor weather the way to the Rotondo hut is marked by poles from Oberstafel (2221m). This can help you escape in poor visibility.

Skiers on the Passo del Sabbione.

About Olly Allen

www.mountaintracks.co.uk
olly@mountaintracks.co.uk

See page 176.

The Albula Alps.

Albula Alps Traverse

By Bruce Goodlad

Tour overview

The Albula Alps in Eastern Switzerland is a stunning range of mountains 'designed' for ski touring. Depending on your exact itinerary you can visit the famous ski towns of St Moritz and Davos, but don't worry, just because these towns are full of people wearing fur coats it doesn't mean that the huts are expensive. You just need to plan your accommodation at the beginning and end of the tour.

Our itinerary goes more or less south to north, so you should get some great skiing on the north-facing bowls. Given the quality of the skiing, the area is surprisingly quiet, so while not guaranteed, you should be able to get some fresh tracks. When planning the tour you need to consider the timing, as the lift in Bergün can close in early April; so you need to check with the tourist office before you set off. You can still skin instead of using the lift, but it is good to know that this is your plan before arriving and discovering the lift is closed.

Albula Alps Traverse

Grade
PD S2 BS

Season
March is the usually the best month as the lift in Bergün (which saves an awful lot of effort) is often closed in April. It is worth checking this with the tourist office in Bergün when planning.

Maps
Swiss Topo 1:50000 ski maps are the best. To cover the whole tour you will need:
Swiss Topo 1:50000 Julier Pass 268 S
Swiss Topo 1:50000 Bergün / Bravuogn 258 S
Swiss Topo 1:50000 Ofen Pass 259 S

Kit
Standard ski touring kit for hut-to-hut touring. You will be skiing on a glacier so you will need ropes, harnesses and crevasse rescue kit. You will also need to bring an ice axe and crampons.

Weather forecast
www.meteoswiss.admin.ch

Avalanche forecast
www.slf.ch

Hut information
Jenatsch hut – www.chamannajenatsch.ch – +41 818332929
Kesch hut – www.kesch.ch – +41 814071134
Grialetsch hut – www.grialetsch.ch – +41 814163436

Useful information
Saint Moritz Tourist Office – www.stmoritz.ch
Bergün Tourist Office – www.berguen-filisur.ch
The youth hostel in St Moritz – www.youthhostel.ch – offers a well-priced half board option and is a good place to gather for the start of the tour. They can arrange a taxi for you to get to the Julier Pass

Alternative guide book
The Swiss Alpine Club guide to *Graubunden South* by David Coulin covers this area.

Albula Alps Traverse

Leaving the Jenatsch hut.

Day 1 – Col d'Agnel – Jenatsch hut

| Grade PD S2 BS | Starting altitude 2200m | |
| Aspects S and N | Ascent 940m | Descent 540m |

The best way to reach the Julier Pass, the starting point for our tour, is by taking a taxi. It is possible to get there by bus, but it is nice to start a tour without the hassle of fitting round a bus timetable. The ascent to the col is a nice introductory skin of about 800m up a wide valley. It is south-facing so it is worth starting as soon as you can in the morning if the forecast is for warm temperatures.

When you are ready to ski at the col you head pretty much due north. The best way to reach the hut is to ski all the way down to the stream junction at point 2496m, then put skins back on and climb the 150m to the hut. This gets you a few extra turns on the way. There is a traverse line marked on the ski map but this is really horizontal, so hard to ski along, and feels harder work than skinning 150m.

Day 2 – Val Mulix – Bergün

| Grade PD S2 BS | Aspects S, E and N | Ascent 430m | Descent 1300m |

This can be a bit of a make-or-break day on the tour. The initial traverse from the Jenatsch hut is pretty steep and exposed, as is the ascent to the Fuorcla Lavina and some of the sections on the descent. So you need to make sure you have stable snow conditions with a low avalanche risk.

Leave the hut heading north-east and traversing round the shoulder at the end of the south-east ridge that drops from the summit of Piz Jenatsch. Climb the west side of the broad valley that heads

Albula Alps Traverse

Crossing under Piz Laviner.

for the col between Piz Jenatsch and Piz Laviner. Just below Piz Laviner at about 3000m, a shelf leads eastwards under the peak and round into the top of the Fuorcla da Beverin. This is quite difficult navigation in anything but good visibility as you are right on the junction of two maps, and the tops of the two valleys look very similar in poor visibility. I'm not just saying this, because two mountain guides and one aspirant guide (myself included) stood here and skied down the wrong valley. We did realise pretty quickly, and we did get some great powder, but we also had to buy the beer to make up for the extra skinning.

Assuming you are in the right valley, head north passing through a narrow section before traversing east to avoid a cliff band. Once you are clear of the cliff band head north through Alp Mulix following the valley to Naz. You can get the train from Naz to Bergün where you will stay for the night. The train journey, though short, is one of the engineering marvels of the Alps, as the train does a complete circle as it winds its way down to Bergün. If you are late in the season and the lift is closed, some of the hotels may be shut too, so it is worth knowing that the Hotel Preda Kulm in Preda is open later in the season.

Day 3 – Bergün – Kesch hut

Grade PD S2 BS **Aspects** SE, N, E and W **Ascent** 800m **Descent** 760m

Assuming the lift is running, this day requires some careful route finding. From the top of the lift, skin onto the summit of Piz Darlux, then ski down the south-east ridge for a short way before skiing down and across the Murtel dla Muotta. The map makes it look like you can make it round and onto the traverse under the Piz Fregslas without putting your skins on. You can't! So enjoy the skiing, then put your

Albula Alps Traverse

skins on and climb north-east round to the Murtel dla Crappa where you can transition back to ski mode. The line here follows a shelf skirting above a steep slope to the shoulder on the north-east ridge of the Piz Fregslas at approximately 2300m. Ski east down some nice, open slopes to Alp Digl Chants, where you cross the stream, put skins back on, and climb east about 600m to the wonderfully-positioned Kesch hut, where you can spend two nights. Having two nights in the hut allows you to have a day tour with a lighter pack or, if conditions allow, climb Piz Kesch.

Alternative

An alternative to the traverse under the Piz Fregslas is: from Piz Darlux you can carry on along the exposed ridge to the Tschimas da Tisch, then ski east down into the Val Plazbi. Here you turn north and ski down to the Alp digl Chants and so to the Kesch hut. There are a few steep sections on this variation as well so, like the rest of the tour, you need to be sure of the avalanche conditions.

Day 4 – Day tour from the Kesch hut

| Grade PD S2 BS | Aspects N, NE, E and SE | Ascent 900m | Descent 900m |

There are a number of options from the Kesch hut. If you are an experienced mountaineer and conditions allow, then an ascent of Piz Kesch is a wonderful mountaineering objective. If you just want a good ski tour, then skinning up to the ski depot below Piz Kesch gives a great north-facing descent. You can get a second ski in by putting the skins back on at about 2700m and skinning west on to the Kesch Pitschen. If conditions are stable, there is a great north-facing descent from here, but it is quite steep so ask the hut guardian about conditions. Alternatively, there is a really nice east-facing bowl that drops from below the summit before the valley leads you back north to the hut. There is also a great north-facing bowl on the north end (point 3040m) of the ridge that leads north from Piz Porchabella.

Day 5 – Kesch – Grialetsch hut

| Grade PD S2 BS | Aspects N, NE and S | Ascent 950m | Descent 1025m |

We have a downhill start today which can be really cold, as you have to be out early enough to climb the south side of the next pass before you get cooked. Leave the hut and ski down the Val Funtauna to the Alp Funtauna at 2192m, from where there are a number of possibilities. If the weather and conditions are good, the most interesting way is to climb almost to the summit of the Piz Grialetsch. Just below the summit you cross over the shoulder on the south side to reach the top of the Vadret da Grialetsch. Ski north-east down to about 2700m, then contour north-west until you can ski down to the hut. If the conditions aren't quite so good, head north from the Alp Funtauna to the Scalettapass then ski north and slightly east to about 2300m, where you can put the skins on and climb the east-facing valley to the hut.

Albula Alps Traverse

Day 6 – Grialetsch – Davos or Zernez

Grade PD S2 BS   **Aspects** NW and NE   **Ascent** 775m   **Descent** 1752m

There are two main options depending on the weather:
1. If it is poor, then you can ski north down the Dischma and out to Davos, where you can catch a train to anywhere in Switzerland.
2. If the conditions and weather are good, then a great end to the week is to head east and climb through the Fuorcla Sarsura, then turn south and climb to the summit of the Piz Sarsura, where the view is amazing.

You now have 1700m of skiing ahead of you to get to the road. The descent starts with wide open skiing on the Vadret da Sarsura. At 2773m leave the glacier and head east, then south-east, into the Schneister da Sarsura which has some great, steeper skiing. Keep following the valley past the Alp Sarsura and into the tree line, you will now be following tracks, and the best snow that will eventually lead you to the road. Unfortunately, you are now positioned equidistant between two train stations both 2.5 to 3km away. You can either walk this, which is no fun, or call a taxi (the hut will have some numbers they can give you). If you started in St Moritz it might be worth getting a cab all the way back, depending on the train timetable.

Fantastic skiing down the Vadrot da Sarsura.

Possible variants or alternatives

On Day 3, instead of going to the Kesch hut, you can ski off the end of the Tschimas da Tisch then turn south down the Val Plazbi, then east to the Fuorcla Pischa, then a long traverse to the Es-Cha hut. On the following day you can traverse the Porta d'Es-Cha and descend to the Kesch hut. The pass is steep and will often involve the use of a rope, definitely an ice axe and crampons, and there are chains in place in summer that may be visible depending on the snow cover. When you have crossed the pass, if the conditions are good you could climb Piz Kesch or follow any of the other tours suggested above.

About Bruce Goodlad

www.mountainadventurecompany.com

See page 132.

Mark Chadwick on the Albula traverse.

Andy Nelson heading for the Passo di Zebrù Sud.

Ortler: The Cappuccino Tour

By Mike Austin and Bruce Goodlad

Tour overview

This fantastic touring area isn't on the radar of most British skiers, yet oddly it is frequently visited by groups of guided American parties. Initially attracted by the idea of completing the Chamonix-Zermatt Haute Route, they often conclude that the spartan food and lodgings, and lack of summits, that the standard Haute Route offers isn't the holiday adventure they were looking for. Enter the 'Cappuccino Tour'.

Located at the junction of Italy, Austria and Switzerland, the area has possibly the finest huts in the Alps. The standing joke is that when they built these huts they helicoptered in huge coffee machines and built the huts around them!

Private, small group bedrooms with en-suite bathrooms and hot showers? Check!
Central heating and wood burning stoves, complete with boot warmers? Check!
Affordable four-course Italian dinners with wine? Check!

Now add into the mix large glaciated peaks, mostly skiable to their summits and generally stable weather.

The range offers plenty of challenging terrain on a variety of aspects that allows for either classic hut-to-hut touring via high mountain cols or, as with the below itinerary, you can base yourself in a couple of the huts from where you can cherry-pick classic ski peaks that rise to 3700 metres. The terrain is big, so basic ski mountaineering and glacier skills are a part of the mix required to negotiate these mountains – although there are often easier route options available. It's easy to see why our American cousins are willing to travel halfway around the world for the skiing here. Bruce and Mike have skied together in the Ortler on many occasions and have pooled their knowledge of the area to share this tour with you.

Ortler: The Cappuccino Tour

Grade
PD-AD S3 TBS

Season
The principal huts open in early March, but April is the best month to visit to allow the glaciers to fully fill in, mitigating crevasse hazard and providing longer days.

Map
Tabacco – Carta Topografica 1:25000 Ortles Cevedale Sheet 8
This is the ski touring map of the region and all the classic ski lines are depicted on it with a dashed blue line.
Garmin's TransAlp and Italian Topo cards can be quite useful as their key details are accurate, providing a useful navigation backup and route planning options, especially if starting and ending your journey from Sulden, as returning to this valley crosses a complex high mountain col that is potentially disorientating in poor visibility.

Kit
Classic ski touring kit including an ice axe, ski crampons, boot crampons and glacier travel / crevasse rescue kit.

Weather forecast
www.meteo.it
www.snow-forecast.com
www.meteoblue.com

Avalanche forecast
www.aineva.it/

Hut information
Rifugio Branca (2487m) – www.rifugiobranca.it/
Rifugio Pizzini (2700m) – www.rifugiopizzini.it/
Marteller hut (2610m) – www.martellerhuette.com/

Useful information
Bormio is the nearest large town to the range on the Italian side. It has plenty of good value accommodation and is about three hours from Milan airport by rental car.
If travelling from the Austrian side, then Sulden is the best place to park up and spend a night, before heading up the lift system to start your tour. A single up, ski touring ticket is available.

Ortler: The Cappuccino Tour

Rob Biggle and team on the Pizzo Tresero.

Day 1 – Bormio – Branca hut

Grade PD S2 BS **Starting altitude** 2158m
Aspects S, E and NE **Ascent** 940m **Descent** 610m

Car rental is really the only option to access the Ortler. Milan is the best international airport if accessing the range from the Italian side, which has the greatest concentration of the high peaks. Access to the mountains is from Bormio through Santa Caterina, then up the Forni valley to park in the large car park below the Forni hut. There is now a small charge for parking payable at an automatic machine just before you leave Santa Caterina.

The Branca hut is then signposted from the car park. There is usually a marked skin track along the valley floor, or you may choose to take the rising traverse line of the summer road. This option is more exposed in avalanche conditions or in hard snow.

Arriving at the Branca hut early allows a short afternoon tour up the Val di Rosole directly behind the hut. By climbing into the east-facing bowls above the small lake at 2888m, the ridge dividing the Val di Rosole and the Val di Cedec can be gained at a few places, and gives good views of routes that are to be climbed later in the week. It also gives a nice little ski to warm up the legs.

Ortler: The Cappuccino Tour

Day 2 (day tour) – Pizzo Tresero

Grade PD S2-3 BS-TBS   **Aspects** N, E and SW   **Ascent** 1400m   **Descent** 1400m

This is an out-and-back day tour, but you still need full glacier travel kit and an ice axe and crampons. From the hut, don't be tempted to follow the groups heading high directly south from the hut. Contour back into the valley floor southwards and gain the toe of the glacier on looker's right close to the cliffs. Climb steeply at first, but soon the angle eases as you gain the glacier and a steadily-rising skin to the broad, flat col between Tresero and Cima San Giacomo. Follow the shoulder, bypassing the steeper ground by trending left to the south-east ridge beneath the summit, and so gain the summit via a narrow ridge.

The fall line skiing options from Tresero's high shoulder above Cima San Giacomo are obvious and often hold excellent, cold snow due to its northerly aspect. If the effects of altitude or deteriorating weather become an issue, an excellent option is to cut around the summit of Cima San Giacomo and down the Vedr di San Giacomo and into the wide Canal di San Giacomo. Although complex-looking on the map, the terrain is surprisingly reasonable on these lower slopes, and offers good, sheltered skiing where the rock walls provide contrast and protect the snow from Alpine winds.

Andy Nelson and team approaching the summit of the Pizzo Tresero.

Day 3 (day tour) – Palon de la Mare

Grade AD S3 TBS   **Aspects** W and S   **Ascent** 1300m   **Descent** 1300m

Another day trip out of the Branca allows for a light pack (same kit as yesterday). Just as well, as the vertical ascent to the summit is another 1300m day. The route-finding crux of the day occurs low down, just a kilometre south from the hut, and feels rude so early in the day. After following an old lateral moraine, turn the lower slope by cutting north-east towards the glacier. The skinning here quickly becomes steep. It is useful to have ski crampons handy, and consider setting your own fresh track. Either of the two couloirs leads to the glacier where the travel turns mellow – it's a simple glacier, and what few crevasse hazards exist are obvious and avoidable in good visibility. The final pull along the gentle summit ridge offer spectacular views across the entire range.

Descend as for the ascent.

Day 4 – Branca hut to the Pizzini hut

Grade AD S3 TBS   **Aspects** SW, S, N and W   **Ascent** 1070m   **Descent** 850m

From the Branca hut follow the Val di Osole easily north. An early start is recommended as the headwall leading to the Col Pasquale gets the full force of the sun; wet avalanche hazard is a concern in the afternoons here. The route to about 3200m is straightforward. Above, the terrain steepens and some

Ortler: The Cappuccino Tour

kick turns are needed. The last 50 metres may require a transition to crampons and axe depending on snow conditions.

The broad col feels spectacular and exposed and with the hard work done for the day an ascent to the summit of Monte Pasquale is a must. It's a great introduction to true ski mountaineering, providing easy, mixed rock ridge climbing in crampons with skis on your back. The climbing is straightforward (approx. 75 metres of gently rising PD), but the altitude and exposure give it a bark greater than its bite. Once through the difficulties, a short skin leads to the remote summit cross. Depending on the snow conditions you may be able to get back to the col on skis, but if not put them back on your pack and climb back down to the col.

The route now skirts right of the col to an obvious drop onto the Cedec Glacier. This area is quite heavily crevassed, but skiing past the seracs of blue ice is one of the more memorable descents of the range, and usually holds excellent snow. The descent to the Pizzini hut down the Cedec Glacier (don't be tempted onto the steeper Vedretta del Pasonal Glacier – its very heavily crevassed) is straightforward and again often holds excellent cold snow.

You can admire your descent from Pascale and the Cedec sipping an espresso from the veranda of the Pizzini hut before going for a pre-dinner sauna. The Pizzini is a gem of a hut – the two brother guardians are huge characters and a good source of route information and current conditions.

Alternative

If the weather is too poor for the above option, travelling from the Branca hut to the Pizzini hut via the low-level valley route is simple, and free of avalanche hazard once in the flat-bottomed Pizzini valley. It's a good semi rest day option if any of the team are feeling tired.

Day 5 (day tour) – Passo di Zebrù Loop

Grade PD S2 BS	**Aspects** all	**Ascent** 700m	**Descent** 700m

An easy day with limited vertical height gain but great skiing. It's a good bad weather option and can be extended to provide additional and steeper skiing. Work the easy-angled slopes west of the Pizzini hut up to the broad Passo di Zebrù Sud. From here drop easily north onto the pocket glacier and continue on the low-angled fall line into the valley. There is good skiing down to about 2600m. Skin up to the Passo di Zebrù Nord, and east down a nice-angled slope back to the hut.

Doing this route in reverse offers a very good steepish ski from the Passo di Zebrù Nord (38°) which is fun to do laps on. Steeper still is the north-facing shot off the summit shoulder of Orientale (3243m), a short skin to the west of Passo di Zebrù Sud and a favourite of the Pizzini guardians.

Dave Crichton skiing down from the Passo di Zebrù Sud.

Ortler: The Cappuccino Tour

Andy Nelson skiing great snow from the Passo di Zebrù Nord

Day 6 – Monte Cevedale

Grade AD S3 TBS   **Aspects** S, NW and W   **Ascent** 1000m   **Descent** 1060m

Monte Cevedale – the highest peak in the range. From the Pizzini hut head towards the toe of the Cedec Glacier before cutting left at 3000 metres into a small impressive bowl. Join the south-west ridge of the bowl at a low and obvious weakness in the ridge (you often need to boot for 50 metres to gain the ridge) and begin to skin steeply, directly up the ridge to the Rifugio Casati. In places the ridge narrows, and the ability to kick turn efficiently is a must here. Ski crampons are often required on the upper section of the ridge. The remnants of barbed wire and gun fortifications from World War I are still evident at the col.

Stop off for a coffee at the Rifugio Casati. It's a huge building that is principally used in the summer months as a stop-off point for mountaineers heading up to the summit of Monte Cevedale, but it's not recommended to overnight there in the winter due to their lack of running water. They always have a good fire in their bar to warm up by with a hot chocolate. From the Casati hut skin easily up the glacier in a south-westerly direction directly towards Monte Cevedale. The terrain steepens gradually and, as the peak is often hammered by the wind, at some point ski crampons or a transition to boot crampons will likely be required to reach the summit.

Ski back to the Pizzini hut down the now familiar Cedec Glacier, threading through obvious, large crevasses up high as you drop onto the glacier. After packing up your personal belongings in the Pizzini hut (time for a final round of espresso and cake), follow the marked 4 x 4 track easily down the valley and back to your car to end the week.

Alternative

A shorter final day that can often give great, spring snow skiing is to ski to the Col Pale Rosse. There is a really nice pointy summit just above the col which is a fun scramble.

Ortler: The Cappuccino Tour

Possible variants or alternatives

The classic tour of the region that encompasses the complete range starts from the north in Austria, from the ski resort of Sulden, where you can visit the excellent Reinhold Messner Museum. Use the ski resort lift system to access the Madritschjoch, then down to the excellent, small and cheerful Marteller hut for your first night. From here large glacier travel is the order of the next day – most parties heading to the Pizzini hut. The end of the week involves crossing the Suldenspitze, past World War I gun emplacements which dominate the valley into Italy below, and involves good navigational planning if the cloud is down.

The Punta San Mateo is also a great option from the Branca hut. It is of a similar scale and difficulty as Pizzo Tresero.

About Mike Austin

www.avalanchegeeks.com

Mike Austin is an AMGA Assistant Ski Guide. He is the co-owner (with Bruce Goodlad) of Avalanche Geeks, an avalanche education company that provides courses for both the public and mountain professionals in the Alps and Scotland. Mike has guided on ski for over 20 years, primarily on the west coast of North America from Alaska to California as well as Norway, Iceland & Antarctica.

He has made winter ascents of prominent high altitude peaks in Alaska and Antarctica and first ascents in the Pakistan Karakoram and the Cordillera Blanca of Peru. Mike and Bruce have skied together many times in the Ortler.

Approaching the Passo Pisgana with the Lobbia Mountains behind.

Adamello

By Cain Olsen

Area overview

Ski mountaineering on the largest glacier in the Italian Alps.

"It is a huge block, large enough to supply materials for half-a-dozen fine mountains. But it is in fact only one. For a length and breadth of many miles the ground never falls below 9500 feet. The vast central snow-field feeds glaciers pouring to every point of the compass. The highest peaks, such as the Carè Alto and Adamello, are merely slight elevations of the rim of this uplifted plain. Seen from within they are mere hummocks; from without they are very noble mountains falling in great precipices towards the wild glacier-close glens which run up to their feet. Imagine an enormous white cloth unevenly laid upon a table, and its shining skirts hanging over here and there between the dark massive supports."

This is how D.W. Freshfield described the central Adamello massif when he first sighted on it on 25th August 1864. The famous British mountaineer was standing on the summit of Presanella and had just carried out the first ascent of this mountain. In almost a century and a half this white cloth has shrunk. It measured 30 square kilometres at the end of 1800, 25 during the 1920s, 17 in 1997, and a mere 13 square kilometres at the last measurement in summer 2009. The message is clear; if you want to see this giant before it melts away, make sure you come quickly. If the glacier continues to shrink at this rate, in about 30 years it will disappear altogether.

In this chapter I have described some daytrips and a hut-to-hut four-day tour.

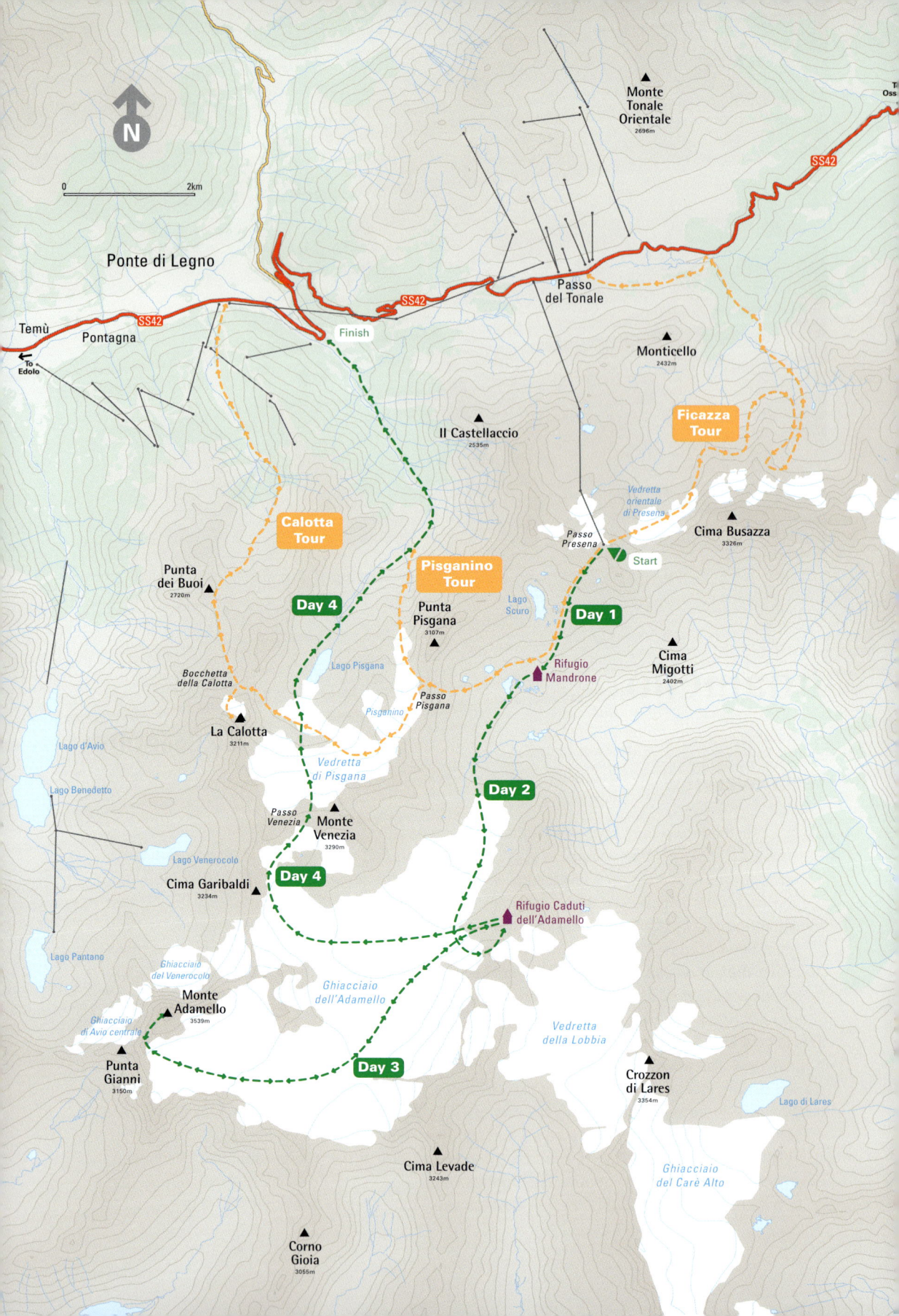

Adamello

The daytrips
The daytrips are the classic outings in this area. The famous Pisgana is described, as well as its smaller brother, Pisaganino. Calotta feels like a step back in time.

All of these have little elevation gain, thanks to the Adamello ski lifts, and massive descents. A 'ski touring pass' has been created specifically for the needs of ski mountaineers who wish to ski Pisgana or Pisganino, and this ticket enables you to use a total of five lifts: the Ponte di Legno-Tonale and Paradiso cable cars, the Presena and Val Sozzine chairlifts, and the Presena lift. This means you can set off from either Ponte di Legno or Passo del Tonale, use the lifts and then ski all the way back to your car.

The Ficazza daytrip is pretty new and offers fantastic snow, far from the crowds in a wild mountain environment ... all the right ingredients for a grandiose outing.

The tour
Then there is the Adamello Tour – a four-day ski trip to discover the scene of World War I, with nights spent in the mountain huts. This is a true Haute Route with numerous variations, meaning that your stay in these marvellous mountains can be extended further still, and careful transport planning will enable you to discover magnificent traverses far from the crowds. Val Adamè, Val Salarno, Val Miller and Val d'Avio are all ideal valleys for single day itineraries thanks to the Paradiso – Presena ski lifts.

Season
January to May depending on conditions, hut-based tours from mid March when the huts open.

Map
Edizioni Tabacco, Adamello Presanella 1:25000 – this map covers all the tours.

Kit
Standard glacier ski touring kit; axe, crampons and glacier travel equipment.

Weather forecast
www.arpalombardia.it/siti/arpalombardia/meteo/previsionimeteo/meteolombardia/Pagine/default.aspx
www.meteotrentino.it

Avalanche forecast
www.arpalombardia.it/siti/arpalombardia/meteo/previsionimeteo/bollettino-neve-valanghe/Pagine/BollettinoNeve.aspx
www.meteotrentino.it/bollettini/today/valanghe_it.aspx?id=9

Hut information
You need to **keep the '0'** of the area code when calling Italian phone numbers.
Rifugio Città di Trento (Mandrone) – www.sat.tn.it/default.aspx?fn=loadarea&idarea=405 – +39 0465 501193
Rifugio ai Caduti dell'Adamello (Lobbia Alta) – www.rifugioaicadutidelladamello.it/ – +39 0465 502615

Useful information
Links to accommodation etc. – www.pontedilegnotonale.com/

Alternative guide book
Scialpinismo nel Trentino. Vol. 3: Adamello, Presanella, Brenta, Ortles, Dolomiti, Lagorai, Alto Garda,
Ulrich Kössler, Editore: Tappeiner

Adamello

On the way to the Rifugio Mandrone with the Adamello Glacier behind.

Day tour 1 – Pisganino and Calotta

Grade PD S2-S3 BSA	**Starting altitude** 3016m		
Aspects all	**Ascent** 450m	**Descent** 1800m	**Season** January to May

What can be said about one of the most famous ski touring trips in the Alps? A mere 400m ascent is followed by more than 2000m of descent, and on busy Sundays during March and April there are literally hundreds of passionate mountaineers enjoying this famous outing. In good conditions this itinerary can be done twice, even three times in a day! A perfect introduction to the area.

From Ponte di Legno get the gondola to Passo Tonale (1800m) and then to Passo Presena (3000m). Enjoy the grandiose panorama onto the Vedretta della Lobbia and Mandrone. To the left you can make out the Crozzon di Folgarida chain, Crozzon di Lares, Corno di Cavento and Monte Carè Alto. In the centre there are Lobbia, Cresta Croce, Dosson di Genova and Monte Fumo, while to the right lie Monte Mandrone and Corno Bianco.

Descend diagonally right towards Lago Scuro. From here continue diagonally right or enjoy a second breakfast with a fantastic slice of cake made by Flavia at Rifugio Mandrone (2449m, mid March to beginning of May).

Put the climbing skins on and ascend west to Passo Pisgana (2933m). From here, after the ritual photos and a sip of hot tea, a 1800m descent awaits! The first section leads to Vedretta del Pisganino and powder snow can be found even late in the season. The route then joins Pisgana and traverses a 'ski cross' across fun and varied terrain. This leads to the 'little road' (take care on the tight hairpin bends) which leads to the Pegrà piste; ski down this to reach the lift which leads to the Corna d'Aola piste. Ski this, down the legendary black piste, to reach the start of the cable car Ponte di Legno – Tonale.

Adamello

Calotta extension

This is a great alternative to skiing down the Vedretta del Pisganino, if you are fit and the weather and conditions are good.

When you arrive at the Passo Pisgana traverse left towards Passo di Bedole (3150m). Take your skins off and descend down the Vedretta di Pisgana. Reach the point where you join the tracks coming from Passo Venezia at about 2740m and continue traversing leftwards. Without losing height, head to Bocchetta della Calotta (2958m), and the small Bivacco Regosa hut. From the hut descend a couple of metres and then continue ascending west, traversing the entire south face of La Calotta. Now ascend the right-hand side (facing the mountain) by making numerous diagonal tracks to reach the summit (3211m).

During the north-facing descent, after a couple of fantastic curves, head south at Bocchetta di Valbione (2813m) and try not to lose too much height. Put climbing skins on for the third and final time and ascend the 100m up to the col. From here enjoy the grandiose ski down the valley all the way to Rifugio Valbione and then, on the piste, to Ponte di Legno. Take great care when crossing from right to left on the 100m drop after Conca di Pozzuolo, where there are numerous icefalls.

Day tour 2 – Ficazza

Grade PD S2-S3 BSA	Starting altitude 3016m		
Aspect N	Ascent 900m	Descent 2000m	Season January to May

A unique place, never crowded and with heavenly snow. It's well worth the effort skinning up 900m, to then trace massive curves down some of the most beautiful snow in the entire Adamello group. This itinerary is special due to its north-facing aspect and the fact that it is never too crowded. The surroundings are grandiose, set beneath the north faces of Busazza and Monte Cercen, wedged between two moraine crests which seem to indicate clearly which direction to head in. There is no summit to be reached, nor is there a precise target to head for, and at a certain point the way forward seems to be suddenly barred by two great rock bastions. But you're not here for a summit, you're here to enjoy everything else possible from a spectacular outing. Finding the right way in poor weather may prove difficult, and attention must be paid in the gullies and slopes in Val di San Giacomo, which can be avalanche prone.

From Ponte di Legno take the gondola to Passo Tonale (1800m) and then to Passo Presena (3000m). From the top of the lift, cross the barrier which cordons off the piste and, descending rightwards off-piste, enter the upper part of Val Presena (also called Cantiere). This section of the valley is wide, meaning there is ample room to choose a good line but keep as high as possible to cross the valley skier's left to right, traversing beneath the west face of the Cima Busazza. Try to lose as little altitude as possible and head to a rocky outcrop located at 2705m (marked on the map). Put your skins on here and continue upwards beneath the north face of Busazza for about 100m continuing east to reach a col.

From here, ski down the series of gullies and fun hillocks for about 800m. When you reach the first larch trees put the climbing skins on once again and ascend first east, then north-east, towards Monte Cercen for about 700m through the wild and solitary San Giacomo valley. Reach the steep and rocky north face of Monte Cercen where the way onwards is barred. All that remains to do therefore is to take the skins off and enjoy the 1000m descent to the bottom of Val Presena. On the valley floor cross the wooden bridge, put the skins back on and ascend the gentle forest path back towards Passo del Tonale.

Adamello

On the east ridge of the Adamello.

Adamello – four day hut-to-hut tour

Grade PD S2-S3 BSA

The Adamello Tour is a magnificent journey into the very heart of the Adamello mountain chain and its imposing glacier system (at 13 square km the largest in Italy). The tour begins at Passo del Tonale, which gave the name to the magma rock which constitutes the backbone of this massif – tonalite.

The mountain huts Caduti dell'Adamello (Lobbia Alta) and Città di Trento (Mandrone) are open from mid March to the start of May. Booking in advance is obligatory and the wardens Romano at Rifugio Lobbia Alta and Carlo and Flavia at Rifugio Mandrone have become synonymous with great tradition in a profession which is by no means easy. They all offer perfect hospitality, excellent cuisine, a warm smile and professionalism.

Day 1 – Passo del Tonale – Rifugio Mandrone

Starting altitude 3016m   **Aspect** S   **Ascent** 600m   **Descent** 1100m

From Passo del Tonale (1800m) reach Passo Presena (2997m) with the gondola. From here, ski south-west down to Rifugio Mandrone (2500m). After a break to leave your overnight gear and enjoy an espresso, you could ascend the 400 metres to Passo Pisgana and enjoy a great ski back to the hut before dinner. This hut has the best food in the Alps!

Day 2 – Cresta Croce

Aspects E, N and NW **Ascent** 900m **Descent** 400m

Today you will skin all the way up to Cresta Croce (3300m) also known as the Cima Giovanni Paolo II and the nearby World War I cannon called 149G or Hippopotamus. From this ridge you can enjoy and exceptional panorama of the Adamello Glacier.

Leave Rifugio Mandrone and skin south-west passing Lago Mandrone to join the snout of Vedretta del Mandrone at 2650m; head south across the glacier to its east side. Skin up the east side passing where you will climb to the Rifugio Caduti dell'Adamello later in the day, then climb more steeply east into the back corner of the glacier bowl under our summit. A ramp leads left, then back right to the ridge and top. If the snow is hard you may need crampons for the last section. Ski back down to the main glacier, then a short climb leads to the Rifugio Caduti dell'Adamello (3040m) at Passo della Lobbia Alta for the night.

If you still have the legs, the south-west ridge of the Lobbia Alta is a worthwhile outing and only a 100m climb from the hut.

The Lobbia hut.

Day 3 – Monte Adamello

Aspects NW and S **Ascent** 600m **Descent** 600m

From Passo della Lobbia Alta, ascend the highest peak on the glacier, Monte Adamello (3554m), by crossing the entire Pian di Neve. (This is the name given to the glacier and literally means 'snow plain'. The ice is 250m deep here.) Leave the hut and head south-west passing the very faint col (barely recognisable as such) Passo Adame at 3128m, then curve west heading for the summit block of the Adamello. As you get closer, ski to the west of the summit (there is a small bivouac hut, the Bivouac Ugolini, just to the west on the ridge crest). Now follow the south-west ridge (usually possible on skis) to the summit. Descend the way you climbed up and head back to the hut.

Day 4 – Passo Venezia

Aspects S, SE, N and NW **Ascent** 350m **Descent** 2100m

Leave the hut, head west and go around the rocks marked at point 3082m on the glacier on the west side (it may be possible to pass on the east depending on the snow cover). Curve round these rocks then climb north-east to the Passo Venezia. The fine summit of Monte Venezia is just to the east and it would be a shame to not to climb the extra 60m to the summit.

You now have 2000m and 13km of north-facing skiing all the way to the bar. Head down the Vedretta di Pisgana passing the lake on the west side, follow the valley north-east then north. At about 2100m you will join the tracks coming down from the Pisganino tour which is followed to Ponte di Legno. You can then get the ski bus or use the lifts to get back to your car.

Adamello

Skiing down great snow towards Ponte di Legno.

About Cain Olsen

www.mountainguidesitaly.com

Cain was born in England, then from the age of 10 grew up on a farm in Northern Tuscany, where his family made wine and olive oil. He has spent the last 30 years hiking, climbing and skiing in the Alps and is extremely knowledgeable about their flora, fauna, history and traditions. Cain gained degrees in Physical Education and Sports Management at Florence and Newcastle Universities, and successfully completed a selective UIAGM/IFMGA mountain guide course (the highest internationally recognised qualification for instruction and guiding in rock and ice climbing, mountaineering, off-piste skiing and ski touring) in Italy. He has been guiding in the Alps since 2002, and has professionally lead treks and climbing expeditions in Asia, South America and the Middle East. He lives between Ponte di Legno in the Central Alps and Finale Ligure on the Italian Riviera with his wife Alice and three sons.

Summit of the Zuckerhütl.

Stubai

By Andy Perkins

Tour overview

Austria is one of the finest countries of the Alps in which to ski tour. The mountains are big enough to get good 'vertical' without being so high that acclimatisation is an issue. The glacial terrain is limited, so we don't need to play crevasse roulette too often. The accommodation, whether in valley hotels or mountain huts, is phenomenally good value for money … and you can't go wrong with weissbier, schnapps and apfelstrudel!

The start of this itinerary near the Alpine crest will be known to some English-speaking ski tourers; this glacial area is spectacular and has overshadowed the rest of the massif to the north. Working our way from the Alpine crest back towards the Inn valley gives two main advantages: we are more likely to be skiing north faces, with increased fluffiness potential (though avalanche risk will as a result be higher, especially in early season); if the föhn wind (strong warm southerly wind) kicks in, the weather will be significantly more amenable just a few kilometres from the crest. On a related note, this tour is escapable from most points in all but the most lethal of conditions.

When I first started to visit Austria, 95% of ski tourers stayed on the dotted line shown on the map. While this has changed a little, there are still loads of variants to go at, so use this description as a guideline but keep your eyes open for all sorts of magic lines and variations.

'Viel spass' (Have fun), as we say in German.

Stubai

Grade
PD S2-3 TBS

Season
End of February until mid April

Map
Alpenvereinskarte 1:25000 Hochstubai Sheet 31/1
Alpenvereinskarte 1:25000 Sellrain Sheet 31/2

Kit
Hut-to-hut ski mountaineering kit, including gear for a very small amount of glacial terrain.

Weather forecast
www.meteoblue.com
www.yr.no

Avalanche forecast
www.lawine.at (the best avalanche forecast in the Alps)

Hut information
Dresdner hut – www.dresdnerhuette.at/
Amberger hut – www.ambergerhütte.at/
Winnebachsee hut – www.winnebachseehuette.com/
Schweinfurter hut – www.dav-schweinfurt.de/huetten/schweinfurter-huette/

Useful information
Bus and train timetables from the excellent https://tickets.oebb.at/en/ticket

Stubai

Ascending the Pfaffenferner en route to the Zuckerhütl.

Warm-up (day tour) – Stubaiergletscher ski area

I always try to have a warm-up day on my tours. It's useful as a physical warm-up, remembering which end of the skis point forward, and as a get-to-know-you session with the terrain and conditions. We can test our kit and iron out any issues, and a team transceiver practice session is always time well spent.

Having met in a hotel in Innsbruck and sampled the delights of this vibrant Austrian city, you take the ski bus from the railway station to Mutterbergalm, which is the base station for the Stubaiergletscher ski area. Depending on conditions and weather, you can do anything from piste skiing to off-piste itineraries to a day tour. Whichever combination you choose you finish at the Dresdner hut.

Day tour

Grade PD S2 BS	**Starting altitude** 3158m	**Aspects** all
Ascent 510m	**Descent** variable, depends on how much lift-accessed off-piste you choose	

The Zuckerhütl, the highest peak in the area at 3505m, is a popular classic. Use the lift system to access either the Eisjoch or the Fernaujoch and then ski to the base of the draglift on the Gaisskarferner. Leave the ski area and continue south-east for 1km. Skins on and head up the Pfaffenferner to the Pfaffenjoch. (**Note** – do not follow the line on the Alpenverein map on the right bank, but take a more central line). Avoid too much faffing and head east to the base of the east ridge of the Zuckerhütl, the summit of which is gained by a short scramble. You may need a rope, ice axe and crampons or all three. Then reverse the route back to the ski area with a couple of very fine pitches. You spend the night in the Dresdner hut, which is often full of piste-skiing beer drinkers on corporate nights out. Embrace it while you can.

Day 1 – Leave the lunacy: Dresdner hut – Amberger hut

| Grade PD S3 TBS | Aspects N and NE | Ascent 150m | Descent 1200m |

This is a relatively short day, so you can ski for the morning in resort and then head over, or use the extra margin to pop through the weather window if things are iffy.

Resort skiing is all very well, but there's only so much oompah Eurodisco one can tolerate. You leave the Dresdner hut and either take the lift system to the Daunscharte if you're feeling flush (about 45 minutes), or skin if you're feeling thrifty. (I don't know how long, I've never done it, but it's about 4km and a 1000m vertical – say 3 hours?) Boot up 50m behind the top of the draglift, and then go left along the ridge to a drop-in point onto the Sulztalferner. Drop in (35° for a short way), and then when it flattens out head almost horizontally across the top of the Sulztalferner at about 3000m to its left bank, passing above a crevassed zone. Once you reach the immense wall of the Wüutenkarspitz, you can head up to the Wütenkarsattel in good weather, or handrail down the left bank to about 2650m in bad weather, before dropping into the main Sulztal valley.

Once in the main valley, at 2400m head north towards the Amberger hut. (**Important** – at 2293m, stay on the left bank. Do not drop into the gorge.)

Once past the gorge, ski down onto the flats and follow the marked trail to the awesome Amberger, one of the best huts in the Alps. It has a perfect blend of comfortable dorms, great food and welcoming staff, but nevertheless feeling wild and remote. Why don't you spend two nights here? Go on – you know it makes sense.

Day 2 – Day tour from the Amberger hut

| Grade PD-AD S3 TBS | Aspects E and N | Ascent 1050m | Descent 1050m |

There are several options from the Amberger hut, depending on weather and snow conditions. I've done the Kuhscheibenspitz several times and it's always been great value. Head south along the flats from the hut for about 1km and then turn right just left of the Wannenbach. The slope is quite steep here and more often than not requires ski crampons. Once it flattens out, head south-west on rolling terrain to point 2708m before turning south and rising gently back left to the Rosskarferner. Gain the ridge to the right of the summit, stash skis and boot easily to the summit of the Kuhscheibenspitz.

From here, there are two options for descent:
1. Reverse the route up.
2. If, and only if, conditions are good and you are comfortable on 40° terrain, the north couloir can be skied. Ski down to point 3035m and locate the entry, most likely on skier's right. Drop in carefully – a technical error or an avalanche, even a small one, will have serious consequences here (and there is no phone signal). A rope might be useful to test the slope. The first 100m has some 40° in it, and then it gradually gets wider and less steep. Re-join the ascent route around 2600m.

Ski back towards the Sulztal (many variants possible) and reward yourselves with some of the finest apfelstrudel mit vanilla sauce on the planet. You could even have a shower if it's that time of year.

The best apfelstrudel mit vanilla sauce on the planet.

Arriving at the ski depot on the Kuhscheibenspitz. Skier – Louise Parkin.

Day 3 – Amberger hut to Winnebachsee hut

Grade PD S2 BS   **Aspect** SW   **Ascent** 720m + 540m to Putzenkarscharte   **Descent** 750m

After a fine 'frühstuck' (breakfast), ski down the road from the Amberger hut towards Gries. About 1km before the village, take a forest track on the right towards the hamlet of Winnebach. From here, you will most likely need to put skis on packs and walk up a narrow zigzag path in the pine woods until you gain the main valley at a small barrage just below 1900m. This valley rises gently north-east for about 2km until, at just above 2200m, you turn left and head steeply north-west. You may need ski crampons or even have to boot a short way to reach the Winnebachsee hut.

This is one of those lovely huts that look like you could lift the roof off and it would play a tune. Set in grandiose scenery and with a small lake for water supply just behind, it's a stunning spot. In theory you should be here for an early lunch, and there are a few options for afternoon entertainment higher up.

One favourite of mine is the Putzenkarscharte at 2900m, which gives a great north-facing descent in a wild setting. Head east from the hut and after just less than a kilometre turn south towards the Putzenkarferner. The top section should only be attempted in stable snow conditions as the access couloir is in the avalanche gradient zone. Reverse your way back to the hut in a series of very tasteful pitches.

Stubai

Caning it on the apron below Kuhscheibenspitz north couloir. Skier – Tim Woodward.

Day 1 - A journey day: Winnebachsee hut – Schweinfurter hut

Grade PD S2 BS **Aspects** all **Ascent** 926m **Descent** 1200m

There are three potential glacial routes to reach the Schweinfurter hut: the Zwieselbachtal (relatively easy-angled and straightforward), the Larstigtal, and finally the route described – the Grastal. This last variant has the steepest and most complex terrain, but you could pick either of the other two lines if conditions or weather dictated.

From the Winnebachsee hut, head north and then north-west passing the Leschhorn to reach the Zwieselbachjoch. Head WSW up the Grieskoglferner to reach the col just north of the Breiter Grieskogel. A short skin takes in the summit of the Breiter Grieskogel from here, before a wonderful long descent to the Horlachtal.

The terrain is steep and quite complex, so you will need good visibility and conditions. Head right down the Grastalferner to a narrowing. From here you can ski down south-west to the Grastalsee and then follow the Grastal, staying just on the right bank as you descend towards the tree line. At 1850m, pick up a track that zigzags down, before contouring right to hit the Horlachtal at Mooseregg. From here, skin gently up the road to reach the Schweinfurter hut.

Day 5 – From pigs to cows: Schweinfurter hut – Kühtai

Grade PD S3 TBS	**Aspects** S and N
Ascent 750m, 1250m to Sulzkogel	**Descent** 780m, 1280m from Sulzkogel

Leave the Schweinfurter hut and head north-east. Late in the season, this could mean booting up for a while before hitting the snow where the angle eases around 2400m. Head for the Finstertaler Scharte, which is gained by a short traverse to the left. From here you can quickly bag the summit of the Schartenkopf. Returning to the col, prepare for the descent.

The first section is steep, north-facing and with cliffs below it, so you should be very sure of your stability assessment before dropping in on a rightwards traversing line. If you are unsure you will have to go back the way you came then out to the road. Once into the main bowl, follow your nose down and left towards the Speichersee. If you're still feeling energetic at this stage of the week, the Sulzkogel gives a fine addition to this day.

Around 2500m, traverse west to the valley that leads towards the Gameskogelferner. Gain this via a short steep climb, then head west and slightly north to the col at the head of the valley. From the col, a short scramble with skis on packs leads to another small saddle, and from here the summit can be gained by a short bootpack.

Retrace your steps and ski down to the Speichersee. Hold your height as much as possible on the right bank until a final short skin to the dam wall. Skins off, and then ski the dam wall – yes, really – before gradually easing slopes lead to the fleshpots of Kühtai and a well-deserved beer. From Kühtai, buses can be taken to Ötztal-Bahnhof and from there the train gets you swiftly back to Innsbruck.

Possible variants or alternatives

Day 1
Glacial recession has been making the drop-in to the Sulztalferner bigger and steeper over the years. In the lifetime of this guidebook, it will almost certainly get more feisty. An alternative way to the Amberger hut is to take the Daunjoch lift, boot up the SSW ridge of the Hintere Daunkopf, and then ski north down a series of bowls to about 2850m before turning north-west into the bowl of the Bockkar. Ski down this and exit left before dropping down to hit the Sulztal around 2500m. Good visibility and stable conditions required for this descent.

Day 4
The Zwieselbachtal or the Larstigtal provide more straightforward ways of getting to the Schweinfurter hut if conditions and / or weather are proving challenging.

About Andy Perkins

www.andypmountainguide.com

See page 100.

Adam skiing back to the Fanes hut.

Circuit of the Tofana – Dolomites

By Martin Chester

Tour overview

Ski touring in the Dolomites is a dramatic and rewarding experience. Huge limestone cliffs and towers glow against a backdrop of winter snow. Surprisingly, amidst this rocky scenery, superb slopes and couloirs of pristine snow carve their way from valley to valley. The area is most famous for these off-piste descents and itineraries, particularly those around the popular lift system of the Sella Ronda. But with so many huts within easy reach of the lifts and pistes, it is possible to devise endless combinations of overnight stops to link numerous days into rewarding tours.

This tour takes us away from the crowds of the Sella Ronda into the Fanes, Senes, Braies National Park. The huts are more remote and more traditional than those next to the pistes, albeit with the high standards you would expect in Italy; small rooms, showers, and excellent dining. While you could whip round the entire route in a couple of days, you could also extend your stay in each hut to make a longer tour – and still only scratch the surface of this great area. The following is a suggested itinerary for a rewarding week of ski touring that will leave you wanting to return for more!

Circuit of the Tofana – Dolomites

Grade
F-PD S1-S2 MS

Season
From the first snow of the winter to early Spring. January to March is ideal.

Map
Tabacco1:25000 Cortina D'Ampezzo e Dolomiti Ampezzane Sheet 03

Kit
These peaks are not glaciated, so lightweight ski touring day packs are adequate. Mountaineering equipment (rope, harness, crampons, axe, etc.) can be added to suit the requirements of any mountaineering or steep skiing objectives.

Weather forecast
www.provinz.bz.it/weather/home.asp in English

Avalanche forecast
www.provincia.bz.it/valanghe/home.asp (in German or Italian)
+39 0471 270555 or +39 0471 271177
You need to keep the '0' of the area code when calling Italian phone numbers.

Hut information
Rifugio Averau – www.btorri.it/rifugio-averau
Rifugio Scoiattoli – www.rifugioscoiattoli.it/
Rifugio Col Gallina – www.cortinadolomiti.eu/EN/rifugio-col-gallina/
Rifugio Lagazuoi – www.rifugiolagazuoi.com if you book early!
Rifugio Fanes – www.rifugiofanes.com/en/dolomites-hut.htm
Sennes hut – www.sennes.com/
Rifugio Ra Stua – www.malgarastua.com

Useful information
Cortina tourist office – www.cortinadolomiti.eu
Cortina Express – www.cortinaexpress.it/?lang=en – direct bus to Cortina from Venice and Verano airports
Kobe Sport in Cortina – www.kobesport.it

Alternative guide books
Freeride in Dolomiti, Francesco Tremolada, edizione Versante Sud, ISBN 9788887890938, in Italian and English. This book gives additional information on off-piste itineraries around Cinque Torri for Day 1 and steeper descents, which can be woven into the journey to the Fanes hut on Day 2.

Circuit of the Tofana – Dolomites

Stunning evening light on the Tofana Circuit.

Warm up day – Cortina into the Cinque Torri system

Grade PD S2 BS **Starting altitude** 2413m **Aspects** all

This first day is entirely optional (and can be circumvented with a ski bus that takes you directly to the Passo Falzarego), but it is a great way to start the tour and savour some of the great off-piste skiing on the doorstep of Cortina.

Wherever you stay, you can quickly work your way through the lift system (or directly by bus) to gain the Bai de Dones lift to the Scoiattoli hut (possible overnight stay). From here, the Averau chair will whisk you to the Forcela Nuvolau. Committed ski tourers will don skins for a quick trip up past the Rifugio Nuvolau to the Ra Gusela. Those with an appetite for more skiing will savour the delights of the off-piste on both sides of the col – around the Fedare bowl and lift (see itineraries 80 to 82 in *Freeride in Dolomiti* by Francesco Tremolada). Eventually, make your way through the Passo Grau via the Croda Negra lift to access the slopes (and savour the last few runs of the mellow off-piste here) above Col Galina. If late in the day, this makes an ideal overnight for a sharp start in the morning. If you booked early, as the hut can be really busy, get to Passo Falzarego in time for the last lift to Lagazuoi and the highest sauna in the Dolomites.

Circuit of the Tofana – Dolomites

Skinning above the Fanes hut.

Day 1   Lagazuoi – Fanes hut

Grade PD S2 D5   **Aspects** N, NE and S   **Ascent** 500m   **Descent** 1100m

Whether you stayed in the hut up here the night before, or took the first lift in the morning, the day starts from the lofty vantage point of Lagazuoi. A quick coffee in the hut will allow you to check conditions with the guardian, as you have two options:

1. Head down the Armentarola piste until the junction, then head off-piste (roughly following the trail of the Alta Via Dolomites) following the fall line on skier's right of the valley. Follow this classic off-piste run to traverse above the lake Lagacio. Put on skins and a short, sharp kick turn ascent (about 300m – south facing) leads to the Forcela di Lech (or Lago in Italian). You can check the conditions of this gully with the hut guardian (it is visible from the viewing platform at the lift station), before committing as it is often stripped of snow. Once through the col, the day can be extended with more skinning to gain height towards Cima Scotoni before a long descending traverse to the valley as for option 2.
2. The more simple and dependable bet (especially in poor weather) is to start off down the same piste, but fork left on the classic Armentarola run towards Capanna Alpina. There are numerous opportunities to duck off the side of the piste in the gently-wooded slopes. Soon after passing the Scotoni hut, the piste flattens and you reach a large flat area. Put on skins and turn right to the Col de Locia. Skinning out of the trees into a glade, you will see the twisted path cut into the cliffs above. It looks unlikely, but you can often skin further than you think. The last couple of hundred rocky metres may require a quick boot until you are through the gate at the top. The stunning winter vista opens out as you follow an undulating trail along the river.

Both options converge at Le Gran Plan and you snake your way along the river, then on down to the Ucia

Circuit of the Tofana – Dolomites

Adam making late afternoon tracks above the Fanes hut.

de Gran Fanes. Again, the route follows the Alta Via Dolomites (the trail may even be evident in a lean winter) with a short climb over the Ju de Limo. From here the super-fit and keen can add a short side excursion to the Col Bechei Dessora, if the south-facing slopes are still cold enough in the early season. Most will be content to pick up the switchback descent down the track to the Fanes hut. With all the best skiing done first thing, followed by a long flat journey, this essential link is like an upside-down touring day, but once you arrive at the Fanes hut it is all worth it.

In total the day gives a minimum of 500m ascent with at least 1100m of descent, with more possible depending on route choice and extra skinning.

Day 2 (day tour) – Sasso Delle Dieci Zehner

Grade PD S2 BS	**Aspects** S and E	**Ascent** 1000m	**Descent** 1000m

You could spend a week at the Fanes hut exploring the wide range of options – and many guests in the hut will be doing just that. Most begin by traversing the plateau to the Lavarella hut before heading north through a faint valley. Climb 150m, picking your way through rocky steps and remember these for later. They are not serious – but bad for your skis! When the slope eases, turn left (W) and skin over undulating terrain through twin bumps, then turn north-west towards Ciastel de Fanes. Leave this on your right as you continue west and ascend the steep, southern ridge (beware avalanche risk on this steep-ish south slope) to below the summit, where you can leave your skis. Many skiers will call this the top, but the real summit requires a short scramble (one tricky step and fixed equipment) for those equipped with rope, harness and crampons.

Return via the same route.

Circuit of the Tofana – Dolomites

The Sennes hut.

Day 3   Fanes hut – Sennes hut

| Grade PD S2 BS | Aspects all | Ascent 1000m | Descent 900m |

In perfect conditions the Forcella di Ciamin (2395m) and descent of the Gran Vallun is one of the finest classic tours of the area.

Ski down the main access track from the Fanes hut to reach the lake (Lago Piciodel, 1819m). Put on skins and climb eastwards (NW to W facing slopes) that gradually steepen to the col of the Forcella di Ciamin. There is an option to boot up to the summit of Ciamin, or continue a rising traverse to the ridge of the Croda Rossa (red rocks). Either way, aim for the second col (at c. 2500m) to find the best way into the Gran Vallun below. This section requires care as, very rapidly, you switch from west, through south and east, onto north-facing slopes. Once in the Gran Vallun, this stunning north-facing bowl leads down to 2190m where the slope eases and it is imperative to turn right (east). Keeping right, pick up the tracks leading to Fodara Vedla (1966m). From here a straightforward skin up a good track (summer road) leads to the Sennes hut (2116m).

Bad weather option

In poor conditions it is possible to complete this journey by skiing out to Pederu down the access track, and skinning up the access track to the Sennes hut. Hut transport (snow-cat) is also available by arrangement with the guardians.

Circuit of the Tofana – Dolomites

Day 4 – A Sennes hut tour and out to Ra Stua

| **Grade** PD S2 BS | **Aspects** SE, E and S |
| **Ascent** 700m | **Descent** 700m (+ 450m from Sennes hut to Ra Stua hut) |

The Sennes hut is another gem worthy of staying for a few days, as it is surrounded by a cirque of inspiring peaks and a variety of day tours. The Munt (or Muntejela) de Senes is the jewel in the crown. This tour describes both options on the peak, by going up one way and down the other. In reality, you may have to select the best combination of ascent and descent options to suit the weather and snow conditions as they are completely interchangeable.

From the Sennes hut skin up the covered road, over the brow, to gain the plateau of the Ucia Munt de Senes. From here, the terrain is undulating for a while, but it is rarely worth taking the skins off for the short descents. Take a moment to choose the best line for ascent and descent – paying particular attention to the presence of cornices on the summit ridge for later. Skin up the left flank of the broad ridge, passing point 2361m and heading between points 2421m and 2437m. Here the terrain steepens as you skin up the south-east, then south-facing slopes to gain the hanging broad ridge toward the summit (2787m).

For the descent, you can take the alternative route, swinging left (east) to gain access to the appealing east-facing bowl. Beware; this often has a corniced ridge to cross, so gain entry by the safest line (and check this out earlier in the day on the ascent). The open skiing leads down to the valley of San Berto, leading quickly back to the main plateau. From here you will almost certainly have to put the skins back on for a short climb over the brow of the bowl, to regain the original track back to the Sennes hut.

After a short break in the hut (and collecting any 'left luggage'), you can skate and pole down the track – first east, then south-east. This is usually easy going and may even be pisted. Cruise easily and quickly down the Val Salata to the Rifugio Ra Stua. Just be aware of the increased risk late in the day, if it's especially hot, or the day after fresh snow.

Day 5 – A final tour above Ra Stua and back to Cortina

| **Grade** PD S2 BS | **Aspects** W, SW and S | **Ascent** 700m | **Descent** 900m |

From the Ra Stua hut, set off back up the track you came down the day before, and quickly turn east up the forest track (signed to Forcella de Lerosa). The route more or less follows the summer track and is usually well travelled by skis and snowshoes alike. Coming out of the trees into meadows at 1904m, turn left to skin north-east over open slopes, passing the chalets of Cason de Lerosa. Curl right round the blunt ridge, before a final steepening climb brings you to the subsidiary peak of the Valbones (2300m).

From here, the views are incredible, and you have a choice of descents. For those with a taxi number and a good command of Italian, you can continue the journey past Castel de Ra Valbones over the Forcella Colfiedo to ski out to Cimabanche. This descent ends at just 1530m so it is a great option early in the season – check the snowline if it is lean, late or hot. For the more conservative, a great descent can be had back over the meadows and through the trees parallel to the skinning line. The mature forest has well-spaced trees and is a joy to ski. Head back to the Ra Stua hut for a coffee, where the guardian will order a taxi when you depart. Ski out down the snow-covered road (the shade of the trees keep it snowy for further and longer than you might expect) and your taxi will be waiting when you arrive at the road head.

Possible variants or alternatives

This is just one itinerary in an area festooned with great options. As a consequence, there are numerous opportunities to extend this tour. Examples include:
1. Combining this trip with a longer entry through the Sella Ronda (a great area for a ski safari of lift-served access to classic off-piste itineraries and easy-access huts).
2. Stay at each hut for longer – both the Fanes and Sennes huts are great bases for a number of day tours.
3. Extend the tour over the Forcella Crocodain to Pratopiazza and even to the Tre Cime and beyond ...

About Martin Chester

www.martinchester.co.uk

See page 44.

Making fresh tracks above the Fanes hut.

APPENDIX 1 – VARIATIONS ON THE MANUEL GENSWEIN TRAINING MODULE

The object is to train people in 15 minutes to be able to perform a companion rescue.

1. Ask everyone to pull out their probe and assemble it. Take it apart and repeat a total of three times. Research has shown that much time can be wasted not knowing how to assemble a probe. When they have done this get everyone to gently probe each other to see what a body feels like.

2. Ask everyone to pull out their shovel and assemble it. Again, do this three times for the same reason as above. You can make this a race to introduce the concept of urgency.

3. Basic transceiver handling. As a group get everyone to turn their units from 'off' to 'send' to 'search' on command. Repeat at least three times so everyone is comfortable with the operation of his or her unit. Also check that everyone knows how to get their unit out from under their clothing in an incident.

4. Practical search of one buried unit at 35m distance. Talk the group through the search as everyone performs it. Whole group on receive, then follow their unit to the buried unit. Focus on following the unit walking in a curve, distance number decreasing.

5. At 10m slow down and, following the arrow, bring the unit in closer to the snow, slowly and accurately. Find the lowest distance reading and mark that point in the snow.

6. Pinpoint search using a probe in a spiral fashion.

7. Repeat the search again, but start far enough away that a signal search is required.

8. Short explanation of tactical / conveyor shovelling, then get the group to start shovelling in formation. Practise rotation.

9. If time allows use two buried transceivers so that the concepts behind multiple burials can be covered.

APPENDIX 2 – KIT LIST

Day tours non-glacial personal

- Skis and bindings – hard to forget the bindings I know
- Skins
- Ski crampons
- Boots
- Poles
- Rucksack
- Avalanche transceiver
- Avalanche probe – 2.4m minimum
- Metal shovel
- Boot crampons – itinerary dependent
- Ice axe – itinerary dependent
- Mobile phone
- Sun cream – for skin and lips
- Knife / multi-tool
- Water bottle / flask
- Personal first aid – blister kit, painkillers
- Insurance
- Camera

Clothing

- Base layer bottoms
- Softshell or Gore-Tex trousers
- Base layer top
- Softshell top with hood
- Waterproof jacket – as light as the forecast will allow
- Waterproof trousers if wearing softshell – as light as the forecast will allow
- Synthetic insulated jacket with hood
- Down jacket – if really cold this and the previous item can be interchanged
- Thin gloves
- Thick gloves
- Warm hat
- Sun hat
- Sun glasses
- Goggles

Appendices

Glacier tour personal

Harness
Personal or group glacier travel / crevasse rescue kit

Hut-to-hut

Headtorch
Book / Kindle
Toothbrush and toothpaste – some huts have showers, but some don't even have running water
T shirt to wear at the hut
Sheet sleeping bag
Change of socks depending on the length of the tour

Group kit

Group shelter
First aid kit
Map
Compass
GPS
Brooks sledge – depending on venue
Spares kit (see Appendix 4)

Crevasse rescue kit

There should be TWO of these in the party, even if it's a party of just two
2 x ice screws – one long about 22cm and one shorter about 17cm. These should be clipped together with a snapgate karabiner, and should have rubber caps on the teeth to protect the teeth and your trousers
2 x 8ft slings (120cm doubled length)
3 x screwgate karabiners, at least one should be an HMS (pear-shaped) design
2 x prusik loops and 1 mechanical device such as a Wild Country Ropeman or Petzl Micro Traxion
1 x pulley-style karabiner – such as a DMM Revolver
30m of 8mm rope – there should always be two ropes in the party
I usually add 5m of 6mm cord, which can be used in anchor creation, but also can be used to help reading the terrain in poor visibility

Personal crevasse rescue kit if not carrying above

1 x ice screw – about 17cm in length
1 x 8ft sling with two screwgate karabiners

APPENDIX 3 – FIRST AID KIT

- 2 pairs non-latex surgical gloves
- 1 face shield to act as a barrier if giving CPR
- 1 pair tough-cut scissors
- 2 triangular bandages
- 2 large wound dressings – Israeli bandages are best
- 2 10 x10cm non-adherent dressings – if you use Israeli type they are part of the system
- Roll of surgical tape
- Small selection of plasters
- A few antiseptic wipes
- 1 100mm-wide crepe bandage
- 2 packs steristrips to close wounds
- Personal painkillers – paracetamol / ibuprofen

APPENDIX 4 – SKI TOURING SPARES KIT

Rubber ski straps x 4 – 30cm ones work bestCable ties – a selection of lengths and thicknesses

Metal scraper

Small block of wax

Binding mounting screws

Physio-type tape – much better than duct tape in the cold

Spare transceiver / GPS batteries

Screwdriver

Emergency skin glue

On longer tours I add:

Araldite

Index

A

Äbeni Flue 151
Abriès 53
Adamello 201
Adamello Tour 203, 206
Aiguille de la Bérangère 96
Aiguille du Midi 104
Aiguilles Rouges, refuge / hut 155, 157, 158
Aiguillette des Houches 111
airbags 15
Albula Alps 185
Aletschfirn 151
All'Acqua 182
Allalinhorn 175, 176
Allen, Olly 176
Alphubel 175, 176
Amberger, refuge / hut 211, 213, 214, 216
Aminona 143
Ammertetali 143
Andermatt 180, 184
Anker, Daniel 137
Argentière 121
Argentière, refuge / hut 120, 121
Armentarola piste 221
Arolla 153, 159, 160
Arpelistock 133, 137
Arpitetta, refuge / hut 163, 166
Arpont, refuge / hut 74, 76
Audannes, refuge / hut 136, 139
Aussois 71
Austin, Mike 200
avalanche forecast 26
avalanche rescue, companion 24
avalanche rescue kit 15
avalanche safety and rescue 23
Averau, refuge / hut 219
Avérole, refuge / hut 61, 63, 66, 67
axe, ice 17
Ayas, refuge / hut 171, 172, 173

B

Baird, Jonny 116
Bardonècchia 59
Bardoneccia 55
Barrhorn 168
Barrloch 165
Baud, Anselme 103
BCA Shaxe 20
Bella Tola, refuge / hut 163, 165
Benevolo, refuge / hut 83, 84, 86
Bergün 185, 187, 188, 189
Bernese Oberland 145
Bertol, refuge / hut 155, 159
Bessans 61, 69
Bezzi, refuge / hut 83

bindings 14
Binntal 177
Binntal, refuge / hut 180, 181
Bishorn 166
Bivacco Regosa, refuge / hut 205
Bivouac des Dorées 120, 121, 122
Blakemore, Tim 80
Blanchère, grading scale 12
Blatten 151
Blinnenhorn 182
Bocchetta della Calotta 205
Bockkar 216
Bonneval-sur-Arc 61, 64
boots, ski 14
Bormio 195, 196
Bourg-Saint-Pierre 130
Bourg St Bernard 122
Branca, refuge / hut 195, 196, 197, 200
Breiter Grieskogel 215
Breithorn 172
Briançon 45
Bric Boscasso 40, 41
Britannia, refuge / hut 171, 175, 176
Brunegghorn 165

C

Cabau, Emmanuel 74
Caduti dell'Adamello 207
Caduti dell'Adamello, refuge / hut 203, 206
Calotta 203, 204, 205
Cantiere 205
Cappuccino Tour 193
Carro, refuge / hut 61, 63, 64, 65
Casati, refuge / hut 199
Cason de Lerosa 224
Castor 169, 172
Cedec Glacier 198, 199
cell phone 19
Cervières 49
Chabod, refuge / hut 89, 90
Chamonix 107, 117
Chamonix-Zermatt Haute Route 117
Champagny 79
Chanrion, refuge / hut 120, 123
Charamoi mai en Val Maira 37
Charlton, Mark 60
Chester, Martin 44
Chialvetta 39, 40
Chivasso, refuge / hut 81, 83, 86, 87, 88, 90
Chli Muttenhorn 183
Cimabanche 224
Cima Busazza 205
Cima di Jazzi 175
Cima Giovanni Paolo II 207
Cima San Giacomo 197

Cima Scotoni 221
Città di Trento, refuge / hut 203, 206
Claudio e Bruno, refuge / hut 177, 180, 182
clothing, ski touring 17
Col Bechei Dessora 222
Col d'Agnel 188
Col d'Arbéron 68
Col d'Arnès 68
Col de Beugeant 114
Col de Chardonnet 121
Col de Labby 76
Col de la Cicle 94, 99
Col de la Fenêtre 94, 99
Col de la Forclaz 112
Col de la Gouille 130
Col de la Grande Casse 79
Col de la Grand Lui 122
Col de Launichard 49
Col de la Vanoise, refuge / hut 74, 77
Col de l'Encrenaz 114
Col de l'Evêque 125
Col del Grand Neyron 90
Col de Locia 221
Col de Milon 166
Col d'Enchiausa 39
Col des Autannes 115
Col des Chasseurs 93, 94, 95
Col des Clochettes 49
Col des Dômes 97, 99
Col des Glaciers 97, 99
Col des Pariotes 65
Col des Peygus 49, 50
Col des Thurges 75
Col de Trièves 65
Col de Valpelline 125
Col du Bal 51
Col du Belvédère 112, 114
Col du Galibier 49
Col du Grand Méan 65
Col du Grand St Bernard 122
Col du Lautaret 48, 49
Col du Moine 79
Col du Passon 116, 121
Col du Vallon 59
Col Gallina, refuge / hut 219
Col Infranchissable 97
Colle del Grand Etret 87
Collister, Rob 168
Col Pale Rosse 199
Col Pasquale 197
Combal des Prés 52
Combe de la Lause 51
Combe du Malazen 49, 50
communication 19
companion avalanche rescue 24

Index

compass 19
Conscrits, refuge / hut 91, 93, 95, 98
Corna d'Aola piste 204
Corno-Gries, refuge / hut 180, 182
Cortina 220
Coulin, David 187
crampons, mountaineering 17, 22
crampons, ski 14, 21
Cresta Croce 207
Crête de la Lausette 50
Crête de la Seyte 52
Crête de Reychard 51
crevasse rescue kit 15, 16
Croix de Bron 116
Cumbal Vallonetto 41

D

Daubenhorn 143
Daunscharte 213
Davos 185, 191
Delaperrière, Eric 103, 110
Dent Parrachée 79
Dolomites 217
Dôme de Chasseforêt 77
Dome de Moming 167
Domes de Miage 81, 87, 89
downhill skiing 22
Drayères, refuge / hut 57, 58, 59, 60
Dresdner, refuge / hut 211, 212, 213
Dufoursattel 175

E

Echo 112 33
Engstligenalp 143
Es-Cha, refuge / hut 191
Esquiar en Val Maira 37
evacuation plan 29
Evettes, refuge / hut 61, 63, 65, 66
Evolène 156

F

Fäld 181
Fanes, refuge / hut 219, 220, 221, 222, 223, 225
Fatmap 29
Felikjoch 172
Femma, refuge/hut 74, 78
Ficazza 205
Fiesch 180
Fieschergletscher 149
Finsteraarhorn 150
Finsteraarhorn, refuge / hut 147, 149, 150, 151, 152
Finstertaler Scharte 216

first aid kit 19
Fodara Vedla 223
Fond d'Aussois, refuge / hut 74, 76
Forcela Nuvolau 220
Forcella Colfiedo 224
Forcella Crocodain 225
Forcella di Ciamin 223
forecast, avalanche 26
Forni, refuge / hut 196
Frederico Chabod, refuge / hut 84
Freeride in Dolomiti 219, 220

G

Gameskogelferner 216
Gasteretal 144
Gaudissart 53
Gelten, refuge / hut 136, 137
Gemmibahn 143
Gentilini, Franck 103, 110
Glacier d'Armancette 99
Glacier de Ferpècle 159
Glacier de la Mahure 76
Glacier de la Plaine Morte 141
Glacier de Moming 167
Glacier de Moncorve 88
Glacier de Mont Miné 159
Glacier des Evettes 66
Glacier des Grands 116
Glacier du Trô la Tête 96, 97, 99
Glacier de Tsantleuron 137
Glacier de Valsorey 131
Glacier de Vouasson 159
Glacier di Tsanteleina 85
Glacier d'Otemma 124
Glacier du Colerin 67
Glacier du Grand Méan 65
Glacier du Mulinet 65
Glacier du Pelve 79
Glacier du Tseudet 130, 132
Glaciers de la Vanoise 76
glacier skiing 22
glacier travel kit 16
Gnifetti, refuge / hut 171, 173
Goodlad, Bruce 132
GPS 19
grading, ski tour 12
Grande Aiguille Rousse 64
Grands Mulets, refuge / hut 103, 104
Gran Paradiso 81, 87, 89
Gran Paradiso National Park 81
Gran Vallun 223
Gran Vaudala 86
Grastal 215
Graubunden South 187

Grenz Glacier 174
Gressoney valley 171
Grialetsch, refuge / hut 187, 190, 191
Gries 214
Grieskoglferner 215
Grimentz 164
Grindelwald 148
Grosses Wannenhorn 150
Grossstrubel 143
group kit 19
group shelter 19

H

Hagenmuller, Christophe 110
Hagenmuller, Jean-François 110
Haute Maurienne 61
Haute Route, Chamonix-Zermatt 117
Haute Route Imperiale 161
Haute Route, West Oberland Ski 133
help, calling for 32
Henderson, Paul 57, 63
Hintere Daunkopf 216
Hohsand Glacier 182
Hollandiahütte 147, 149, 151
Hospice du Grand St Bernard 120, 122
Hotel Weisshorn 163, 165
huts, mountain 88

I

ice axe 17
ice screw 16
I Re Magi, refuge / hut 57, 59, 60

J

Jenatsch, refuge / hut 187, 188
Julier Pass 188

K

Kandersteg 133, 136, 141, 144
karabiners 16
Kesch, refuge / hut 187, 189, 190, 191
kick turn 21
kit, first aid 19
kit, group 19
kit, hut trips 18
kit, mountaineering 17
kit, ski touring 13
kit, spares 19
kit, specialist 20
Konkordiaplatz 148
Konkordia, refuge / hut 147, 148, 149, 152
Kössler, Ulrich 203
Kranzberg 148
Kuhscheibenspitz 213
Kühtai 216

Index

L

Labande, François 93, 110
La Bandia Longa 40
La Caffe 112
La Cassorte 157
Lacs de Jovet 98
La Fouly 122
La Gardiole 53
Lagazuoi 221
Lagazuoi, refuge / hut 219, 221
La Giète 112
La Lauzière 53
L'Albaron 66, 67
Lambronecca, refuge / hut 171
Lämmeren, refuge / hut 136, 137, 141, 143
Länglfue, refuge / hut 171, 175, 176
La Pointe de Vouasson 158
Larstigtal 215, 216
La Tresenta 90
Lausetto 38
Lauterbrunnen 144
Laval, refuge / hut 59
Lavarella, refuge / hut 222
Le Bettey 111, 112
Le Brévent 111
Leckihorn 183
L'Écot 64
Le Cugnon 95
Le Gran Plan 221
Le Mourre Froid 52
Les Classiques de Randonnée à Ski 129
Les Classiques de Randonnées à Ski de Suisse 147
Les Contamines 91
Les Diablerets 133, 136, 142
Les Faverges 143
Les Plus Belles Randonnées a Ski 163
Les Plus Belles Traces du Mont Blanc 110
Les Praz de Chamonix 113, 114
Les Prioux 75
Le Tour 115
Levanna Occidentale 65
L'Eypiol 53
Lobbia Alta, refuge / hut 203, 206, 207
L'Omen Roso 165
Lötschental 151
Ludvigshöhe 174

M

Madritschjoch 200
Mandrone, refuge / hut 203, 204, 206, 207
Mantova, refuge / hut 171, 173, 174
maps 11
Margherita, refuge / hut 171, 174
Marteller, refuge / hut 195, 200

Matterhorn 125
Mauvais Pas 95
Mezzalama, refuge / hut 173
Miage 91
Mittelgipfel 141
Mittlebarg, refuge / hut 177
Mittlenberg, refuge / hut 180, 181
Modane 71
Mont Blanc 101, 105
Mont Blanc and the Aiguilles Rouges: A guide for skiers 103
Mont Blanc Ski Tours 103, 110
Mont Collon 159, 160
Monte Adamello 207
Monte Cervet 43
Monte Cevedale 199
Monte Eighier 43
Monte Estelletta 41
Monte Freide 43
Monte Midia Sopra 41
Monte Pasquale 198
Monte Rosa 169
Monte Rosa, refuge / hut 171, 174, 175
Monte Ruissas 38
Monte Soubeyran 42
Monte Venezia 207
Montjoie valley 91
Mont Pucel 138
Mont Thabor 55, 58
Mont Thabor, refuge / hut 57, 60
Mont Vélan 127, 130
Mota Rota 159
mountaineering kit 17
mountain huts, using 30
Munt de Senes 224
Munter, Werner 28
Mutthorn, refuge / hut 144

N

Nant Borrant 95
navigation equipment 19
Naz 189
Névache 55

O

Ofenhorn 182
Olsen, Cain 208
Orestes, refuge / hut 171
Ortler 193
Ouille d'Arbéron 68

P

Pain de Sucre de Mont Tondu 98
Palanche de la Cretta 157
Palon de la Mare 197

Passo Adame 207
Passo della Lobbia Alta 207
Passo del Naso 172
Passo del Sabbione 182
Passo del Tonale 203, 206
Passo di Zebrù 198
Passo Falzarego 220
Passo Grau 220
Passo Pisgana 204, 206
Passo Presena 204, 205, 206
Passo Tonale 204, 205
Passo Venezia 207
Pederu 223
Perkins, Andy 100
Petersgrat 144
phone, cell 19
phone, satellite 19
phone, smart 19
Pian di Neve 207
Piansecco, refuge / hut 177, 180, 182, 183
Pic Blanc du Galibier 48
Pic d'Artsinol 156
Pigne d'Arolla 124, 160
Piramid Vincent 174
Pisgana 203, 204
Pisganino 204
Piz Darlux 189, 190
Piz Grialetsch 190
Piz Jenatsch 189
Piz Kesch 190, 191
Piz Lucendro 184
Piz Sarsura 191
Pizzini, refuge / hut 195, 197, 198, 199, 200
Pizzo Rotondo 183
Pizzo Tresero 197
Plan du Jeu, refuge / hut 120, 122
plan, evacuation 29
planning, ski tour 27
plan, rescue 31
Plateau du Couloir 123
Pointe de la Sana 78
Pointe de l'Observatoire 76
Pointe de Terre Rouge 60
Pointe de Tourtemagne 164
Pointe Marie 69
Pointe Ronde 107, 112
Pointes des Grands 116
poles, ski 14
Pollux 172
Pont 81, 88
Ponte di Legno 203, 204, 205, 207
Ponte Maira 41
Ponte Soubeyran 43
Powell, Al 54
Pralognan-la-Vanoise 71, 75

Index

Prarochet, refuge / hut 136
Pratopiazza 225
Prats Hauts 52, 53
Preda 189
Presanella 201
probe 15
Punta Calabre 85
Punta della Paletta 84
Punta del Sabbione 182
Punta Galisia 86
Punta Nera 57
Punta San Mateo 200
Putzenkarscharte 214
Puy-St-Vincent 51

Q

Queyras 45
Queyras – Toponeige 48
Quintino Sella, refuge / hut 171, 172, 173

R

radio, VHF 19
Ralphs, Terry 144
Ra Stua, refuge / hut 219, 224
Regosa, refuge / hut 205
rescue kit, avalanche 15
rescue kit, ski tour 15, 16
rescue phone numbers 20
rescue pack 21
Rifugio Vittorio Buzzi 91
Roc de la Pêche, refuge / hut 74, 75
Roc du Blanchon 75
Roche Château 60
Rocher de la Grand Tempête 60
rope 15, 16
Rosano, Bruno 37
Rotondo, refuge / hut 180, 184
Ruisseau d'Arnès 69

S

Saas valley 175
safety and rescue, avalanche 23
Sanga, Georges 129, 155
Santa Caterina 196
Sasso Delle Dieci Zehner 222
satellite phone 19
Savoie Ski de Randonée 74
Scalettapass 190
Schartenkopf 216
Schnegg, Ralph 137
Schnidehore 133, 140
Schwarzhorn 143
Schweinfurter, refuge / hut 211, 215, 216

Scialpinismo nel Trentino. Vol. 3: Adamello, Presanella, Brenta, Ortles, Dolomiti, Lagorai, Alto Garda 203
Scoiattoli, refuge / hut 219, 220
season, ski touring 10
Sella Ronda 225
Sennes, refuge / hut 219, 223, 224, 225
Séracs de Tré la Grande 95
Sex Rouge 137
Shahshahani, Leïla 74
Shahshahani, Volodia 74
Shaxe, BCA 20
shelter, group 19
shovel 15
Signalkuppe 174
Silbersattel 175
Simmefäll 143
ski crampons 14, 21
Ski de Randonée Haute Alpes 48
Ski de Randonée Bas-Valais 129, 155
Ski de Randonée – Haute Savoie – Mont Blanc 93, 110
skiing, downhill 22
skiing, glacier 22
skiing, skills 21
skiing, uphill 21
ski mountaineering 17
skins 14
Ski Randonnée Alpes Fribourgeoise et Vaudoise 107
skis 13
Skitouren Berner Alpen West 137
Ski Touring 21, 22, 23, 107
ski tour planning 27
ski tour timings 28
slings 16
smart phone 19
spares kit 19
Speichersee 216
Stechelberg 144
Steghorn 141
St Luc 164
St Moritz 185, 191
Stockhorn 175
Strahlhorn 175
stretcher 20
Stubai 209
Stubaiergletscher 212
Sulden 195, 200
Suldenspitze 200
Sulzkogel 216
Sulztal 213, 216
Sulztalferner 213, 216
Swiss Alpine Club, grading scale 12

T

Tardivel, Pierre 93
Tassan, Lionel 93
Teasdale, Andy 70
Tête Blanche 159
Thabo, refuge / hut 57
Three Valleys 71
Thumel 84
Ticino / Mesolcina / Calanca 180
timings, ski tour 28
Tofana, circuit of 217
Toponeige Mont Blanc 93
Tour de Soleil 177
Tour du Ciel 161
Tracuit, refuge / hut 163, 165
transceivers 15
travelling to the Alps 10
Traynard, grading scale 12
Tre Cime 225
Tré la Tête, refuge / hut 95
Tremolada, Francesco 219, 220
Trient, refuge / hut 120, 121
Truc di Tsanteleina 84
Trugberg 148
Turtmann, refuge / hut 163, 165
Turtmannspitze 164
Turtmanntal 161, 165

U

Université du Genève 221
uphill skiing 21
Üschenetal 141

V

Vadret da Sarsura 191
Val Adamè 203
Valbione, refuge / hut 205
Val Clarée 55
Val d'Anniviers 161, 164
Val d'Avio 203
Val d'Hérens 153
Val di Rhêmes 81, 84
Val di Rosole 196
Val d'Isère 71, 78
Valfréjus 55, 57, 60
Val Funtauna 190
Valgrisenche 81
Valle d'Apsoi 39
Valle Enchiausa 39
Vallon de Combeynot 49
Vallon du Timorion 90
Val Maira 35
Val Miller 203
Val Mulix 188

Index

Val Plazbi 191
Val Presena 205
Val Salarno 203
Val Salata 224
Valsavarenche 90
Valsorey 123
Valsorey, refuge / hut 120
Vanoise Ice Cap 71
Vanoise Ski Touring 57, 63
Vanoise Toponeige 74
Vanoise traverse 71
Vedretta del Pisganino 204
Vedretta di Pisgana 205, 207
Vélan, refuge / hut 120, 123, 129, 130
VHF radio 19
Vignettes, refuge / hut 120, 124, 125, 155
Vittorio Emanuele II, refuge / hut 81, 84, 87, 88, 90

W

Wannenhorn 150
West Oberland Ski Haute Route 133
when to ski tour 10
Wildhorn 133, 138, 139
Wildhorn, refuge / hut 136, 138, 139
Wildstrubel 133, 141
Wildstrubelgletscher 141
Wildstrubel, refuge / hut 136, 137, 140
Winnebach 214
Winnebachsee, refuge / hut 211, 214, 215
Witenwasserenstock 183
Wütenkarsattel 213
Wyssnollen 149

Z

Zermatt 117, 125, 171, 172
Zernez 191
Zinal 164, 167
Zuckerhütl 212
Zwieselbachtal 215, 216

frost guiding

British Mountain Guides for Ski Touring and Off-Piste

Telephone +41 788 74 78 31
www.frostguiding.co.uk

AvalancheGeeks

WE TAKE AVALANCHE EDUCATION SERIOUSLY

www.avalanchegeeks.com

AMERICAN AVALANCHE ASSOCIATION
PROFESSIONAL MEMBER

Bruce Goodlad and Mike Austin are Professional Members of the American Avalanche Association

from Pesda Press

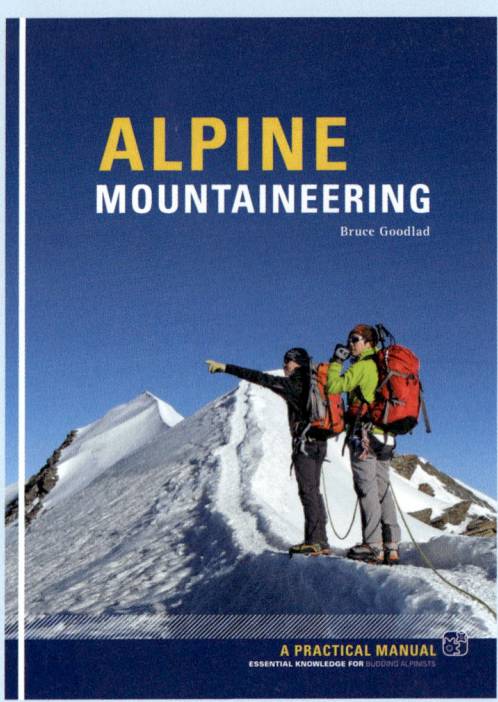

www.pesdapress.com